2.

Chicken Soup
for the Soul®

The Gift of Christmas

Chicken Soup for the Soul: The Gift of Christmas
A Special Collection of Joyful Holiday Stories
Jack Canfield, Mark Victor Hansen, Amy Newmark.

Published by Chicken Soup for the Soul Publishing, LLC   www.chickensoup.com
Copyright © 2012 by Chicken Soup for the Soul Publishing, LLC. All Rights Reserved.

CSS, Chicken Soup for the Soul, and its Logo and Marks are trademarks of
Chicken Soup for the Soul Publishing LLC.

The publisher gratefully acknowledges the many publishers and individuals who granted Chicken Soup for the Soul permission to reprint the cited material. Front cover illustration courtesy of iStockphoto.com/CSA_Images, Vetta Collection (© CSA_Images). Back cover illustration courtesy of iStockphoto.com/mstay (© Mark Stay). Interior illustrations courtesy of iStockphoto.com/Magnilion, and, /mxtamaview (© Megan Tamaccio)

Cover and Interior Design & Layout by Pneuma Books, LLC
For more info on Pneuma Books, visit www.pneumabooks.com

Distributed to the booktrade by Simon & Schuster. SAN: 200-2442

Publisher's Cataloging-in-Publication Data
(Prepared by The Donohue Group)

Chicken soup for the soul : the gift of Christmas : a special collection of
  joyful holiday stories / [compiled by] Jack Canfield, Mark Victor Hansen,
  [and] Amy Newmark. -- [Trade pbk. ed.].

     p. ; cm.

First published as a proprietary ed. in hardcover in 2010.
  A collection of true personal stories about Christmas and the holiday season. Stories range from serious to thoughtful to heartwarming to funny.
  ISBN: 978-1-61159-901-5 (pbk.)

  1. Christmas--Literary collections. 2. Christmas--Anecdotes. I. Canfield, Jack, 1944- II. Hansen, Mark Victor. III. Newmark, Amy. IV. Title: Gift of Christmas V. Title: Special collection of joyful holiday stories

PN6071.C6 C451 2012
810.8/02/03942663   2012936142

PRINTED IN THE UNITED STATES OF AMERICA
on acid∞free paper
21 20 19 18 17 16 15 14 13 12   03 04 05 06 07 08 09 10

The Gift of Christmas

A Special Collection of Joyful Holiday Stories

Jack Canfield
Mark Victor Hansen
Amy Newmark

Chicken Soup for the Soul Publishing, LLC
Cos Cob, CT

Contents

❶
~All I Want for Christmas~

❷
~Love Actually~

❸

~Close Encounters of the Santa Kind~

❹

~Deck the Halls~

❺

~It's a Wonderful Life~

❻
~A Few Good Elves~

❼
~I'll Be Home for Christmas~

8
~Toy Story~

9
~There Will Be Family~

10
~A Christmas Carol~

⓫

~Good Gift Hunting~

⓬

~The Star of Bethlehem~

Introduction

Merry Christmas! We are so pleased to bring you this special extra-large collection of Christmas stories. We had so many fabulous stories to choose from that we couldn't narrow the list down to our normal 101 stories, so you are getting an extra twenty in this book.

It was "Christmas in July" in our offices, with Christmas carols playing as we read the thousands of stories submitted for this book, most of which were submitted during June and July. It just shows that the Christmas spirit lives in all of us year-round. Wouldn't it be nice if it were Christmas all the time?

We hope you will enjoy reading this collection as much as we enjoyed making it for you. I am writing this in August, with 96-degree heat and 100 percent humidity outside, and December sure sounds appealing right now.

Curl up in front of the fire and have a good read. And remember that our Christmas books are always appropriate for young readers or listeners—we work closely with Santa to keep the magic alive.

~Amy Newmark, Publisher

Chapter 1

The Gift of Christmas

All I Want for Christmas

Special Delivery

The happiest moments of my life have been the few which I have passed at home in the bosom of my family.
~Thomas Jefferson

My mother rounded up my brother and me and sat us beside the Christmas tree. "Listen kids," she said, "this year there won't be a gift package coming from your Aunt Hilde."

We looked back at her, mouths agape. "No package?" we replied in unison.

My mother shook her head, somber-faced. "Nope," she said. "No package."

Each year, beginning the Friday after Thanksgiving, the anticipation began. Christmas carols playing on the radio, the decorating of the tree, and the scent of my mother's once-a-year cinnamon cookies baking in the oven all foretold the one object we waited for like none other during the holiday season: our annual Christmas gift package from Aunt Hilde. My brother and I would race each other to the mailbox after school, hoping to find the large square box wrapped in brown paper and secured with a web of rough twine before my mother had a chance to lay hands on it. Invariably she would retrieve the box before us, only to taunt my brother and me by placing it under the Christmas tree with the warning not to touch.

Mom insisted she had to first check the handwritten customs declaration, which lay sealed in a plastic pouch on the side of the box. Only then, she said, could she determine if the package needed to be opened immediately should there be something of a perishable nature inside. My brother and I would pray that in addition to our gifts Aunt Hilde had sent something like a dozen fresh eggs or a raw pork chop that required the package's immediate opening. Yet the customs declaration never revealed any such item and we were forced to wait until Christmas Eve for the contents of a package sent from a faraway place called Munich, Germany to be revealed.

After a few years' worth of packages, we knew to expect certain perennial items: cookies, chocolates, a particular brand of European hand cream for my mother. But each year, in Aunt Hilde's infinite thoughtfulness, she included a special souvenir for my brother and me from one of her many travels throughout the world and it was the expectation of those unknown items that whipped our imaginations into a near frenzy. We'd trace the words on the customs declaration with our fingers to try to decipher the names of the gifts described in their native languages.

"What is a wooly-bello?" "What is a Floh-spiel?" we'd ask each other. And why did the box growl one year, each time we shook it? It wasn't until my mother pulled out her heavy-duty shears from the kitchen drawer after Christmas Eve dinner and released those treasures from their cardboard cocoon that we learned those items were a fuzzy toy dog for me and a game of tiddlywinks for my brother. Only then, too, did we learn that the growling emanated from a talking teddy bear who held a note in his paw declaring that he came from a gift shop located on the outskirts of the Black Forest.

Aunt Hilde, actually a third cousin, was widowed at a young age and had no children of her own. She had been particularly close with my mother; they had shared an apartment in Connecticut as young women when my mother first immigrated to the United States. Both cousins were heartbroken when Hilde found it necessary to return to Germany to care for her aging mother. Shortly after, my parents married and had children and it was then that Hilde, in her generous spirit, adopted our family as her own. To my brother and me, who had never met her, she was like some kind of mythical fairy godmother who thought about us and loved us from afar. Those annual gift packages were the only tangible proof we had of her existence and love. And this year, there would be none. I felt tears well in my eyes. Didn't she love us anymore? "Why?" I asked my mother. "Why isn't Aunt Hilde sending a package?"

She only waved her hand in a dismissive fashion, "She's just too busy this year."

Christmas Eve came and with it the acute realization that something was missing from our celebration. As our family sat around the Christmas tree, I silently scolded myself for being so spoiled. There were plenty of gifts from Mom and Dad. I really had no right to expect a woman who I didn't even know to give me gifts as well. I mean, we had never even met for goodness sake. Certainly, she didn't owe me anything; I wasn't entitled to any gifts from her. Still… I felt sad.

Suddenly, my mother abandoned her seat on the couch and pushed the drapes aside to peek out our living room's wide picture window. "Did I hear a car door slam?" she asked. My mother looked back, motioning my brother and me toward the window. "There's a taxi in the driveway."

My brother and I jumped up to see for ourselves what was happening outside. There was a taxi in our driveway and from it emerged a woman with a round mane of silver-gray hair: Aunt Hilde. She grabbed her two suitcases from the driver's hands and stalked up our walkway, climbed up the front stairs, and walked straight into our living room. And just as if she had done this every Christmas for the last twenty years, she took off her coat, hung it on the coat rack, hugged us, and sat down with us next to our Christmas tree. Immediately, she began speaking in a mixture of German and English with a little Italian added for the benefit of my father who had come to the U. S. from Italy as a child. After inquiring about the family, she detailed the accounts of her latest vacations to Majorca and the Ivory Coast while handing souvenirs and gifts to each of us. My brother and I could only stare. Our Aunt Hilde was like an apparition: tall, sturdy, and commanding, with the largest bosom we kids had ever seen. Later, my mother said that God must have given Aunt Hilde such a large chest to house her great, big heart.

I believe my mother was right about that because those gift packages so lovingly wrapped in brown paper and twine kept coming each year for the next forty years of Hilde's life. In fact, they have continued to arrive each Christmas season even after her passing eight years ago. You see, Aunt Hilde left a provision in her will that her heir, another distant cousin, was to continue her Christmas package tradition as long as she was able, and in line with Aunt Hilde's generous spirit she has done so. Yes, my mother was right. Only a chest so ample could house such an enormous heart.

~Monica A. Andermann

Molly Passes the Torch

There is no psychiatrist in the world like a puppy licking your face.
~Ben Williams

Dad passed away, leaving Mom alone. She traveled from her home in Florida to South Carolina to be with my brother's family the week before Christmas. While there, Molly, the family's Westie, adopted Mom. Wherever Mom seated herself, the furry white bundle of love made sure she was by her side. When Mom rested her head on the guestroom pillow at night, she'd find one of Molly's bones tucked under her pillow. Arriving at the breakfast table each morning, there was Molly's favorite pink sock resting on Mom's chair.

All too soon it was time to return to Florida. Mom was lonelier than ever.

My brother Dave called to check up on her. "Mom, you never did let us know what you really want for Christmas this year. Did you think of any ideas?"

"I guess what I'd like more than anything in the world is a little white Westie like Molly to love. I'd name her Kati with an 'i' at the end."

"We'll have to see what we can do."

Christmas arrived in sunny Florida with palm trees blowing on a warm breeze. Mom was cleaning up breakfast dishes when she heard the doorbell ring. She hurried to answer it. In walked my brother Dave and his wife Andrea carrying a miniature version of their dog Molly. Mom immediately buried her face in Kati's fur. My brother set to work assembling the puppy's crate. Andrea filled the doggy dishes with clean water and puppy food.

Later, as everyone was settling down for the night Mom noticed a familiar pink sock inside Kati's crate.

"Isn't that Molly's favorite sock?"

Dave rubbed his chin thoughtfully before answering.

"Funny thing about that sock… We were getting ready to leave the house for our trip here. Molly was sticking to Kati like glue. Andrea knelt down to give Molly a hug, explaining that we were bringing Kati to you. Suddenly, Molly raced off, disappearing upstairs. Seconds later she came barreling back into the kitchen. In her mouth was her favorite pink sock. She placed it directly in front of Kati as if to say, 'I took care of Grandma while she was here with us. It's your turn now, Girl! Take good care of Grandma. I'm passing the torch to you.'"

Kati's favorite toy has been the pink Christmas sock to this day… and Mom and her sidekick, Kati, are inseparable.

~Mary Z. Smith

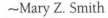

A Christmas Accident?

As each day comes to us refreshed and anew, so does my gratitude renew
itself daily. The breaking of the sun over the horizon is my grateful heart
dawning upon a blessed world.
~Terri Guillemets

"Now here's the part I hate. I-85 and the trucks." Were my mother's words to determine our destiny that fateful day in December 1998? Was it fate that brought us face to face with a careening, brakeless eighteen-wheeler? Our lives changed on December 21. Old Man Death had his eyes on us but God had other plans, for there are no accidents with Him.

Mother and I and our Maltese, Noël, were on our way home from Florida to South Carolina. Seventy-nine miles separated us from home. A brief eighty minutes and we'd be pulling into our driveway after a long journey. The day before our trip, I handpicked a bushel of ripe tomatoes from a local Florida field. I remember giving several of them to an older man parked next to our car at the hotel where we stayed the previous night.

When we got to Commerce, Georgia, I related to my mother how I wanted to stop at an outlet store and buy some undergarments. Besides, Noël had to take a little walk before the final leg of our trip. We were eager to get home. This knowledge caused me to scurry through the store and in the back of my mind I thought I really needed to buy some slips but due to our desire to get back on the road, I decided not to.

Snugly tucked into our seatbelts, we headed toward the nearby Interstate. Moments later, my mother screamed, "Oh, Marilyn! There's a truck!"

The split second before impact afforded me no defense as I saw the massive truck grill literally inches from my face—separated only by a thin piece of glass. Upon impact—confusion, a spinning sense, a brief vision of grass and glass flew everywhere inside our car. A momentary burst of white dust—air bag explosion—then a wire fence next to me in the field where we landed. Something wet and warm oozed all over my face—blood. My right eye closed quickly as I felt intense scratchiness. I closed my left eye to immobilize it. In my blindness, I groped my way over the console and heard myself say, "We've got to get out of here in case the car explodes!" I pushed my seventy-nine-year-old mother out her door as hard and fast as I could. This whole scenario lasted only moments and I felt no pain as the adrenaline kicked in. Only a sincere desire to escape and be safe.

The next moments seemed surreal. Help had come from everywhere. It seemed like only minutes from the time we were laid on the ground until we were safely strapped onto stretchers and headed for the hospital. We later found out this took about an hour and a half in real time.

I was very concerned about Noël and the fact he was diabetic. We told everyone to look for our dog and about his health needs.

Once inside the ambulance, my head securely held by a neck brace, I began to quiet myself as much as possible. The EMTs asked me many questions. Since I wasn't talkative, they told me they were just making sure I was still with them. I responded by saying, "I'm trying to calm myself by praying."

At the hospital, Mother and I were finally released from triage to a private room. Most of our injuries were due to our seat belts and air bags. Mother had six broken ribs, and I had a hairline fracture in my lower jaw. I was plenty sore and bruised all over. From all the flying glass, my face had about seventy-five tiny cuts which healed and left only a few small scars. Fortunately, my eyes didn't get cut at all and the glass was flushed from them completely.

The first three days afterward, both of us stayed in bed and slept. Complete exhaustion filled every cell of my body. Nurses and doctors came and went, food trays were brought and left, and all the while the most wonderful Christmas shows on TV played in the background. As I dozed, I heard strains of the Mormon Tabernacle Choir as they sang their melodic carols. I heard the lines, "Dear George, remember no man is a failure who has friends. Thanks for the wings, Love Clarence," and reruns of countless past Christmas concerts pervaded our room.

One dear nurse brought her children to visit us, and a small Christmas tree. Since we had no ornaments, we used wrapped peppermint candies someone gave us, secured with bobby pins from my mother's hair.

When the fourth day arrived, even though very stiff and sore, I attempted to care for my mother when the nurses weren't in the room. My spirit was bright. Mother kept telling me I shouldn't be so happy. But I was! Inside I was elated our lives had been spared even though our car and its contents, including the bushel of tomatoes, were totaled and our dog was at the clinic in serious condition. My heart was peaceful. I knew our guardian angels had been working overtime.

I healed quickly and wanted to walk the halls for exercise. Christmas Eve, as I walked, I approached a woman's room, and she motioned for me to step inside. Elderly and lonely, I discovered that she checked herself into the hospital every Christmas week so as not to be alone. Her room was decorated with all sorts of homey furniture and knickknacks. We sat and talked for quite a while that evening.

On discharge day, I hired a taxi and checked on Noël at the vet's office. I was saddened when I saw him because he didn't know me, and I could tell he barely clung to life. With paralyzed legs and glazed-over eyes, I could not, in good conscience, have allowed him to live another day. It was a difficult phone call to my mother, and we both openly cried at the decision that had to be made.

I've often thought — if I had taken the time to look for the slips, our destiny might have been different. However, we were told later if the unharmed trucker hadn't hit us, the impact of the accident would have probably killed him and for that I'm very grateful. I was also told by a police officer our car changed the truck's direction from smashing into a gas station and its pumps. He told me if that had happened, the gas would have caused a major fire for maybe a block.

I can honestly say, Christmas 1998 was very special to me. We were given the best gift of all — our lives.

~Marilyn Shipe

The Red Bank

There is not a more pleasing exercise of the mind than gratitude.
It is accompanied with such an inward satisfaction that the duty is
sufficiently rewarded by the performance.
~Joseph Addison

The most anticipated highlight of my grade school years was the annual Christmas gift exchange. Hearts raced as our small hands reached into the box that held the names of every student written on small strips of paper. Our hope was to draw the name of our best friend or to have our best friend draw our name. Sometimes we traded names, and we were not above bribery to obtain the name of a special friend.

No matter how many people I asked, I was unable to discover who had drawn my name my fifth grade year. I hounded all my friends, but even with their help, it was hopeless. No one was telling.

The final December day of school dawned upon a fresh snowfall, a perfect setting for our Christmas party. The cookies and Kool-Aid provided by room mothers were the appropriate colors of Christmas, and our teacher, Mr. Brehm, brought his banjo to accompany our rousing renditions of carols and "Rudolph, the Red-Nosed Reindeer." Mr. Brehm, handsome as a movie star, actually played quite well.

I don't remember who was appointed to distribute gifts, but I could hardly wait to discover what my, no doubt, wonderful gift would be and who would be the giver. When the square package was placed on my desk, I had to swallow a lump of disappointment. From the gift wrapping, I was fairly certain that it had not been wrapped by a girl.

Squeals of delight, laughter and gaiety filled the room around me. Carefully I pulled the tape from the wrapping paper, prolonging the suspense as long as possible. The box inside was unremarkable, white with no lettering. I opened the lid and tried to keep my face from registering the dismay I felt.

The box held a small, mantle-clock-shaped bank with a coin slot large enough to accommodate a fifty-cent piece. A bank! For a ten-year-old girl who wanted a new box of crayons, or a glass bottle of cheap cologne, or a movie star coloring book, maybe even some pretty hair barrettes. I seldom had any money, so what would I do with a bank? I lifted the small scrap of paper inside the box. The block print said: From Johnny.

Oh, no! The gift was from a boy! A boy I scarcely knew! One thing I did know was where he sat in the classroom. Slowly I swiveled my chair toward his desk. Johnny was looking right at me. Young as I was, I recognized the look of nervous anticipation on his face. His blue eyes bored into mine, while my mother's words of warning that very morning echoed in my head.

"Even if you don't like the gift you receive, you say 'Thank you' and say it like you mean it!"

So I took a deep breath, smiled, held up the bank and did my best. "Thanks, Johnny." A smile that threatened to split his face was my reward. I remember thinking that Johnny was really kind of cute, for a boy!

"I thought you'd like that!" he said. I blinked at the thought that he might have actually chosen the bank for me, instead of relying upon his mother to buy it. In fact, my mom had always bought the small exchange gifts that I gave each year. I placed the bank back into its box and enjoyed the rest of the party.

That evening, I examined the bank carefully. The metal front and sides were painted bright red, and the numerals were black. The hands that could be spun to any time I chose were shiny, silver-colored metal, as was the removable back. I supposed, as clock banks went, it was okay.

During the next few years, my family moved three times. I went to a new grade school in the seventh grade, and I attended two high schools. The bank remained among the possessions that moved with me. It went with me when I got married and began a new life with my husband. For years, I kept it in my dresser drawer, a receptacle for all my loose coins. When the bank was full, I deposited the money. It easily held a hundred dollars worth of change.

One day, as I dropped some quarters into the bank, I realized that I could not remember another single gift I had received during all my school exchanges. Nor could I remember any gift I had given on those occasions. In fact, except for a special doll, a birthstone ring and my bicycle, I could scarcely remember any other gift. Johnny's gift was the only serviceable, lasting one.

The night our house was burglarized was frightening and traumatic. I was livid! Just the thought that someone had rummaged through our things, tossed aside items and took others infuriated me! Guns, jewelry, a hard-won WWII German dagger, money, small things that a smash-and-grab thief found easily, disappeared as if they had never been in our house.

It was a few days before I realized that the red bank was gone, and then only because I meant to drop some change into it. At first I thought it had shifted to the back of the drawer. My heart sank when I realized that it was gone from my life. Everything else that was stolen had been acquired during our marriage, but I had taken care of that bank for forty-five years! I felt as if a piece of my childhood had been stolen, too.

When I think about the bank, which is at least every Christmas, I'm reminded that expensive, material gifts do not reflect the essence or spirit of Christmas giving. The simple things, little things, sometimes even practical things given with a loving heart are the gifts that we remember, as well as those who gave them. Although I have not seen him for fifty-eight years, I will never forget Johnny Gibson, the fifth-grade classmate who gave me a memorable gift, a red clock bank with black numerals, a silver back and silver hands.

Thanks, Johnny.

~Barbara Elliott Carpenter

Our Spirit of Christmas

When you are sorrowful look again in your heart, and you shall see that in truth you are weeping for that which has been your delight.
~Kahlil Gibran

I was not looking forward to Christmas that year. My mother had been gone less than three months and she had been our family's Spirit of Christmas. Without her, I couldn't imagine how any of us, especially my dad, would find any joy in it.

She had delighted in her role of gift giver. On Christmas morning, we were always amazed at how she knew just what we'd hoped for, or how she'd chosen some special trinket we'd treasure but hadn't expected. She would begin shopping early in the year, stowing away gifts in perfect hiding places. For hours in December, behind closed doors, she'd surround herself with colorful rolls of paper, spools of ribbon, package decorations and tape, turning ordinary boxes into artistic creations begging to be opened.

The most vivid memory of my parents' pre-Christmas arrival at our home was their car's backseat and trunk, overflowing with all shapes of wrapped surprises. Once they'd been added to our own gifts around the Christmas tree, the result was a room that looked like Santa's workshop before his annual deliveries.

It was early October as I sat in my parents' guest bedroom, dreading the upcoming holiday season. Through the windows, the steaming rays of the afternoon sun reminded me why I hated Florida weather. I longed to be home in Virginia where the temperatures were cool, the tree leaves a fall rainbow. But I hadn't been able to refuse my dad's request of help.

After nearly sixty years with my mother, he found it impossible to think about getting rid of anything in the house that had meant something to her. He wanted me there to decide what to do with it all. Since my arrival several days before, I had put off the task, afraid of how I would handle my own unending grief as I attempted to empty drawers and closets. In truth, I wanted to avoid it as much as my dad did.

I decided to start with the drawers of the guest room dresser, remembering they held little-used scarves, gloves, jewelry, odds and ends. Perhaps, I reasoned, if what I unearthed at first was less than precious, I could then move on to facing the more difficult decisions. By the time I reached the bottom drawer, my self-assurance about completing this task had emerged—until I slid that drawer wide and gazed upon its contents.

Minutes slipped by as my tears blurred the details of the unwrapped gifts my mother had hidden there. One by one, I opened the boxes and turned back the tissue folds, all holding riches far beyond monetary worth. I recognized a pair of earrings I'd admired in a store window months earlier. There were specific items for every member of the family.

My mind struggled to comprehend how my mother had managed, in her last painful months of cancer, to shop for, choose and hide away these most special expressions of her love. It was so like her, though, that in her last days, when her body had given up its fight, her resolve had still been to put her family first. And, I realized that she'd been hoping to celebrate just one more Christmas with us all.

I carefully packed each present before I left for home. On Christmas morning, with my dad joining our family in Virginia, everyone received those final gifts from my mother. They weren't wrapped as beautifully as she would have done, but that didn't matter. She had found a way to give us her Spirit of Christmas that year, the year we needed it most.

~Suzanne Rowe Ogren

The Christmas that Never Was

Christmas, children, is not a date. It is a state of mind.
~Mary Ellen Chase

'll never forget the moment that celebrating Christmas ended for me, forever. The year was 1978. It was the strangest sensation when I stopped—heartbreaking and yet strangely liberating and exhilarating at the same time.

When I was a kid, my parents used to call me Little Miss Merry Christmas. My mother didn't like Christmas. She didn't know how to cook so she despaired every holiday when cookies or turkeys were needed. She hated decorating the house. Couldn't stand shopping for Christmas presents and she complained about nearly every present she received. They weren't thoughtful enough or too practical. And Lordy how she hated trimming Christmas trees!

The only real festive moment my mom enjoyed was making fudge—a recipe she and her friends had learned during World War II. They'd made batches and batches of the confection and sent them to soldiers fighting in that war. Fudge was the big Christmas tradition for Mom that she absolutely had to do. But if the fudge didn't turn out just right, she'd end up in a fit of tears.

Mom also loved being with her family even though she and her sisters usually fought whenever they were together. Christmas Eve was spent with her siblings and their kids.

I was the opposite of my mother. I loved everything about Christmas. When I was ten, I took over decorating the house and setting out the Christmas cards we received. By the age of twelve my father and I made the Christmas turkey. I found a farm in the country where we could cut down our own Christmas tree. My dad and I went every year and chopped down the biggest tree we could find. I'd spend the rest of the day decorating it while listening to Christmas carols and drinking homemade eggnog.

By the time I was eighteen I had pretty much taken over the preparations for Christmas, even baking cookies. All Mom had to do was make the fudge.

Then I went into nursing school and stayed in residence. My mother bought a fake tree. We argued about it. Fought. Battled as if it were World War III, but my mother was determined to have a fake tree so she could put it up December the first and not worry about needles falling.

No more garlands of holly, no more putting out the Christmas cards. It was too much for her to do without me. But there was still fudge.

I had been a nurse on a chemotherapy unit for two years when my mother pulled me aside one Christmas Eve and showed me a wound on her shoulder. I recognized it immediately. It was a secondary metastases from a tumour in her breast.

Some things just don't need to be said between mothers and daughters. We both knew in that moment that there would not be very many Christmases left for my mother.

I didn't sleep that night, just couldn't, and I watched the sun rise and kiss the sugary snow with its brilliant light. After a moment's hesitation I donned a sweat suit and my running shoes, went outside, and began to run. Within minutes I found myself running through a woodland nestled at the end of my street. I ran past a herd of deer, bunnies, squirrels. I felt as if my lungs would explode from the frigid morning air, but I still ran.

I ran along the river and mountains of piled ice on the frozen bank.

And then I ran past our neighbourhood church and stopped. Long icicles hung all along the side of the roof. They were prisms for the sun and rainbows danced on the wall.

"All right," I whispered. "If You are going to take her, all I ask is that it be swift and without pain."

As I walked home I began to think of my patients. Four of them were stranded at the hospital for Christmas because their families couldn't or wouldn't take them home for the day. None of them would live to see another Christmas.

"Dad," I called when I returned home. "How big is our turkey?"

"Why?"

"Do we have enough for four more people?"

"Sure."

"Good. We're having company."

After setting the table and making sure everything was prepared, my father and I signed my four patients out and brought them home. Two were in wheelchairs, one had oxygen. The fourth one, Mrs. M., my father and I had to carry inside.

We ate turkey, pumpkin pie, sang carols, and settled around the tree with hot cocoa and—my mother's fudge.

"I used to make this fudge for my husband when he was a soldier overseas," said Mrs. M. with a wistful smile on her face. "He hated it. He didn't tell me that until twenty years later, God bless him."

After several heartfelt thank yous were made, my mom made "care" packages for our four guests and we returned them to the hospital.

Three weeks later Mrs. M. died. The others were gone shortly after that.

That was the last year Mom made fudge. She didn't have the strength anymore. Dad and I tried to make it under her supervision but Mom was never satisfied with the texture.

The following year the Christmas tree went up in November and remained until February. Not only did Dad and I make the fudge, we tried our hand at Divinity, a confection my grandmother had made. We failed miserably at that as well.

I knew my mom was doing poorly; she didn't even get together with her family anymore. In August of 1978 my mother died. She was fifty-four.

Strangely enough I was okay. God did as I had asked of Him. She awoke one morning not knowing where she was. The cancer had spread to her brain. She was afraid to leave her home so I nursed her there.

She smiled at me two weeks later as I tucked her into her bed. "I'm tired," she whispered.

"I know. It's okay if you let go, now. I'm okay; so is Dad."

Mom died in her sleep that night.

I had realized on that Christmas day with our four guests that there were a lot of "forgotten" people around, especially senior citizens. After my mom died I found myself spending more and more time with my cancer patients, giving them simple pleasures like afternoon teas, picnics in the warm sun. Pumpkin carving. Homemade fudge. Holidays weren't really necessary anymore. I had learned to cherish each moment of each day.

My dad took my mom's death much harder than I had imagined he would. I tried to spend as much time as I could with him. In December I asked if he had set up the Christmas tree yet and he shook his head no. Three days before Christmas I tried to help him, but his heart wasn't in it.

"Dad, if you don't want to do this, it's fine by me," I said. "You and I can change the traditions, you know. We can do Chinese food and see a movie. Or go on a vacation."

"But what about your mother's tree?"

"I know what we can do," I said cheerfully. "Come on."

We packed up the tree and all of the decorations and drove to the hospital where we gave it a new home on one of the chronic care units that didn't have a tree. The patients and staff were thrilled.

My dad gave me a nervous glance. "You're really okay with this?"

And that was the moment I knew I'd never celebrate Christmas again. Didn't need to. I was celebrating life every day.

I smiled at him. "Yeah, Dad. I'm doing great."

~Pamela Goldstein

The Unexpected Gift

It's not what you look at that matters, it's what you see.
~Henry David Thoreau

Standing upon a hill, the small, one-room school I attended as a child served less than twenty students. Pine trees reflected on the windows from every hillside—each one ready to be a perfect Christmas tree. It was early December 1951, and my sister Frances and I anxiously awaited our school Christmas program, an event anticipated by the whole community since September. We would wear our Sunday best and bring a gift for a secret friend whose name had been drawn from a box earlier that month.

On the morning of the program, a minister from the community would read from the Book of Luke about the birth of Jesus and then Santa Claus would visit. I memorized a poem that began: "Winds through the olive trees softly did blow, around little Bethlehem long, long ago." Frances memorized "What Can I Give Him?" by Christina Rossetti. Frances was in the first grade; I was in the third. I loved memorizing poetry and receiving my gift, but it was the clothes we wore that year and the generosity of my mother that stand out most in my mind. Though not wrapped up in a package, her ingenuity taught me to appreciate the best gift I would ever receive.

Our biggest concern was about the outfits we would wear to the program, since the tobacco crop, our family's main source of income, was late.

"We have no money for new clothes this year," my mother, who was raised during the Great Depression, said. "But I will work out something." She always did.

We lived in a farmhouse about a mile from the school. In one corner of the living room, in front of the window, sat an old Singer sewing machine in an oak cabinet.

"Come with me," she told us, as Frances and I followed her up the stairs and into one of the bedrooms where an old box of clothes sat. The only time they had been worn in years was when we played dress up.

"Hold on to Frances," she told me as she carried a red gabardine jumper in one hand and a navy woolen coat in the other.

When Mom reached the bottom of the stairs, she said, "Stand on the chair in the living room one at a time."

I went first, as she unwound a tape and began to measure the length of my torso from my waist to knees. In the same manner, she made calculations for Frances. She wrote down the figures for both of us and began to draw a pattern on an old *Grit* newspaper.

Next, she laid the jumper down and began to cut pieces. She followed the same procedure with the navy coat. Having no zippers, Mom left a slit where she used a zigzag stitch to make a buttonhole by hand, its beauty unequaled today by any buttonhole crafted on a modern machine.

When I arrived home the next day, the rhythm of her feet on the pedal was like music to my ears. Holding up my finished skirt, she said, "I hope this fits."

Likewise, she did the same to Frances. We tried them on; they both fit perfectly, but Mom was frowning.

"These skirts need new blouses," she told us.

With both of us following behind her, she went to the dresser drawer.

Pulling out an old muslin sheet, she said, "I believe I can spare this one."

Thus, the cutting and measuring began all over.

We came home the next day to find the white blouses finished and laid out on her bed. Down each side of my blouse, Mom had sewn a row of pink lace. Frances's had light blue. These pieces of lace, which Mom had saved for years, gave a perfect touch to our outfits. The handmade buttonholes fit the buttons perfectly, showing the same degree of excellence as the work done on the skirts.

Not only were our outfits finished, but the blouses were washed, starched and ironed with the sad irons heated from the wood stove. The skirts were cleaned and pressed, each pleat standing out. She had pressed and tied a satin hair ribbon for each of us.

The program day finally came. Our poems were memorized, and we were dressed in our "new" clothes. Inside the school, we saw our secret Santa gifts lying under a decorated pine tree that, mere hours before, had only been a reflection in the school window glass. The smell of the fresh-cut pine wafted through the air as the sun glistened on Christmas card cutouts tied to the branches with red ribbon.

It's been almost sixty years since the Christmas that my mother breathed new life into an old box of clothes. The day of the Christmas program I received a store-bought gift from one of my classmates. I don't remember what it was or who gave it to me. I don't remember if the minister spoke eloquently or if anyone applauded when I recited my poem. But I do remember the gift my mother gave me—the knowledge that human generosity cannot be measured with a price tag.

Six years ago my mother celebrated her last Christmas with us. But her creativity has extended into my own life, especially when financially hard times have come my way. I remembered my gratefulness to her each Christmas when I made my own children's Christmas pageant costumes, baked from scratch, helped my husband cut pine logs for our Christmas Eve fire and decorated the house with holly sprigs from the bush I planted in my yard. I did all of this so my own family could have Christmas traditions. With many people cutting back, my mother's determination to always "work something out" has served me well in recent years. The gift of finding a way to make Christmas special, even when the means are limited, was given to me by my mother, unexpectedly, years ago. It has been the greatest gift of all.

~Janet N. Miracle

Where Are My Christmas Cards?

We make a living by what we get but we make a life by what we give.
~Winston Churchill

Who doesn't like getting cards in the mail? Real cards—not e-cards or virtual cards that say, "I was thinking of you, just not enough to spend money on a stamp." Christmas is the one time of year to catch up with friends and family we don't see often enough, receive a card, sometimes a handwritten note and hopefully some pictures of their growing children, their dogs, or even their vacations.

The anticipation of finding a Christmas card in the mailbox is comparable only to finding a new present under the tree every day during the month of December. In a tiny metal box, that typically receives monthly greetings only from the electric company or Publishers Clearing House, news arrives of babies, new jobs, college graduations, and photos of smiling faces. The month of December delivers the promise of holiday messages, of tradition.

Every year I mail dozens of Christmas cards, mostly to people with whom I've been exchanging yearly greetings for as long as I've been married. When I separate them for the post office each year, the stack going to people out of state is as big as the stack staying in town.

I send them to relatives I haven't seen in ten years, to friends who've moved away, to a soldier overseas, to friends of my aging parents—these all make sense. It stops making sense when I send one to my mother (who I see almost every day) and to my next-door neighbors. Nonetheless, I send them, because I hope that the recipients get as much joy as I do finding Christmas cards in the mailbox.

One year was different. My holiday joy took a nosedive the year it seemed like everyone had decided to boycott the Christmas card tradition. I'll always remember it as the year that cards trickled in slowly and painfully, like receiving a million dollars in the mail one dollar at a time; I was grateful for each one, but just one a day seemed like a cruel joke.

I waited. My kids noticed.

"Mom, didn't you send out Christmas cards this year?" asked my sixteen-year-old daughter as she looked through a stack of mail.

"Yes, of course I did. Why do you ask?"

She pointed to an empty red and green wicker basket on the counter. "Where are all our Christmas cards?"

That was the big question, wasn't it? It was already the second week of December and the only cards I'd received were from our insurance agent and tax preparer. It was starting to become a twisted and backward version of "The Twelve Days of Christmas," except that in this version, my True Love gave me bills on the eighth day and junk mail on the ninth.

I thought the weekend of the 15th would be productive for the people who hadn't yet sent their cards, so on the following Wednesday I expected my mailbox to be full. Wednesday came and went; I received two cards.

"Unbelievable!" I complained as I walked inside from getting the mail.

On Thursday, I was excited to see three cards in the mailbox—until I realized one of them was my own, returned to sender for an outdated address.

Where were my Christmas cards? I love getting the ones that include pictures, and the cards that include a yearly "This is what we've been doing" letter are a beloved bonus. I tape any pictures to my refrigerator so we can enjoy them until New Year's Day, but this particular year my fridge was nearly bare.

I don't know what changed from all the years past. One friend sent out a Facebook message to let people know that, while she was enjoying everyone else's Christmas cards tremendously, she wouldn't be sending out cards this year because she was too busy.

Too busy. Maybe that's the culprit. Too busy to bake, too busy to write cards. Maybe this is a sign of how overextended we are with our jobs, kids' activities, and social commitments. We all complain about how busy we are this time of year, especially my husband, who doesn't buy my gift until the weekend before Christmas because he can't believe "how fast Christmas came this year." December does have a way of using eleven months to surprise us.

Perhaps it is the economy. If you buy the boxed cards the day after Christmas, you can get two boxes for the price of one, but stamps get into people's wallets. Even though mailing a letter through the post office is still the most cost-efficient method to get something across the world, when you're mailing sixty-plus of those "somethings," the cost may become an issue.

"Why do you keep mailing them if it makes you so upset?" asked my husband one night as he listened to me list everyone who hadn't sent a Christmas card that year.

"I've asked myself that same question!" I said. "And I've decided that I'm finished with the whole tradition. People just don't send Christmas cards anymore, I guess."

Christmas came and went. A few cards arrived after December 25th. Such blatant lack of Christmas spirit disillusioned me. What was next? Too busy to decorate a tree? I allowed the shortage of Christmas cards to damper the last vestiges of my holiday spirit.

Then, not long after Christmas, a special card arrived in the mail that caused my shrunken grinchy heart to grow three sizes that day.

"Loved ones," it read, "I can't tell you how much we look forward to receiving your Christmas card every year. The kids are growing too fast, and we are getting old, so your yearly holiday greeting is better than any monetary gift. We read your letter at least three times and find pleasure in every detail you take the time to write. We love you and hope that you know that our love travels the miles to reach you, just as your card has traveled miles to reach us. Much love."

My grandparents are both gone now, but I still have that card. It is the first card I put in the wicker basket each year to remind me that the true spirit of Christmas is giving, not receiving. And every year, I continue to mail Christmas cards to everyone on my list.

And it's okay if they don't mail one back. The holiday tradition continues.

~Dana Martin

Christmas Keepsake

Gratitude is the memory of the heart.
~Jean Baptiste Massieu

My son's freshman year at college proved financially difficult. When he entered college, his father was out of work. I did not work outside of our home because of being a full-time caregiver for my father-in-law.

A boy with whom my son attended high school was on his way to the junkyard and stopped at our house so my son could say good-bye to the car filled with memories. Instead of seeing the memory-filled car go to its fate, my son offered to buy it. The purchase took place with the exchange of one dollar. When his father came home to this *fait accompli*, he told him, "If the car breaks down on the highway, take the plates off and leave it. It won't be worth the money to tow it."

Our son became the king of cheap dinners — Asian noodles or macaroni and cheese. Every few weeks he and his roommate would pool their money to make spaghetti with homemade meat sauce as a treat.

When Christmas came I suggested that he dispense with gift giving as we knew he couldn't afford purchases. "People will be giving you gifts because they love you and want to be supportive of your educational efforts," I told him. "They won't expect gifts from you."

As our family gathered on Christmas morning the usual chaos

ensued as the many gifts were opened. Most of the gifts my son received were practical, such as socks and shirts. Among his gifts were a basket of snacks and, of course, boxes of macaroni and cheese.

When I said that it was time for me to serve brunch, my son announced, "We're not finished. It's my turn."

He handed everyone a homemade Christmas card. Inside was written a special memory. On some cards, he wrote about an event or activity he shared with the recipient. On others, he penned something he had learned from that person.

To one grandma who knew he was interested in finance, he wrote, "You taught me to read the stock market and financial page of the paper." For my husband's father, he wrote, "We used to fish with toy fishing poles using real hooks to catch little fish under the dock."

He recalled for his other grandma, "You would invite me and my sister to bake cut-out cookies and decorate them so Mom could Christmas shop for us." Since she also made special birthday cakes each year, he wrote, "I remember the train cake with the engine, car, and caboose."

For my father, he wrote, "Grandpa, you taught me to play pool in your basement. You also helped me with my stamp collection." To his own father he wrote, "I broke a window playing driveway hockey. I was afraid of what you'd say. You looked at me and said, 'Every kid is entitled to one broken window. I guess this is yours.' I still think about our good times playing hockey and chess. You were never too busy for time with me."

"Mom, there are too many things I could say about how important you are. You are always there for me. We were headquarters for all the kids in the neighborhood and the taxi that took us places."

From the tears that filled the eyes of the grandparents, I guessed that they were touched to learn that things they had done had become living memories. I don't remember the other gifts I received that year. But my son gave me living memories to cherish as well.

And I felt great pride at his valuing the people near to him.

~Judith H. Golde

Whistling Dixie

There are no seven wonders of the world in the eyes of a child.
There are seven million.
~Walt Streightiff

Life in the 1950s was gentle and innocent. There was a simplicity and freshness in adults and children alike that carried over into the holiday celebration, as well. I was a young mother, excited about decorating a real tree the year after our first child, Diana, turned two. After all, what could be more thrilling than seeing Christmas through the eyes of my toddler? No stone would be left unturned, I decided. My daughter would have the best holiday I could create.

Diana greeted the seasonal activities with wide-eyed interest and cheery enthusiasm. She sampled my homemade sugar cookies — but seemed to prefer the raw dough. She admired the tree and left all the shiny ornaments alone — mostly. She helped me tape Christmas cards to the hall mirror — then artfully rearranged them, again and again, proud of each new display that she created. And she endured our lengthy shopping excursions — perhaps in part because we ended each one with a stop at Murphy's, the local five-and-dime in our small hometown of Medina, New York.

"Should we go get our treat now?" I grabbed her dimpled hand and led her to the deep chest cooler against the far wall of the store.

There, squeezed tight against me, Diana stood on tippy-toes, stretching to see while I searched for her favorite: a cardboard Dixie cup of vanilla ice cream. My little daughter's coffee-bean eyes sparkled under the strand of plump red and green bulbs strung overhead while she watched the busy shoppers and waited to savor her icy treat, one bite at a time.

I reached into a box for a small wooden spoon, closed the lid to the freezer, and gave the clerk fifteen cents.

"Wait until we get to the car to open it," I reminded my little one.

As December 25th drew ever nearer, I tucked her into bed one night. Priming her for the excitement of the holiday ahead, I asked, "Diana, what would you like for Christmas?"

She cocked her silky blond head and sing-songed sweetly, "A Dixie ice cream."

I tried to hide my grin as I snuggled the blanket under her chin. "Well, yes," I agreed. But, thinking about the baby doll I'd already wrapped—along with a host of carefully hand-selected items—I pressed her for more. "But isn't there something else you want, too?"

Diana considered the question at length. "Hmmm," she said and then brightened in sudden decision. "Yes," she nodded, "a spoon."

~Marie Stroyan as told to Carol McAdoo Rehme

Chapter
2

The Gift of Christmas

Love Actually

The Christmas Gift

The only gift is a portion of thyself.
~Ralph Waldo Emerson

It was Christmas Day and I was working a flight. Not exactly what I had in mind. I wondered who would fly on Christmas Day. I was surprised to find that lots of people fly on Christmas Day. I suppose the reasons are as varied as the faces I saw while boarding the airplane on that early morning flight.

I was decked out with Christmas pins on my blazer and even a reindeer headband. Everyone made some comment as they saw me.

"Where's your red nose?"

"Does it light up?"

"Are you guiding the plane tonight?"

It made the mood festive and fun.

The plane was full, and it was a job finding enough overhead bin space in which to place all the bags and coats, to say nothing about all the brightly wrapped gifts.

As I walked through the cabin one last time before takeoff, I noticed a young father and his small son sitting in a row together. The little guy was fastened into his car seat, excitedly looking out the window. Dad was pointing to other aircraft on the runway as the little boy's voice echoed through the cabin, "Airplane, Daddy, airplane!"

I wondered, as I sat on the jump seat, where the mother was. It was Christmas Day, after all.

Once we were able to start our beverage service, I walked past the pair again. It was a sight that warmed my heart. Dad was fast asleep with his head resting against the small car seat. The little man was all eyes, taking in everyone and everything, but not uttering a word.

During our beverage service, I handed a soft drink to a very pregnant woman near the rear of the aircraft. We chatted a minute before she said, "Do you suppose you could help me with my heavy bag when we land? My husband put it up for me and I just can't get it down alone."

I told her I'd be happy to help her, but then I just had to ask, "Where is your husband now?"

"Oh, he's sitting up near the front."

I thought their seating arrangement strange but didn't have time for more conversation right then.

By the third trip through the cabin, I had put two and two together. Walking past the pregnant woman again, I stopped at her row and asked her if, by chance, her husband was sitting with a small boy.

"Yes," she replied with a smile.

I couldn't figure out the separate seating, and it kept nagging at me.

"In case you're wondering," I said as I approached her again, "your husband is sound asleep, and your darling little boy is wide awake, watching everything that is going on."

"Oh man," she said with a laugh, "that little guy is always so good for his dad!"

Just a few minutes before we were preparing to land, I noticed the dad was awake. I also noticed that the seat next to him was empty, as it had been the entire flight.

"I told your wife that you had a good nap," I said, goodheartedly.

He laughed and then added, "Is she okay?"

"Oh, she's fine. But... if you don't mind my asking... why isn't she sitting next to you?"

His eyes lit up, and with such love in his voice, he said, "Oh, this is my Christmas gift to her."

I knew just what he meant. She was going to have two hours.... two full hours.... to sit alone. She could sleep. She could read. She could do nothing, but she did not have to worry about her son. She was soon to have another child and time alone is precious. I know. I'm a mom, too.

Christmas gifts usually come wrapped in beautiful, shiny paper topped with a huge bow... usually, but not always.

~Mary Catherine Carwile

A New Beginning

A long marriage is two people trying to dance a duet
and two solos at the same time.
~Anne Taylor Fleming

She removed the top of the gift box, and gently pushed the tissue paper to the side. Her eyes widened. She gasped and threw herself back into the chair, as if she had seen a ghost. Then, my wife, Christine, covered her mouth and started sobbing. I bent down to embrace her, and started crying too.

There had been a lot of tears shed in our home that year. Our children, Patrick and Erin, were concerned to see their mother crying again. But they quickly realized these tears were different. They were tears of joy—and hope.

The present I gave to Christine that Christmas morning three years ago saved a relationship that began when Christine gave me the same gift—albeit in much better condition—fifteen years earlier.

"What's in the box?" Patrick asked after we regained our composure.

"Nothing, sweetie," Christine replied as she put the top back on the box.

"None of your business," I added with a wink.

"Come on, Mom, tell us what's in the box," Patrick persisted.

Christine looked over at me and I nodded my approval.

She motioned for the children to sit beside her next to the tree. Without saying a word, she opened the box and removed the tissue paper to reveal an ordinary piece of lined notebook paper. It was dingy and yellow from age. The writing on the paper was her own.

Patrick leaned in closer and noticed the severely wrinkled paper was covered in tape. At some point, this document had been torn to pieces. A tear fell from his mother's eye, landing near the top of the page where it said, "My Certain Someone."

"I wrote these poems for your father when we were in college to show him how much I loved him."

She lifted the paper out of the box to reveal another poem underneath. It was also stained and covered in tape.

"Your father cherished these poems," she continued. "He is more sensitive than you may realize."

"Yeah, right," Erin said laughing.

"Those poems have always been my most prized possession," I said.

"So why are they all torn up?" Patrick asked tentatively.

I paused, took a deep breath, and hung my head in shame.

"Because I let my anger get the better of me."

"Your father and I were, and still are, very much in love," Christine said. "But, as I'm sure you both know, we have been having a pretty tough time lately."

"We know, Mom," the children replied in unison.

I looked at my beautiful wife. Something in her eyes told me it was time to be honest with the children about all the fighting they had heard in the recent past, and hopefully, reassure them about the future. I walked over to the window and stared at the lightly falling snow for a moment before continuing.

"Kids, you know I have been unhappy for a while now. I really hate my job, and I feel like a fish out of water living in New York. I had hoped to raise my family somewhere else," I said without turning away from the window. The dancing snow was peaceful and hypnotic. Somehow, it was helping me discuss this difficult subject with my children. "I blamed your mother for my unhappiness because she insisted we move here to be closer to her family.

"We started having terrible fights almost every night. After you kids went to bed on Thanksgiving, we had our worst fight ever."

"That was when your father tore my poems to shreds right in front of me," Christine said, pausing to dab her eyes and blow her nose. "He threw the pieces in the garbage and stormed out the door. I wasn't sure if I would ever see him again, but I was certain I would never see these poems again."

"It's okay, Mom," Patrick said as he put a comforting arm around her shoulder, and glared at me.

"So, what happened?" Erin asked.

"I came home late that night after a long walk and a lot of soul searching," I said. "Everyone was asleep. I stayed up the rest of the night picking every piece of paper out of the garbage and taping the poems back together."

"You did a pretty good job," Christine said, holding the paper up to the light of the Christmas tree. "But why did you wait until today to give them to me?"

I walked over to the Christmas tree and stared up at the serene angel perched on top. Then, I turned my attention to the angel comforting her two children. I sat down on the floor facing her, and took her hand in mine.

"My walk took me to the center of town on Main Street. I found myself standing in front of the nativity scene they had just set up in the park."

"Oh, my God, you went that far?" Christine said. "That has to be at least five miles from here."

"I had a lot to think about. As I stared at the manger, I recalled how I used to thank God for the gift of you every night when I prayed. I began to wonder how I went from thanking God for bringing you into my life, to blaming you for all of my unhappiness."

Christine gave my hand a gentle, reassuring squeeze as I paused to collect myself.

"I closed my eyes and remembered many of the wonderful times we have shared, and I found myself unconsciously reciting your poems," I continued. "When the enormity of what I had done finally sank in, I almost got sick on one of the wise men."

Patrick and Erin laughed.

"I ran all the way home. After I finished taping the poems back together, something inside me said to save them for Christmas morning. I wasn't sure why, but it felt right."

"It may be because when Jesus was born, it symbolized a new beginning," Christine said. "And I think it is time for our new beginning."

~Ron Geelan

When the Time Is Right, You'll Know

Love one another and you will be happy.
It's as simple and as difficult as that.
~Michael Leunig

As the holiday season of 2003 approached, my girlfriend Kerri couldn't stop yammering on about Christmases at home. I remember becoming increasingly annoyed with her stories, and although she never noticed, I'm sure she would've understood.

On November 30, 1995, years before she met me, my father and half-brother left this world. And with that tragedy being so close to December, it really cast a dark cloud over the holidays for me. I also always spent them alone until now. This Christmas however, I had Kerri and her joy for the holidays, her love of her family, and her giddy excitement over what had become just December 25th to me.

Although I was depressed, I was still very much in love, and I didn't want to ruin our first Christmas living together. That's when I bought us two bus tickets from Baltimore, Maryland to Charleston, South Carolina. Sure the Scrooge in me wanted to see just how great these Christmases at home were, but also Kerri couldn't have been happier, and I enjoyed making her happy. After all, this was the woman I planned to marry.

Speaking of marriage, we had been talking of getting engaged for months, so I told her, "Maybe this Christmas I'll talk to your father in person about marrying you."

She replied, "This is going to be the best Christmas ever!"

I was hoping she was right. Because unbeknownst to her, I had already bought an engagement ring.

It was now two days before Christmas and that 600-mile ride on the bus was everything you'd expect it to be: cramped, stuffy, long, and kind of miserable. For me, you can add "nerve-wracking" to that list, as my mind was focused on "the talk," then the proposal if "the talk" went well, and the fact that the ring was in my duffel bag under the bus. You had better believe that whenever passengers were beginning or ending their bus trip during our eighteen-hour ride, and bags were coming on and off of the bus, I was pressed against that window watching like a hawk.

That night when we finally arrived in Charleston, and we pulled up to Kerri's parents' house, I saw bright, shiny Christmas lights and lit-up reindeer. We walked inside and everything Kerri spoke of in her many stories was there. And I tried to be as excited as Kerri, but after being on a bus since 5 AM, I was only interested in one thing: sleep.

Christmas Eve was a blur of catching up with Kerri's family, calling her friends to let them know we were in town, and then visiting with some of those friends. Later that night, when Kerri and I were lying in bed, I told her that I thought that tomorrow morning I would finally "talk to him." She cuddled up close, and while still clueless about my plan, she sensed my nervousness and said, "It'll be fine. I love you."

On Christmas morning I woke up before Kerri and made my way to the living room. Just as Kerri said last night, her father, an early riser, was awake. I took a seat on the couch and asked him to sit in his recliner. He smiled at me while doing so, which led me to believe that he already had a clue about what was about to happen. Or maybe he found it humorous to see a twenty-five-year-old say to him, "Please, Sir. Sit."

Whatever his reason, had he not smiled I don't believe I would've found the courage to continue.

"Your daughter and I have been living together for a while now and I hope you knew this day was coming. I love your daughter very much, and I want to marry her, and I want to know if that would be okay with you."

This big mischievous grin rolled across his face.

"What would you do if I said no?" her father replied.

"I, well, I guess I would have to respect that...." I stammered out before getting cut off by his laughter.

"Welcome to the family. We'd be happy to have you as a son-in-law," he said as he shook my hand.

Relieved, I confided in him, "Sir, I have the ring in my bag, but I don't know where to propose."

That's when he said something that I will never forget, "When the time is right, you'll know."

"I hope you're right."

I crept back into the bedroom and lay back down in bed to find that Kerri was awake.

"Did you talk to him?" she asked.

"I wanted to, but I chickened out."

"Awww, that's okay, honey," she said with some disappointment in her voice as she hugged me tight again. I spent the next hour thinking of how to propose.

After Christmas dinner, Kerri's father gave her mother her anniversary gift. Their anniversary is the 26th, and her gift was an amethyst set of earrings and matching necklace. As the women in the family all gathered around her gift like moths to a porch light, Kerri's father looked over at me with a look that can only be described as, "Don't you have some jewelry that you want to give?"

I nervously mouthed, "Now?"

And he just shrugged his shoulders, with a look of, "Why not?"

I got up, and as I quickly made my way for my duffel bag, I thought to myself, "Oh, 'when the time is right you'll know?' Right, it's more like 'I'll tell you when the time is right.'"

I found the ring and came back into the kitchen looking very nervous and pale. Kerri took one look at me and asked a very concerned, "What's wrong?"

I grabbed her hand and put it to my chest. "Feel my heart. I'm so nervous right now."

That's when I dropped to one knee in front of her whole family as she covered her mouth and said a muffled, "No, no, no."

Certain that her "no's" were from "No, I can't believe it!" and not "No, I don't want this." I proposed.

"Kerri, I knew I was going to love you forever from the moment I met you, and now I can't imagine my life another day, another minute, without you in it. Will you marry me?"

"YES!!" she screamed as her family cheered. And with Kerri's emphatic response, with that one word, Christmas for me was saved. It turned the holiday I once dreaded, nearly destroyed by a family tragedy, into the holiday when I took the first step in starting a family of my very own.

And it's with misty eyes that I'm reminded of this story every year as Kerri and I sit together watching our son Benjamin open his gifts on Christmas Day.

~Ben Kennedy

Silent Home, Quiet Night

Love is like dew that falls on both nettles and lilies.
~Swedish Proverb

I hang up the phone and blurt out, "They're not coming."

My husband, Craig, looks as concerned as I feel, but says, "Don't panic."

"But we'll be all alone on Christmas Eve!"

He frowns.

"No kids." My voice nearly breaks.

"First time in thirty years."

We stare at each other in disbelief until I have a brilliant idea. "Let's invite someone else."

"Who?"

I shrug, "I don't know." Then I reach for the church directory. "I'll look in here."

Craig shakes his head. "It's too late. Service starts in an hour."

A silent dread hangs between us. He beckons me to sit on his lap. I go to him and settle down. It feels safe here, but my world is threatened.

It's the night before Christmas. We drive to church while visions of our children dance in my head. I tell my memories to stop stirring and settle down. It's a natural part of the cycle of life. We raised them to be independent.

Craig's touch on my arm breaks into my thoughts. "What?" he asks.

"I guess I should have expected this. We always prayed that the Lord would give each of them a soul mate."

"He has."

"That part is good. I like it. I just didn't figure it meant sharing them on the holidays."

"I know."

I'm wondering if Craig feels the strangeness as much as I do, like things are out of order. I don't mention that I'm worried that this holy night won't seem as special.

We share a magnificent time of worshiping with our friends at church. But as the service ends and the lights dim we all switch on our new, safer, battery-operated candles while singing "Silent Night." My head knows that this change makes sense but my heart misses the smell of dripping wax and heat of tiny flickering flames. Then, it's over. After hugs and waves to those around us, Craig and I head home alone.

Standing at our stove, I carefully stir the potato-leek soup. Next, I remove the bread from the oven and place it on the table. Craig takes my hand and offers thanks for our traditional meal. We sit side-by-side at the table where our little ones went from high chairs to high school to hightailing it out of our home to form families of their own. My heart trembles.

That's when something wondrous happens. It's not as glorious as an angelic choir or as world changing as our Savior's birth, yet it holds its own mystery. Slowly, softly, in the stillness, we smile into each other's eyes.

Craig says, "It's quiet."

I nod. "It's sort of nice."

"The soup's delicious as always."

"Thank you. I'm glad you like it."

"I like you."

"I like you, too."

He leans in for a kiss.

I kiss him back. And in the silence I sense that this is still a very special, holy night after all.

~Sue Cameron

Christmas Again

There is no surprise more magical than the surprise of being loved.
It is God's finger on man's shoulder.
~Charles Morgan

Each time my husband went out to his truck he brought in another empty box. My heart was being torn into a million pieces. "Oh, please, stop. This hurts so much." But he just continued as he hummed the tune of our wedding song. I couldn't believe how cruel a person could be, especially to move out on Christmas Day! My two sons were busy in the basement playing with all of the new toys that Santa had brought while their father packed up his belongings. He was leaving! This time it was for good. He even took his stocking that was "hung by the chimney with care." My husband often equated himself to the "Grinch" and now he was stealing Christmas from us! Would Christmas ever be the same again?

I spent a year and a half working hard to keep my two sons in the beautiful two-story colonial home that we had just bought before their father left. It had been quite unbearable and I tried keeping a positive attitude, which wasn't always easy.

Finally, we did have to move out of our home into an apartment building. This was an enormous transition for all of us. We had lost many of the material things that we had worked hard to obtain. We had also lost our yard and our freedom to live within our own boundaries. Now we had rules and many guidelines, like: "No riding bicycles on the property. No nails or holes in the walls. No noise after 8 PM." That was especially hard for boys!

But the biggest adjustment was yet to come. Somehow, by my husband leaving, our family unit was broken. Dinnertimes were no longer the same. Birthdays and holidays were now shared or split. This was the most painful part of all in the divorce.

It was Thanksgiving of 2006 and we were celebrating at my brother's home. His house was filled with wonderful smells and each couple looked so happy together. The children were running around in their "Sunday Best" and excitement was in the air for the upcoming holidays. I tried to keep myself together, but then the basket with a pen and paper was handed off to me. "Here, this is for the Pollyanna." This was our family's gift exchange for all of the nieces and nephews. I immediately began shaking and ran upstairs. I found a quiet place and sobbed my heart out.

I couldn't even bear the thought. I was struggling so desperately financially and emotionally. I needed to figure out how to get through the next few weeks and survive Christmas.

Each night, I got on my knees in prayer. "Lord, help me to get through this. Give me the strength I need to be alone. Guide my ways and the path I take. And God, if there is someone out there especially designed for me, please send him to me. I promise not to look myself."

I came up with the idea to bake cookies and make homemade candies during the weeks approaching Christmas. I could give them as gifts and when my boys were with their father on Christmas Day, I would visit neighbors and friends and deliver some joy.

The door closed as my boys ran out. "Bye, Mommy, Merry Christmas, See you later!" My countertops were filled with baskets and plates all wrapped in cellophane and big red bows waiting to be delivered. Tags marked, "Merry Christmas, Enjoy! Love, Marisa, Colin and Jacob."

I took a quick shower and refused to cry. My first stop was one of my upstairs neighbors whom I knew on a first-name basis. I knocked on the door and a beautiful young lady answered it. Surprised at her appearance, I said, "Merry Christmas, these are for Ricky."

"Oh, Daddy... someone brought you cookies!"

She was smiling at me as her father walked to the door.

"Merry Christmas, come on in."

"No, no. I have quite a few deliveries to make."

Ricky stopped to introduce me to his daughter. I already knew Kelsey, who lived with him. Amanda was visiting for the holidays.

"You didn't make these yourself, did you?"

"Every one of them. I baked them all with my own hands." With a cracking voice, I blurted out, "My husband left me two years ago on Christmas Day and this is my way of getting through it."

I was quickly given an invitation to join Ricky and his girls for dinner later, but I had too many plans myself. "I'll take a rain check."

"How about we have a cup of holiday cheer later?"

"Maybe. Gotta go. Merry Christmas!"

As it turned out, I did join Ricky and his girls along with my boys. Secretly, Ricky's daughters played matchmaker. They just recently shared their little plot with me almost four years later. Kelsey worked on her father and Amanda worked on me. The girls would not let me be alone anymore. From that Christmas on, I was invited to share in all their plans.

Ricky and I will be married this summer on the beach and Christmas has new meaning for me. Though I had lost so much, I have now gained a wonderful fiancé, two daughters, a new grandson, and lots of love. My prayer was answered and it's Christmas again!

~Marisa A. Snyder

Saving Christmas Dinner

A three-year-old gave this reaction to her Christmas dinner:
"I don't like the turkey, but I like the bread he ate."
~Author Unknown

other passed away in 1996, and our grief was overwhelming. However, not until Christmastime did her death seem to swallow us in despair. Christmas dinner brought back more loneliness and pain than any of her sons, daughters-in-law, or grandchildren expected.

Momma always went overboard during the Yuletide season. She finished all the baking and candy making several days earlier. Containers of divinity candy, peanut brittle, and fudge sat stacked on counters, and on the screened porch sat a coconut cake and a stack cake, both aging and soaking up their own juices. Dozens of sausage balls and Rice Krispies squares were replenished throughout the season.

Christmas Eve began the serious cooking. Mother crammed an enormous turkey into the oven, where she basted it hourly throughout the night, and then made dumplings, yeast rolls, mashed potatoes, green beans, gravy, and best of all, dressing. Folks in the North prepare meals by stuffing some kind of concoction, complete with fruit and nuts, into their birds. In the South, women bake dressing.

The base ingredient of this ambrosia is cornbread or, if that's not available, bread or biscuits. The rest of the recipe is made up of things that each woman decides enhance the taste. The mixture is put into a casserole dish or pans and baked until the top is crisp. That simple food is the most important part of Christmas dinner down here.

Mother made several pans of dressing. In one she laid a bed of oysters, and all but my older brother avoided it. The hope at the end of Christmas Day was that enough was left to take home for late-night snacks or the next day's lunch. After her death, we would eat our meals without Momma's dressing, and facing life without it nearly broke my family's heart. She left us without having ever written her recipe down. She always said, "I use a pinch of this and a tad of that." That's not much for the next generation to go on.

My wife Amy had been a professional for years—a professional mother and a successful woman working in the business world. Her workday began at 8:00 AM and ended sometime around 5:30 in the evening. When she arrived home, her second job started. The kids needed her help, and she had dinner to fix, clothes to wash, and any of a dozen other chores to complete each night before she fell exhausted into bed. Over the years she'd become a wonderful cook who received highest praises from her family and friends for her ability to work all day and prepare a feast for dinner.

Amy understood how important that dressing was to her family. In fact, she craved a piece of it as well. She scoured Mother's cookbooks for an index card or slip of paper, anything that might give a clue to the ingredients. Nothing was ever found. Each time a turkey was prepared for any meal, Amy heard the sad voices of her children as they lamented the lack of good dressing for the feast. I further added to the problem by exclaiming those terrible, inexcusable words, "It doesn't taste like Momma's." I was forgiven for my insensitivity only because Amy loved and missed that holiday dish too.

She set out to find the right mixture of ingredients in Mother's dressing. My overworked wife made batch after batch of the stuff but never asked anyone how it tasted. Her own memory served as the evaluator. Each attempt edged closer to the original, but something was still missing. Amy never gave up, though, and with each failure she became more determined to crack the secret recipe. During those years our family ate Thanksgiving meals with Amy's extended family. At Christmas we shared our meals with my brothers and their families. We ate the dressing that was prepared, but with each bite my brood missed Mother and her magic in the kitchen.

Five years later, Amy served an amazing dinner to our family. Christmas was still months away, but on the table sat a plump turkey breast. All the standard fare, including Southern sweet tea, sat before us. Amy then walked into the kitchen, and she returned holding before her a large pan of dressing. Lacey, Dallas, and I smiled politely at her, but we dreaded what we were sure would be another poor imposter. I dug out a corner piece and placed it upon my plate. The kids and I took bites at the same time.

No way! Impossible! It's a miracle! Before us sat a full dish of what tasted exactly like Mother's dressing. The kids gobbled it up, and I hurriedly ate my first piece and reached for another. We didn't care about the other food; we'd just been reunited with a food that had been missing for too long.

Amy stood and watched as we made pigs of ourselves. Never had she worn such a warm smile. She had worked for years to recreate the dressing her children and husband loved so much. Finally, her hard work paid dividends as my wonderful, loving wife discovered the right quantity of the secret ingredient: sage.

When Momma died, she left behind a loving family. She also left a group who held tradition in high regard. Amy missed Mother too, and she worked hard, harder than most wives and moms would work, to bring one small memory back. Amy's dressing is eaten quickly each time it's served. She has given so much to her family, and in return, we look at her as a woman and mother who works miracles. Her conquering the dressing dilemma brought joy back to meals and saved Christmas dinner.

~Joe Rector

Good Things Come in Large Packages

You know when you have found your prince because you not only have a smile on your face but in your heart as well.
~Author Unknown

"May I stop by? I just happened to be Christmas shopping in your neighborhood." Why was my boyfriend shopping in my neighborhood? There was a perfectly good mall down in his neck of the woods.

"Sure!" I said. "I'll make some hot chocolate."

Ten minutes later he stood on my doorstep holding a huge box that obscured his face. Gingerly, he walked in and set the box under the Christmas tree. It was beautifully wrapped and had a large red bow on the top.

"This is for you," he stated. "You can't open it until Christmas morning."

Christmas was three days away. This was not going to be easy. What in the world could be in such a large package? We sipped our hot chocolate and chatted in front of the fire, all the while keeping one eye on that box. When my boyfriend rose to leave he told me he would be back early Christmas morning. "We'll open our presents together. Won't that be fun?" I nodded in agreement and gave him my word that I would not open the mysterious gift under the tree.

After we parted I returned to the box. Yes, I had promised not to open it. However, nothing was ever said about not shaking it. I lifted the package and was surprised by its lightness. Then I gave it a few gentle shakes. Nothing. No sound of anything moving inside. Apparently, the contents were packed very well.

Throughout the next couple of days I went about my business and tried to ignore the huge gift under the tree. The gift, however, did not ignore me; after all, it literally had my name on it and called out to me. Several times a day I stopped to give it a little shake, straining to hear something move inside. My imagination conjured up all sorts of contents: skis; a bicycle; the complete library of classic literature. I even hoped my two Beagles would tear it open, but for once they decided to be good. They knew Santa Paws was coming and they were not about to take any chances.

On Christmas morning my boyfriend arrived at the crack of dawn, his facial expression one of eagerness mingled with some anxiety. He nervously took the cup of coffee I offered.

"Would you like some breakfast before we open our gifts?" I asked.

"No thanks," he replied. "We can eat later."

We walked to the living room and stood in front of the Christmas tree.

"Wait!" I exclaimed. "Don't you think we should have a time of prayer first? After all, it is Christmas."

My boyfriend sighed heavily. "Okay," he consented.

We sat on the couch and I reached for my Bible. "I'd like to read the Nativity story from the Gospel of Luke." Slowly and deliberately I began the familiar narrative: "There were shepherds abiding in a field, keeping watch over their flocks by night..." When I finished reading I closed my eyes to pray and thanked God for his many blessings during the past year, particularly for the wonderful man sitting beside me. I paused and waited for my boyfriend to express his feelings and thankfulness to the Lord. Instead, I heard, "Okay, can we open our presents now?"

I was incredulous. I knew my boyfriend to be a Godly man, but at that moment his mind was obviously elsewhere. "Don't you have anything you'd like to say?" He bowed his head and muttered a few words that sounded scripted and akin to "Rub a Dub Dub, Thanks for the Grub." I decided to not push the issue and agreed to let the gift opening begin.

We took turns unwrapping our presents to one another. There were the standard yet comfortable gifts: a red sweater and coordinating shirt; pajamas and matching slippers; a pillow in the form of a gingerbread man. Finally, there was one package left, the Big One. My boyfriend set it before me and urged me to open it. I tore away the meticulous wrapping and lifted the lid. Inside was newspaper. Lots of newspaper. I waded through it until I found a photo album. The cover contained a picture of the two of us at our favorite restaurant.

"I put together an album of all the places we've gone and all the things we've done since we met; a year and a half of memories. Go ahead and look at the pictures."

I was touched by such a thoughtful gift, something that had taken time rather than a lot of money. I began to flip through the pages that recounted hiking trips and apple picking, a birthday dinner at an elegant French restaurant, a quiet New Year's Eve in my home. As I turned the fourth page I saw a flash of light and something sparkly. There, nestled in one of the photo pockets, was a breathtaking diamond engagement ring.

My mouth fell open but no speech emerged. I was completely caught off guard. My boyfriend removed the ring from the album and got down on one knee. "Laurel, I love you and I want to spend the rest of my life with you. Will you marry me?"

"Yes!" I managed to utter. "Yes, I will marry you!"

Four months later we were wed in a small but elegant ceremony.

I have experienced many Christmas holidays and, God willing, I will experience many more. None, however, can or will compare to that Christmas, the Christmas of the Large Package that contained an even bigger gift, a gift of the heart.

~Laurel Vaccaro Hausman

In My Father's Eyes

Our wedding was many years ago. The celebration continues to this day.
~Gene Perret

It had been more than twenty years since my father's death, and Christmas loomed a few months away. As always, I missed Dad terribly. Not only did I long for him, I needed to remember—things I was afraid of forgetting.

Dad had a way of making me feel special, smart, pretty—all the things I didn't usually feel around others. The love was always there—in his eyes. And when I saw this, I knew everything was going to be all right.

Knowing Mom would have what I needed, my husband and I went to her place the next day. I hauled out a box of her old pictures, searching for photographs of Dad, while my husband read the paper.

Sifting through the box, I came across an old 5x7 photograph I'd never seen. Dad's classic smile lit up his face. My gaze traveled toward his eyes, until something distracted me—moose antlers.

Seriously.

Huge antlers stuck out, one on each side of his head.

Can you believe that?

I finally figured out, thanks to Mom, that someone snapped the photo at the Moose Lodge with Dad standing in front of the mascot. Antlers and all, I still wanted the picture.

A few hours later, I hopped into the truck and flashed the photo in front of my husband. "Isn't it great?"

"What's up with the antlers?"

I flipped my hand. "Oh, it was taken at the Moose Lodge."

"Oh… that's too bad."

"I still want a copy."

I set the picture on the compartment between the seats. "Whatever you do, do not lose this."

"I'm not going to lose your dad's picture," he said, as if I was accusing him of already having done the deed.

Men.

We arrived home and went into the house. And can you guess who went off and left the picture in the truck?

Moi.

The next day, when I finally remembered, I called my husband's cell phone. "Do you have Dad's photo?"

"Yes, dear, and it's fine."

"Oh, thank God. Where is it?"

"I've already put it inside the compartment, so it will be safe."

"Well, just don't forget it when you get home."

Ahem… like I did.

"I won't."

My husband came home from work, and I bolted into the kitchen, holding out my hand. "Well?"

"It's out in the truck."

"Is the truck locked?"

"Yeah, but I'll get it the next time I go out."

I jiggled my hand. "Give me the keys."

"Oh for Pete's sakes, Deb."

He fished his keys out of his pocket and dangled them in front of me.

I grabbed them, went out and unlocked the truck, reached inside and flipped the compartment open. When I saw Dad and his antlers, relief washed over me.

After I returned to the kitchen, I pulled open a drawer on the china cabinet and slipped the snapshot inside, vowing to copy it later.

Did I mention that I'm a serious procrastinator?

A few days before Christmas, I remembered the snapshot, so I went to the china cabinet and pulled the drawer open.

The photograph was gone.

I fished through papers, trinkets, and more until I finally reached the bottom.

Nothing.

When my husband came home from work, I again bolted into the kitchen. "Have you seen Dad's picture?"

He tossed his keys on the counter. "What are you talking about?"

"You know—the one with the antlers. Weren't you standing here the day I put it in the drawer?"

"I don't know. I don't remember now."

I rolled my eyes. I don't know. I don't remember now.

Men.

A few days later, and still no picture, I made the mistake of saying something to Mom.

"You lost your father's picture?" she said.

Why couldn't I keep my mouth shut?

"No, Mom. I misplaced it is all. I'll find it."

But I didn't.

Ho. Ho. Ho.

I later wrapped the gifts for my husband, his family, my family, and then placed them under the tree. As I stood there, I noticed something.

Why weren't there any presents under the tree for me?

Christmas Eve arrived, and we went to his parents' house, as we did every year, and had a nice time with his family. They gave me gifts.

On the way home, a thought popped into my brain. I'll bet he slipped my presents under the tree before we left for his mom and dad's house.

We arrived home, and like a child, I went rooting under the tree—nothing there. I knew I'd receive gifts when my family arrived Christmas night, but knowing this didn't help. A man should have a gift for his wife come Christmas morning.

Bah. Humbug.

Wait.

Christmas morning.

I slapped my forehead. Of course, he was going to sneak it under the tree before I got out of bed. How silly could I be? I snickered with glee, like the child I used to be.

Christmas morning arrived, and my husband, who looked like the giddy child I was the night before, asked if I was ready to open gifts.

I looked under the tree—still nothing.

How dare he?

I waved my hand. "You mean your gifts?"

I walked over, retrieved his presents, and dropped them on the coffee table in front of him. He patted the sofa. "Aren't you going to sit by me?"

Did he want to survive to see Christmas next year?

I sat down.

He opened his first two gifts, ever so happy, while I sat there and pouted.

Hello? What was wrong with this picture? (No pun intended.)

He paused. "I have to go to the bathroom."

I cradled my head in my hands, secretly hoping he'd fall in. The next thing I knew, a large package came sliding across the floor in front of my feet. I raised my head, and my eyes widened.

He smiled and pointed. "Open it."

I ripped the paper off, gasped, and then bawled.

Right in front of me sat a large framed picture of Dad—the one with the antlers, only the antlers were gone. It looked like Dad had posed in a professional studio—a heavenly one at that.

"How did you do this?" I croaked.

"Thought I didn't get you anything, didn't you?"

His chest swelled, bless his heart.

"Oh, and I had it digitally re-mastered for you," he added.

I stared at the picture. Memories of Christmases past, even those I thought I had forgotten, flooded my heart as I looked in my father's eyes.

"Thank you," I said, suddenly noticing the same love in my husband's eyes as he looked at me.

Men.

I hung the picture, knowing everything was going to be all right.

~Deborah Young Anderson

The Christmas Contest

A wise lover values not so much the gift of the lover as the love of the giver.
~Thomas á Kempis

I suspect that most people secretly dislike Christmas shopping for their significant other. It's not that I dislike shopping. It's shopping for my husband that changes things. And for the record, this has nothing to do with pressure from him because, honestly, the man would be pleased as punch with a greeting card and a kiss. But rather it's the expectation to deliver that "Wow" factor, wanting to choose a gift that combines precisely the right amount of thoughtfulness, usefulness, and oh-that's-so-you-ness—just like he manages to do for me each holiday.

It's enough to drive even a shopaholic like me nuts.

So, one morning in late November, Scott and I were in bed—still in our PJs and watching the Food Network—when we engaged in one of those conversations with no definitive beginning or end. We went from phyllo dough to snowblowers to vacationing in Montego Bay, Jamaica. Finally, the topic turned to Christmas gifts for one another.

"I don't want—or need—anything," I declared. Sure, I couldn't deny that the well-oiled tradition of trading presents was great fun, but I really didn't want anything. "What do you want?" I countered.

"Nothing," he said. "But we could make a deal...."

A deal to not buy one another something? "I don't understand,"

I said, hoisting myself on my elbows. He had summoned my full attention.

"We could impose a limit on spending or something...." his voice trailed off.

"Go on," I urged. I was truly interested in seeing where he was going with this.

"Seventy-seven dollars and seventy-seven cents," he said pointedly. "We'll see who can come closest. That has to include wrapping paper and everything."

"Fine," I replied, feigning confidence. "You're on."

But what I really wanted to say was, "Oh, drat!"

I had to admit it was romantic. We were married on 07-07-07 at 7:07 PM, thus the significance of the number seven. But still. As if buying for the man who has everything wasn't already hard enough. Now he had to go and impose the additional challenge of a price limit.

This was right out of Scott's playbook—I mean that literally, as he is a former offensive lineman for the Detroit Lions. A few Christmases ago, he had the "brilliant" idea of making one another's gifts. Armed with stacks of construction paper, brand new glue sticks, and all of my football paraphernalia, my intention was to capture the depth of his football career with a poignant collage.

Again, that was my intention.

It ended up looking like a fifth-grader's art project.

Not to be outdone, Scott presented me with a watercolor painting that was the spitting image of our first photograph. Show-off.

That portrait currently hangs in our kitchen nook. My shadow-box is in the basement.

Enough said.

And now, once again, I was faced with fulfilling yet another one of his stipulations; it was like déjà vu.

When Christmas morning arrived nearly a month later, I was feeling pretty good about my gift for Scott. True, I had exceeded the price limit by $2.40, but I was certain I would win the challenge.

At 4:30 AM, I shuffled out of bed and quietly scurried to the Christmas tree with the gifts in hand. In the dim glow provided by the tree's bevy of colored lights, I surveyed what was already there. Nothing new had been added. I had beaten Scott to the punch!

With a faint air of cockiness beginning to take root, I returned to bed and the warmth of Scott's presence.

Despite my excitement, I managed to return to a slumber so deep that I awoke only after I had rolled over to Scott's side of the bed and realized that he wasn't there. I ran my hand across the comforter to verify what my eyes already knew.

It was 7:32 AM.

And I smelled coffee.

By the time I had arrived at the tree, Scott was already there, waiting for me, wearing a mischievous grin.

"Coffee?"

"To get you out of bed," he said.

He knew me all too well.

"Let's get this party started," I said, falling to my knees to retrieve his gifts. "Open this one first, then this one," I instructed.

I watched with bated breath as Scott proceeded to open a hard-cover coffee table book about the history of brandy and an Elsa Peretti for Tiffany brandy snifter. The brandy connoisseur that he was, I was certain I had nailed it. I cupped both hands over my mouth and waited for him to speak.

"Wow. I... you won," he said holding the glass to the light before returning his attention to me. "You're amazing." He lowered himself onto the floor and kissed me gently.

I had dreamt of "winning"—whatever that meant—but I had not envisioned what that would actually feel like. The compliment nearly brought me to tears. I bit my lip nervously. "Nope, I went over by $2.40," I admitted, certain that the revelation would somehow encourage him to rescind his praise.

"This," he said gesturing to the items, "is pretty tough to beat. Your turn—look behind the tree."

I did as told and found two packages, a small one and a larger one. I grabbed the small one and ripped the paper dramatically like a small child.

In my hands was a white shadowbox which contained my most prized pair of track spikes, exactly as they were when I had last worn them during my final track meet in high school almost fifteen years ago. The laces were dingy from years of repetitive long jumping, and the right shoe even had the infamous cushion in the sole, a reminder that I had chosen to compete despite having a bruised heel. I made lots of happy memories in those shoes.

"Scott," I said, barely able to speak. "How did you know?" my voice was now cracking, words nearly garbled.

I held the box close to my chest, as if to hug the treasures inside.

"There's more," he said, nodding toward the larger item.

In one fell swoop, I removed the paper from the front and turned the picture around to face me.

That's when the waterworks came.

The top read ROCKETS VARSITY TRACK. It was a 33" x 23" professionally done poster that contained four black and white photos of me long jumping at a home track meet. Below the photo was JOHN GLENN HIGH SCHOOL CLASS OF 1995.

It was hard to believe that the girl in the photo was… me. It all came back. Her passion. Her spunk.

How did Scott know about her?

Come to find out, he had rummaged through several boxes of photos I had tucked away in our basement's furnace room where I had kept nearly every photo from adolescence. Unbeknownst to me, Scott had been poring over them for months.

And his total cost?

A total of $76.25.

"You may have won the challenge," I began, "But I am the recipient of the best gift," I said, smiling.

"I'm glad you like them," he said proudly.

"I mean you."

~Courtney Conover

A Divine Christmas Tradition

Daughter am I in my mother's house, but mistress in my own.
~Rudyard Kipling

A picture-perfect Christmas Eve afternoon—carols drifting softly from the stereo, three lights twinkling, the neighbors' kids gathered to play *Monopoly* in the rec room. A slow all-day drizzle settled in over the Pacific Northwest.

Dad came upstairs from working on his car in the garage.

"Whaddya say you and I try making some divinity?" he asked me while reaching for the double boiler.

"Uh-oh," said Mom. "You're going to attempt making divinity while it's raining?" She got her purse and coat from the hall closet. "I think I'll just run to the store for a few last-minute groceries. I'll be back in an hour or so."

Dad laughed as she backed the car out of the driveway. "Happens every year," he mused.

"Why is that?" I asked.

"Oh, years ago, when your mother and I were just married, we thought it would be nice to start a family Christmas tradition. We decided to make divinity together one damp Christmas Eve."

"Just like you and me today, right?"

"Well, not exactly. You see, we were pretty young and neither of us really knew how to make the stuff. We didn't have a candy thermometer, and we didn't even have a clue what 'hard ball stage' meant."

"So what happened?"

"Let's just say it's a miracle we didn't burn the house down."

"Oh, Dad, you're exaggerating."

I soon finished chopping the walnuts, leaned my elbows on the counter, and watched him pour the cooked corn syrup over the whipped egg whites. We set the light and fluffy candy aside to cool. Then Dad started a second batch.

"Don't you think we've made enough?" I asked.

Dad didn't answer.

"Dad! Wait! You're not even using the thermometer! You're sure to ruin it! It won't set up!"

He smiled. "You just don't understand yet about traditions."

Mom arrived home as I was cutting the first divinity into one-inch squares, placing half a maraschino cherry atop each piece.

"I'm home," she called. "I brought chocolate ice cream."

"Chocolate ice cream?" I asked, taking the grocery sack from her.

"Sure," said Mom. "We'll need something to pour the ruined divinity over."

"But Mom, how did you know?"

Mom laughed. "Your dad always gets too anxious about his candy making. The first batch he makes never sets up, so we pour it over ice cream."

"The first batch?" I asked incredulously, looking quickly at Dad, who was busying himself with the dishes.

"It's kind of a tradition," said Mom. "And after a few years everyone in the house learned to just get out of the way till it's over." She turned to put the ice cream in the freezer.

Catching my eye, Dad shook his head, placed a finger to his lips, and winked.

~Jan Bono

Chapter 3

The Gift of Christmas

Close Encounters of the Santa Kind

The Christmas Eve Race

Blessed is the season which engages the whole world in a conspiracy of love!
~Hamilton Wright Mabie

"You'd better go right to bed when we get home," my mother said, glancing over at me. "Santa can't come until you're asleep."

Or something like that. I wasn't paying much attention. I was four years old, and I was simultaneously cranky, overtired and excited. It was well after dark, and my mother and I were driving home from a Christmas Eve visit with friends. I slumped in my car seat and looked out the windows at the snowy December night.

Everything about the world seemed different on Christmas Eve. There was something that made the trees sparkle under the snow and made the air seem crisp with excitement and anticipation.

I wanted to stay up and savor it all. Even at four, I was a night owl. I didn't like going to sleep while the rest of the world was still up and about, and I was the tiny queen of stalling techniques. Christmas Eve wasn't going to be an exception to that.

As we rounded the corner and began to drive down our street, I noticed some activity at a house near the corner. Under the porch lights, it was easy to see the figure, a tall man who had paused in the doorway. A tall man with a red and white suit that stood out in the dark winter night.

My mother and I shrieked. I knew who that figure was. I'd visited him in a department store a few weeks ago.

All at once the drive home took on an air of urgency. "Hurry!" I shouted. Santa couldn't visit unless I was asleep, but there he was, just down the block! Why had he shown up so early? Was it later than I'd thought it was? The rest of the drive down the block seemed to take hours, and my eyes darted back and forth nervously as I watched for any sign of Santa's arrival.

My mother parked the car and hustled me upstairs. We were trying to beat the clock. I don't even remember how I managed to get out of my boots, coat and Christmas Eve clothes and into my yellow pajamas, but I did, and I did it at warp speed.

As I hurriedly brushed my teeth, my young mind spun on its axis. Which house had Santa been leaving? Was it five doors down? Six? Maybe it was seven. What would happen if I still wasn't asleep by the time he arrived? I all but catapulted myself into bed and squeezed my eyes shut, willing myself to sleep.

As it turned out, Santa didn't miss my house. When I awoke in the morning and walked into the living room, the plate of cookies I had left for Santa was empty and a colorful array of presents greeted me from under the tree. He'd waited up for me.

We never did find out how or why Santa had been leaving our neighbors' house that evening. The gift he gave to me, and to my mother, stayed with us though. For me, he'd brought the spirit of Christmas to life. And for my mum, he'd provided a peaceful Christmas Eve night, with a child who neither stalled nor whined about going to bed. As she's told me several times since then, I'd never fallen asleep that quickly in my life — not before, and not after. Santa had shown us both, for a moment, that sometimes it was worth believing in magic.

~Denise Reich

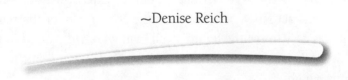

Dog Day Surprise

If you can look at a dog and not feel vicarious excitement and affection,
you must be a cat.
~Author Unknown

With just fifteen shopping days left, the department store's Christmas Wonderland was in full swing with Santa, two elves, and a photographer. Two days during the season were set aside as "Bring Your Pet to See Santa" time, one day exclusively for cats, the other for dogs.

On "dog day," I brought my freshly groomed West Highland Terrier, Skipper, and Portuguese Water Dog, Max, for their annual visit. We joined the other dogs and owners waiting in line and watched Santa give each dog a treat as he greeted them.

When it was their turn, Skipper and Max tugged at their leashes to reach him. Santa handed each one a biscuit and called him by name. Skipper wolfed down his treat, jumped in Santa's lap and sniffed his beard.

"Well, hello Skipper!" Santa said with a laugh. "Have you been a good dog?"

Skipper planted a kiss on Santa's nose.

"I'll take that as a 'yes,'" said Santa. He reached down and scratched Max's ear. "And what about you?"

Max licked his hand.

"Well, my two little angels, it's time for a picture." With Skipper under his right arm and Max by his side, Santa posed for the camera.

Just as the photographer snapped the photo, the dog at the end of the line barked an alert. Skipper and Max snapped to attention.

I followed their gaze and saw a woman cradling a cat in her arms. She must have confused the dates. When the frightened cat wriggled out of its owner's arms and ran for cover, Skipper and Max charged toward the enemy.

"Grab the leashes!" Santa shouted. The elves and I lunged, but the dogs were too quick. Working as a team, Skipper and Max each took off in a different direction as the cat dodged through clothing racks and between counters.

"Skipper! Max!" I called.

"Sophie!" yelled the cat owner.

The fugitives ignored our calls. The dogs still in line jumped and barked in chorus as if cheering on Skipper and Max, drowning out the store's Christmas music. A rack of shirts tumbled to the floor.

"Doggie! Doggie!" shouted one grinning little girl who reached out her hand as Skipper raced by.

I ran after Max, who continued the first floor patrol while an elf chased Skipper who soon bounded up the down escalator. The moving steps were no match for a Westie in pursuit. When Skipper reached the second floor, the elf was out of breath at the bottom, unable to keep up.

Customers and clerks on the first floor shouted, "They're over here!" When I dodged shoppers and clerks staring at a disheveled shoe display, I knew I was on the right path. Max's throaty barks, now in rapid succession like rifle fire, told me the cat was cornered. Looking in the direction of the barks, I saw a cat sitting amidst a rainbow of sweaters on a high shelf. Max jumped, straining to reach her, ignoring the sweaters his scraping paws pulled off the lower shelves and onto the floor. Sophie hissed at both of us when I grabbed Max's leash and escorted him outside to the car. One dog secured, one more to go.

When I returned to the store to search for Skipper, I heard the following announcement: "Will the owner of a small white dog please come to the hair salon on the second floor?" I hustled as fast as I could through the holiday crowd, ignoring the feline perpetrator being carried out by its owner.

As I approached the salon, I heard one stylist say, "What a cute little dog."

"Who does your fur?" asked another stylist as she picked up Skipper and admired his coiffure. Skipper leaned his head back and grinned, soaking up the adoration.

When I retrieved Skipper, a stern-faced manager approached and motioned me aside. Our conversation was brief. Although any jury of dog owners would clearly find the cat to be the guilty party, the manager's unjust verdict was final: Skipper and Max were not to set paws in the store again.

~Janet Hartman

An Interview with Santa

May Peace be your gift at Christmas and your blessing all year through!
~Author Unknown

As I was packing up to leave I spotted the old gentleman kindly smiling at me. He had an indescribable charm about him that made me stop for a moment and talk with him. Let's face it, I am either good at interviews or bad at them, but either way I end up doing them, mostly to the satisfaction of my editors.

One of the simplest ones I have done has turned out to be one of the most inspiring. I got to interview Santa Claus. All I ever knew about Santa was *'Twas the Night Before Christmas: A Visit from St. Nicholas* by Clement C. Moore, *Yes Virginia, There Is A Santa Claus* and the Coca-Cola ads which I was told commercialized Santa.

It was just as the annual Christmas parade was coming together that I had Santa slip to the side for a few quick questions. There he stood in a redder than usual suit with a pure white beard, really shiny black boots and a belt that was obviously too big for him. What was also obvious was the fact that this was all for show.

To his side was an elderly gentleman gently caring for Santa, dusting his shoulders, making sure the suit wasn't dirty, the boots not scuffed, and that all was right in the world for Santa, so that he could dazzle the hoards of kids lining the snow-covered streets, awaiting his arrival. Cool?

I asked Santa the usual questions and in a minute or two the interview was over and I was on my way to my next conquest.

As I was packing up to leave I spotted the old gentleman kindly smiling at me. He had an indescribable charm about him that made me stop for a moment and talk with him. I took the opportunity to ask him a question or two, starting with, "How did you get the privilege of being Santa's helper?"

"Well," he said, "many years ago I was the man who rode on the sled and I could never quite give up the role. I genuinely enjoyed the shiny faces of the kids who came out in the cold to see me."

"Very nice!" I was quick to say.

"So, old timer, then you know the true meaning of Christmas?" I shot toward him.

"I think I do," he quipped with a smile. "You see, I am not advanced in years as much as I am advanced in wisdom."

"Well said!" I proclaimed, remembering something my grandfather always said: "Live and learn, otherwise it's not living."

"So, then, how do you feel about all the commercialization where Christmas is concerned?"

Without blinking, he was quick to state, "It has its advantages as well as its disadvantages."

I couldn't help but chuckle at the truth in his words. "So then the Santa we all know from the Coca-Cola ads got you some fame and fortune as a result of the exposure?"

"Yes, of course and it didn't hurt Coke's business either!" he quipped.

"Oh," I said, chuckling, "I get it! It has to do with give and take, like all business, right?"

"Not quite, it has more to do with communication, reaching out to the people through whatever medium is the handiest."

"So you are saying that Coca-Cola didn't make you famous?"

"Not at all, son. Legend has made me famous; I just used them to promote the love and warmth of Christmas. It must've worked too because people are still searching for posters, calendars and all kinds of remnants from that era and that was over fifty years ago. They tend to reach back to happier times in their lives."

"So then where does one go from here?" I inquired.

"We all long for world peace, for hope for the future and for a safe world to live in, correct?"

"Yes, sir.

"Well you won't find that in a bottle of Coke, but you might find it in the spirit of Santa! Santa Claus has been a representative of love and hope and peace for centuries and I promise not to go away now, just when I am needed the most."

"But Santa, it seems like such a greedy and unappreciative world today. Don't you feel like giving up?"

"Not at all, son, I am inspired by the world around me. I learn from those who have suffered tragedy and yet don't give up. I am inspired by an elephant in India who with three legs walks along with his herd to the watering hole, quite often being helped along by the others in the group. I am inspired by the singing miner from Springhill who when facing his death in the darkness of a mine collapse found comfort singing hymns, and the woman who risked her own life by saving a drowning fawn that had fallen from a bridge into the river below, as well as countless others who continue to show courage and inspire me."

"It seems to me that nobody shows the true spirit of Christmas, like where is God in all this?" I wondered.

"Look closely and you will see love and where there is love, there is God. He will never abandon you either. After all, it's not about the toys as much as it's the anticipation of them. It's not about the family gatherings as much as it is the families, and it's not about who is right or who is wrong as long as one is willing to admit that we are all wrong once in a while. It's about stopping for a moment and appreciating the world around you. About honoring those who have gone on before us and those who are up and coming. We can learn from both you know.

"It's about forgiving ourselves and those we have wronged, it's about pride, friendship and humanity and sharing that love and wisdom and tradition with those around us. My advice to man today is to learn to accept the beauty in this world that has never faded despite wars, weather and loss of faith, I know it's all still in there, it just has to be brought to the surface."

"I have to admit, Santa, you have certainly given me something to think about," I said.

"Well, then I guess I have done my job, haven't I?" Again smiling and winking.

Suddenly, looking into his smiling face, I was able to see the ageless beauty of Santa, the wonders he has performed over the centuries and was reminded as to just how much we love him and how willing we all are to be good boys and girls so that he might not pass us by. Perhaps I just needed a reminder to place a little goodness back into my heart in this holiday season.

As I walked toward my car I couldn't help but look over my shoulder at him, working away behind the scenes so that the man on the sleigh in the parade could have all the glory, and again I was reminded of the real selflessness needed to bring forward the true meaning of Christmas.

~Richard Todd Canton

The Christmas House

Even as an adult I find it difficult to sleep on Christmas Eve.
Yuletide excitement is a potent caffeine, no matter your age.
~Carrie Latet

The Christmas season is steeped in secular tradition for me, as I imagine it might be for many people in my generation. My family never went to church, but Christmas Eve dinner HAD to be hosted at my grandparents' house. We didn't say grace, but my father ALWAYS made homemade Chex Mix for the family—and I wrapped emptied cashew tins with wrapping paper to deliver the stuff in. I painted my fingernails red and green and gold and slipped gaudy pairs of jingle bell earrings in my lobes for weeks on end. And most importantly, every winter, my parents and I drove our boxy 1990 Nissan Sentra past The Christmas House.

The Christmas House was a classic country home planted on the broad side of a T-intersection in Waukegan, Illinois. Eleven months of the year, it was beautiful. In December, its halls were decked out to the nines. You could see it for half a mile as you drove north on County Street.

The Christmas House had a peaked roof perfect for lighting, which the owners trimmed in crystal twinkle lights. Its big, bay windows glowed day and night with the light of candles that never seemed to burn out. The yard, sloped ever so slightly as to give the impression that this house sat on a pedestal (which it deserved), featured every Christmas decoration a kid could hope for: light up snowmen; over-sized candy canes; nine plastic reindeer pulling a sleigh. Somehow, it even seemed to be dusted with a perpetual layer of fluffy snow. It looked like one of those ceramic houses you buy at Hallmark. That's how classic it was.

Driving past The Christmas House was a daily ritual in my family. Heck, it was a daily ritual for the entire neighborhood. Every single day between Black Friday and January 2nd, you could see a line of cars crawling past The Christmas House, parents and kids alike gawking through the windows. Whether on their way to school, on their way to the store or just on their way around the block, The Christmas House warranted a drive-by. The place was famous.

It was also magical.

One Christmas Eve, when I couldn't have been older than nine, we drove past The Christmas House late at night. We were on our way home from my grandparents' house, and even though we'd driven past the place earlier that day—twice—my dad made a detour to visit it one more time.

"Jessica," I heard my dad call out from the front seat.

I was asleep in the back, exhausted from a long night of opening presents from my eight very generous aunts and uncles. It was also way past my bedtime.

"Jessica!" he said, much more urgently this time.

I sat up, unsettled by the anxious tone in my father's normally level voice. Had we hit a reindeer?

"Look!"

My dad pointed out the window. Groggily, I wiped the layer of fog from my window with the palm of my hand, something my dad had always urged me not to do. ("Use your sleeve! Your hand leaves oils on the glass!")

As I blinked myself back to consciousness, I realized what all the commotion was about and squealed: "Santa Claus!"

Santa Claus was darting across the street. To The Christmas House.

"Santa!" my dad echoed, equally surprised.

A second later, the man in red was gone.

We just sat there for a while, stunned. Giddy with Christmas cheer. We'd seen Santa at the mall and on TV, but never out in the wild. On Christmas Eve. In the MIDDLE OF THE NIGHT. Where was the camera when you needed it?

Slowly, after it was clear Santa wasn't going to reappear, my parents and I drove away, jabbering all the way home about our remarkable sighting. How late was it? Where was Santa's sleigh? Did he mean for us to see him? Had he been to our house yet?

To this day, my father swears he can't explain the incident. He didn't know Santa was going to be right there, right in front of The Christmas House when we drove by. He didn't intentionally make a detour because he "knew" something. He had no idea where Santa came from or where he went after he'd finished his work at The Christmas House. My dad, a truly pragmatic man, was as surprised as I was.

That's why The Christmas House is so special to me. It wasn't spotting Santa Claus that excited me so much — although that was exciting. What tickles me pink is that this small moment, those fifteen seconds in a snow-covered compact car in front of The Christmas House, brought a twinkle to a grown man's eye. As an adult myself now, I find fewer and fewer events that impress me. I am awed less. But catching my father in a moment of genuine surprise, witnessing my down-to-earth dad absolutely floored by a Santa sighting, well, that meant something truly unique had just transpired.

That night, The Christmas House lived up to its name.

~Jess Knox

Santa's Gift

Whatever you believe with feeling becomes your reality.
~Brian Tracy

My husband and I both agree that Christmas is one of our favorite holidays. Anyone with children knows that the holiday is even more magical when you experience it through the innocent eyes of your children! Christmas with our four little ones is always exciting! There is never a dull moment.

As our oldest boy has grown, he has sometimes questioned the big jolly man's ability to really pull together all those presents. We have told him that he can believe what he wants, but he better be careful because we'd heard the number of unbelieving children getting coal in their stockings is on the rise. As any nine-year-old boy questioning Santa, he kept his eyes and ears open, ready for any evidence that would prove his theory to his naïve parents.

It wasn't until Christmas morning that he found the evidence he needed. As we were taking turns opening presents, we got to Lissy, our five-year-old daughter. Lissy is an adorable little girl who loves to sing at the top of her lungs. She picked out of her pile her largest, most perfectly wrapped gift with the tag that said, "To: Lissy, From: Santa." Without hesitation, she tore the paper off the gift to reveal the perfect present for our beautiful little performer—a karaoke machine! At that moment, Levi finally got the proof he had been looking for! He stood up and shouted with annoyed confidence, "That's it. Santa

DOES pick out the presents himself! There is NO way Mom and Dad would EVER be dumb enough to get Lissy something to make her even LOUDER!"

~April JaNae Homer

A Pact

Sometimes being a brother is even better than being a superhero.
~Marc Brown

"We have to make sure we're asleep before he comes," I said. My little brother's glance met the floor. I knew he was running something through his head. I was sure of it. It was one of the tiny details that stuck out to me in the four short years since his birth.

We were basically inseparable, me and Nick. It was funny. I was the big brother, the one who was supposed to give him a hard time, beat him up a little, and then abandon him to go play with my older friends. But it never occurred to me. Sure, we fought once in a while, but for the most part we'd been attached at the hip since my parents first brought him home from the hospital.

Of course, things were a little different before his birth. When Mom first told me I was about to get a little brother for Christmas, I told her, and I quote, "I'd rather have a puppy named Brownie." I didn't even bat an eyelash. But the whole puppy idea quickly vanished the first time an infant Nick squeezed my finger in his tiny fist. That's when I knew it'd be my job to protect the little bugger for the rest of my life.

"What time does he usually come?" he asked after mulling my statement a bit.

"I don't know. It's way past bedtime, I know that. But I heard if you open your eyes while he's in your house he'll disappear until next year."

"Really?" Nick sounded pretty alarmed.

"I don't know," I told him, "but if we're asleep then we don't have to worry. Promise?"

"I promise."

"And don't forget, first one awake gets the other one up before he goes downstairs." It was a tradition we'd created together the first year Nick was able to understand the whole concept of Santa Claus. More importantly, it was a pact not to be broken even under the direst of circumstances.

"Got it," he said. "Now, can we put the cookies out already?" I piled an ungodly amount of Mom's mistletoe-shaped butter cookies on a plate and watched as Nick picked all the bits of maraschino cherry off and stuffed them in his mouth. We poured a tall glass of ice-cold milk and placed our offering in the usual spot beside the fireplace. "Don't forget a carrot for Rudolph," Nick added.

When all the goodies were in place for Santa's Christmas Eve visit, Mom and Dad tucked us in for the night and the excruciating wait until morning began. That night, I spent countless hours clamping my eyelids shut as tightly as I could and rolling around uncomfortably in my bed. When that strategy failed, I simply stared blankly at the ceiling and traced the tiny cracks in the plaster with my eyeballs. I was sure Santa would be skipping our house, and it'd be entirely my fault. The glowing, red eyes of the alarm clock glared the numbers three, three, and zero into mine and I once again sewed them up tightly.

That's when I heard something.

It started as some light scratching from the base of the stairs. Then it graduated into a low, raspy creak that sounded like a rusty gate closing somewhere off in the distance. I kept my eyes shut and stayed deadly still in my bed. He couldn't possibly know I was awake if I stayed in this position, could he?

It got quiet again, but only for a moment before the scratching started up again. This went on and off for what seemed like an eternity.

I couldn't take it anymore. I had to at least sneak a peek at the clock. Maybe it was morning. I opened my left eyelid so slightly that everything appeared as one big blur, but I was able to make out that it was now 3:45 AM. Fifteen whole minutes had passed? It was excruciating and there was no sign of the noises stopping any time soon.

Santa couldn't still be down there, could he? I mean, how would he have time to visit all the other boys' and girls' houses if he spent so much time hanging around in mine? And that last question's the one that did the trick.

All of my courage in tow, I crept out of bed without making a sound and slithered past my parents' room on my belly. Then I stopped in front of Nick's room. I knew it was much too early to venture downstairs but I couldn't go another second without discovering the source of the peculiar noises.

So I did the unthinkable.

Maybe I was afraid he'd get us caught. Maybe I was trying to keep him out of trouble, or perhaps I was afraid I'd scare off Santa and he'd be there to witness my mistake. I don't know why I did it, but I broke the pact.

I tiptoed down the stairs and knelt down beneath the Christmas tree, and that's when I found the source of all the scratching and screeching. Santa Claus had indeed paid a visit, and he'd left us the most glorious gift any child could ever ask for. Curled up in his tiny kennel was a sleeping puppy. It should have been the happiest moment in my young life, and it nearly was... except there was something missing.

I knew exactly what I had to do.

I snuck back up the steps and bolted into Nick's room. Then I shook that little kid like I was mixing a can of paint. His eyes shot open like he was in a trance and before he could say anything I blurted out something like, "Santa came! We got a new puppy!"

His eyes, still trance-like, widened to the size of cue balls and then he said the only thing a stunned four-year-old could possibly say when met with such an overwhelming surprise. "Holy crap!" he shouted, which woke up the rest of the house and started Christmas morning just a wee bit earlier than my parents expected.

~C.G. Morelli

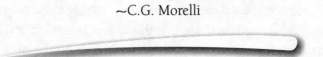

Christmas Magic

*Our hearts grow tender with childhood memories and love of kindred,
and we are better throughout the year for having, in spirit,
become a child again at Christmas-time.*

~Laura Ingalls Wilder

"Can we go see Santa tomorrow?" four-year-old Tami asked, drawing at the kitchen table while I prepared supper. "Jenny's going."

Jenny was Tami's best friend at preschool, and I imagined they chattered nonstop about Santa with Christmas just three weeks away.

"I think we can make time for that."

"Can Daddy go?"

"Afraid not, sweetie. He's working this Saturday."

"We could ask Monty." Tami loved her godfather, who was such a close family friend that when my husband, Tami and I moved to Portland from Los Angeles he relocated too. He had a kind heart and a sharp wit, and had spent many hours helping us make repairs on our fixer-upper house.

How could I explain to Tami that he'd do anything for us but celebrate Christmas? Monty and I had argued about the holiday for eight years and finally agreed to disagree. He objected to the commercialism of the holiday, and wanted no part in it.

"Call him, Mommy. Please," Tami begged when I hesitated.

I punched in Monty's number. Maybe for Tami he'd make an

exception. "Tami and I would like to invite you to visit Santa with us tomorrow," I said after we exchanged hello's.

"You know I won't go near a department store at Christmas," Monty said. "Got a sink that's leaking? A cat up a tree? Glad to help with that."

"Monty's busy," I told Tami. "Let's see if we can go with Jenny and her mom."

The next morning Tami and Jenny held hands as they approached the big, gilded chair where Santa sat. Tami's blue eyes sparkled with excitement as she climbed onto his lap and whispered her dream list in his ear.

"Santa said I've been very good," she confided to me afterward.

"You have been," I agreed, thinking that both Hal and Monty would enjoy seeing her so thrilled.

That night Hal told us he'd spotted a U-Cut Christmas Tree farm just a few miles from our home. "Why don't we cut our own tree tomorrow afternoon?" he suggested.

"Our own tree? Monty will want to do that!" Tami said confidently.

I lifted her into my lap. "Monty doesn't feel like we do about Christmas," I explained, my arms around her waist. "He doesn't want to do special holiday things."

"Why not?"

"People have different beliefs. We believe we're celebrating the birth of Jesus, and it's a special time for families to do things together. Monty thinks stores push the holidays to make money and they've ruined the real spirit of Christmas. He doesn't want anything to do with it."

Tami frowned. "You could at least ask him."

I felt torn between respecting Monty's wishes and honoring my daughter's. Tami's pleading blue eyes won.

"Would you like to get a tree with us?" I asked when I called. "Christmas is very important to Tami and she wants to share it with you."

"I thought we agreed to disagree."

"You and I agreed. Tami didn't."

"Consider this an opportunity for her to learn to respect other people's views."

Chastened, I promised not to ask again.

The next afternoon Hal, Tami and I headed out to the tree farm, all singing Christmas carols. Tami wandered up and down the rows of trees, then stopped in front of a full, seven-foot Douglas fir. "This one!" she cried.

"Good choice," I agreed.

On the way home, the tree tied to the rack on our CRV, my thoughts turned to Christmas Eve. "Wouldn't it be fun to have another family over and act out the Christmas story?" I suggested.

"Jenny'd like being in the play." Tami bounced excitedly in her car seat. "She could be the angel. I could be Mary and Monty could be Joseph."

"I'm not asking Monty again, sweetie. He'll just say no."

"I'll ask him."

"Heavy pressure, having Tami call," I could imagine Monty scolding me. Once again I was torn, but called and handed Tami the phone.

"Will you come be Joseph on Christmas Eve? Please, Monty?" she asked. I couldn't imagine anyone resisting her high, sweet voice.

But Monty was as determined as she was. "He said he'd take me to the zoo after Christmas," she said, shoulders slumping when she hung up.

Jenny's family, including two older brothers, was thrilled to join us for Christmas Eve. After a spaghetti dinner, I pulled out costumes: robes for two wise men and Joseph, a leather vest and walking stick for the shepherd, a small alpaca rug for the sheep now agreeably on all fours, a white polyester dress with a wide blue sash and a blue head scarf for Mary, a similar dress and a princess tiara for the angel. I'd written a simple script for the narrator, Jenny's mom.

"And there were in the same country shepherds abiding in the fields keeping watch over their flocks by night," she began. The shepherd bowed and the sheep baahed. "And lo, the angel of the Lord came upon them."

Just as the angel stepped forward, the doorbell rang.

Carolers perhaps? I motioned everyone to hold their positions and went to the door.

"Ho, ho, ho." Monty stood in the doorway with a self-effacing grin.

"Come in," I beamed.

When he saw our little costumed group, his cheeks reddened. "Don't let me interrupt," he said, backing toward the door.

"Monty." Tami flung herself in his arms. "Come see our play!"

"Please stay," Hal and I chorused.

Monty graciously settled onto the couch and watched our play, applauding at every possible spot. Afterward he visited amiably with everyone and accepted a piece of spice cake. I knew the effort he was making and my heart swelled with appreciation.

When Jenny's family said goodnight and piled into their van, Monty turned to Hal. "I brought something for Tami. Could you help me carry it in?"

"A present?" Tami clapped her hands.

Monty ruffled her blond hair. "I guess it's a present. It's something I thought you could use."

I grinned at his effort to minimize the Christmas part and Hal followed him to his truck. They returned with a vanity dresser that looked to be from the forties. It had been freshly painted a soft yellow with green trim.

I gasped. We had scant furniture and this would be perfect in Tami's room.

"I love it," Tami said, twirling in front of the oval mirror.

"The former tenant of the place I just rented left behind some furniture," Monty said.

"I know," I laughed. "Strictly practical. It took no time at all to sand and paint it."

Tami stopped twirling, raced to Monty, and leapt into his arms.

"You're one of Santa's helpers, aren't you? This is too big for his sleigh."

"Well... no... it's just from me," Monty stuttered.

"You have to be his helper. You come on Christmas Eve, you have a huge present for me, and you're even wearing a red shirt."

Monty seemed surprised when he looked down at his shirt. "It is red," he said softly. "I have some Christmas spirit after all. You must be magic."

Tami snuggled against his shoulder. "Christmas is even better with you here."

"For this year anyway," Monty smiled, tightening his arms around her.

~Samantha Ducloux Waltz

North Pole Bound

I wish we could put up some of the Christmas spirit in jars
and open a jar of it every month.
~Harlan Miller

Snowflakes gently tumble from the dark December sky as my husband parks the SUV outside the train depot. "There it is!" squeals Julia, my seven-year-old, her fuchsia fleece PJ bottoms peeking from beneath her down coat. She points a mittened hand toward a line of boxcars bedecked for the holiday in glittery white lights and strands of pine garland. "Look, it says The Polar Express!"

Julia's preteen sister Emily rolls her eyes towards the line of pajama-clad children clutching train tickets marked "North Pole Express." "Yeah, right. Like we're gonna go all the way to the North Pole in just one night."

Don't ruin this, I want to say. Where's your Christmas spirit?

But I stop, remembering words of wisdom from Chris Van Allsburg, author of the award-winning children's book *The Polar Express*. "The bell still rings for me," I say with a Santa-like wink. "Listen really hard, and maybe you'll hear it too."

Emily's raised eyebrows relax a bit as we move past a line of Santa's elves, outfitted in green pointy-toed shoes, red and white striped tights, and jingle bell necklaces. "Merry Christmas!" they chorus, ringing and jingling with each jolly step.

We hand our tickets to an elderly train conductor, smartly

outfitted in a gray uniform and cap. "Welcome aboard," he says, giving me a hand up the steep steps. "Enjoy your ride."

A ruby-cheeked elf leads us to our seats. "Some elf dust?" she offers, rubbing glittery gel on Julia's outstretched hand. "Would your sister like some?"

"Oh all right," Emily relents, reluctantly agreeing to a dusting of holiday magic.

Then all at once, we lurch forward. Finally, we are North Pole bound.

As the train leaves the station, the smell of chocolate fills the steamy boxcar.

"Cookies and cocoa?" a friendly elf asks, handing us chocolate chip cookies and cups of hot chocolate.

Emily actually accepts this magical offering. I catch her looking up as another elf reads *The Polar Express* and walks up and down the aisles displaying illustrations of enchanted Northern forests, Santa's workshop, and a land filled with boundless, brightly-wrapped gifts.

Lights appear out the windows as the train slows to a stop.

"The North Pole!" squeals Julia, rubbing her hands against the steamy window to get a closer look. "There's Frosty!"

Emily hops up on her knees. "Julia, there's Santa's workshop," she says, pointing to a host of elves hammering away in a wooden shed labeled "Toys." "And over there, you're right—that's Frosty the Snowman!"

We wave at a lineup of costumed figures: Frosty, the Grinch, and a family of elves. Never mind the highway signs that point to Northern Ohio. Tonight, we are at the North Pole—a magical place infused with Christmas spirit.

"Ho, ho, ho!" a low voice bellows, pulling us away from the train windows. "Merry Christmas!"

As Santa enters our train car, Julia's smile flashes bright as a shooting star. "I want an American Girl doll," she says, beaming as Santa offers her a small silver bell.

I hold my breath as Santa nods, then moves toward Emily.

"Have you been a good girl this year?" he asks, pointing a white-gloved finger her way.

Well, she's been pretty Grinchy, I want to say. She thinks she's too old for all this Christmas stuff. Don't be surprised if she doesn't even talk to you, Santa.

Emily stares straight into Santa's white beard with a surprisingly serious expression. "I'd like a DS game."

"I'll see what I can do," Santa says, handing Emily a silver bell. "Merry Christmas, Emily."

"He knew your name!" Julia hops up and down like an excited bunny. "Santa knows everything!"

"That is weird," Emily says, shaking her bell back and forth.

I don't bother to mention her nametag, because I'm too intrigued by the beautiful high-pitched sound Emily's bell makes as she shakes it back and forth.

On Christmas morning, the girls hurry to look under the tree. Tearing into two wrapped packages, they unveil treasure: An American Girl for Julia and a DS game for Emily.

"You have to believe to receive," I say, spying two silver bells hanging from our Christmas tree.

Emily laughs, her blue eyes twinkling with the magic of Christmas.

I reach over and jingle one of the silver bells. "I can still hear it, can't you?"

As the girls play with their gifts, I ring the bell again. What a beautiful sound: the spirit of the season, ringing deep within all of us. Hopefully, that's a sound my girls will never outgrow.

~Stefanie Wass

Through the Eyes
of a Child

Try to look at everything through the eyes of a child.
~Ruth Draper

As the New England air began to get colder, and my mailbox began to fill up with Christmas cards and Christmas lights seemed to grow overnight on bushes all around the neighborhood, I knew this only meant one thing—Santa Claus was coming to town.

In the past, Christmas had meant fun, family and holiday cheer, but I knew this year was the big leagues, and I had to get my game face on very soon if I was going to start answering questions and planting the seed of belief, faith and fairy tales in our "newest addition." Two years ago my boyfriend and I got custody of his two-year-old grandson and this was the first year that AJ was really focused on the man in a red suit who would come down our chimney with presents, eat cookies, drink milk, and then, with a twinkle in his eye and a touch of his nose, join his posse of reindeer on our roof again. At four years old he seemed to know much more than I ever did about this jolly old red-faced guy. Or perhaps he knew what I had forgotten.

As more and more lights appeared on random shrubs, and Christmas songs played on the radio, the overwhelming fact that it was up to us to make this year magical was apparent. I was nervous since I had thought I was too old for this. At forty, I had already stopped putting up a big Christmas tree due to the mess, no more lights, and who needed decorations… really? Who sees them anyway?

This year it would all happen: decorations, the Christmas tree, a special night of hanging memories on mostly low branches, Christmas movies, Rudolph the Red Nosed Reindeer song rehearsals nightly, and cookies that were most carefully chosen for Santa Claus. We made reindeer food (a special recipe of oatmeal flakes and glitter dust saved from the wand of the Tooth Fairy) and gently sprinkled it on the front lawn. After all, the reindeer need snacks too. After a few days, and a beautiful winter snowstorm that blew through most unexpectedly, I began to think to myself that this might even be fun. There was one last event though, the infamous sitting on Santa's lap.

A few days before Christmas, on a sunny Saturday afternoon, Santa was to make a stop in our town for the annual parade. I was filled with excitement, as this was no ordinary stop, and no ordinary Santa Claus. This particular Santa Claus arrived on a giant fire truck courtesy of the Springfield (Massachusetts) Fire Department and had a certain twinkle in his eye that was very familiar to me. As the lights flashed atop the truck and the firemen proudly helped Santa off the huge, shiny ladder truck, hundreds of children poured out of the American Legion Post 420, to meet their new white haired friend, and our "grandson" held tightly to my hand in awe of what he was seeing. Pride in the firemen and in Santa took over, and my eyes began to well up with tears of joy, delight and honor to know these people. The kind of people who would give of themselves freely and openly to children they didn't know, and in a way that was so completely full of honor and respect—it left me speechless. Thankfully, just then Old Man Winter blew a strong gust directed right at me and my tears froze in place before spilling down my cheeks.

As AJ carefully and a little nervously made his way over to Santa to get a candy cane, he whispered to me, "I wish Papa could see this!" Little did he know that his Papa (my father) *could* see him.

Soon, Santa Claus made his way into the hall of the American Legion and began handing out huge bags of presents to all the children! AJ looked on, from a safe distance at all that was going on and little by little began to trust in the pure enjoyment and spirit of the day and moved a little closer to Santa. As I looked on with my boyfriend and my father's good friend, we began to wonder if this man who we had all come to know and love really *was* Santa Claus. Although his costume was flawless, something else was swirling around this wonderful man on this day of enchantment. Something more than magical, more than mystical, and something that usually only exists in the hearts of children. Pure hope. Pure joy. Pure faith. Pure love. And pure pride.

As the children clapped and laughed in delight, and told this magical man their deepest dreams and wishes, I began to see life just a little differently. Although pure chaos existed all around... right there, on that special day, that one meeting, one twinkle and one candy cane had certainly set life in motion. The cosmic pendulum of tradition, faith and belief in something that others may eventually say isn't real, began to swing.

As I smiled, laughed, sang and watched a small boy let go a little, believe a lot, and trust in the magic of Christmas, I also saw a grown man do the same. Across the crowded hall, I made eye contact with Santa Claus. For one second, our eyes locked and I knew that all the weeks of preparation, all the songs, decorations and tales of elves and toy making had done something more than I expected. Somewhere between the verses, ornaments and painting of our beloved "love rocks" I had managed to smile a little more, laugh a lot more and earn the trust and unconditional love of a small child. I had gotten everything I had asked for, and for the first time in a long time, I had no doubts as to whether Santa was real. He was real. Although my father played his part in making Santa come alive that day, I know the spirit of Santa was also there and if you don't believe me, the Springfield Fire Department, some members of the Springfield Police Department and American Legion Post 420 would all swear to it. Even though Mrs. Claus, we heard, could not make the trip due to a mishap in the toy factory that caused a broken foot, she too was there in spirit and in the minds of all who attended.

Christmas will come and go, always. The feeling of excitement

and the hope of a new friend and the love of family is year-round...
as it should be.

~Christine A. Brooks

The Gift of Christmas

Deck the Halls

Mistaken Identity

Perhaps the best Yuletide decoration is being wreathed in smiles.
~Author Unknown

A domestic goddess I am not. The only time that our home is redecorated is well, actually never. Yes, I do the semi-annual spring and fall housecleaning. I move things to clean around them, but then I put them back right where they were to begin with. Even the landscaping is the same except for a few additional weeds that I haven't gotten around to pulling yet.

So, at the age of thirty-seven, when I found out I was pregnant, my angst was high for several reasons, the least of which was my perceived ineptitude with anything requiring familial skills. And, to make the cosmic joke even greater, I was blessed with a daughter who, by the age of two, was far more talented in arts and craft efforts than I thought I ever was.

Whether it was the creative spirit of my mother or simply the grace of God, I learned quickly how to come up with ideas to keep my toddler entertained. The projects I conjured allowed her the freedom to express herself, keep her mind challenged, and, as it turned out, I was quite the recycling queen. They say desperation is the mother of invention, and with limited funds, I could not run to the local craft store daily to buy this, that and the other thing for her undertakings. You would be impressed with what I did with empty milk cartons, creamer bottles, cereal boxes and more.

For the first seven years of her life, my daughter was accustomed to going with me to thrift stores to hunt for the great treasures we would find for under a dollar. We also went to the end-of-season clearance sales, bargain bins and dollar stores searching for just what we needed to put the finishing touches on her latest great artistic creation.

Each school year, I would volunteer in the teachers' workroom twice a week. This is where I met Maria, the true maternal idol. If you needed 125 little booklets printed, collated, laminated and assembled, you gave the job to me. But, if you wanted a cute seasonal bulletin board, or theme-based art projects that coincided with the science or history lesson, you went to Maria. She was so creative that if she wasn't the sweetest person ever, I could have easily been jealous.

Week in and week out, we would collaborate on giving the students the most imaginative and well-assembled projects that they will probably ever encounter in their entire school career. As the holidays were approaching, I started asking Maria for some ideas to decorate our home in a manner other than what we had been doing for the past several years (reused Christmas decorations bought from the discount stores—purchased in late January, of course). She came up with some great ideas that I knew would make even my "perfect" neighbor pleased. I have to take a moment here to tell you about my neighbor, whose house and yard have probably been photographed in every home and landscape magazine in the country. To say that she takes pride in her decorative skills is a vast understatement, but it is her syrupy sweet condescending approach to me that really gets me going. "Dahling (we live in the South), did y'all know that mowing your grass each week not only helps keep those dreadful dandelions you have at bay, but makes the grass more healthy."

I never thought I was the type of person to compete with someone over something as superficial as holiday decorations, but this year I felt armed and ready to go. I was even practicing my feigned humble description, "Well, my dear neighbor, I never dreamed that I could create such a dazzling display, I guess the festival fairies guided my hand." But what I never expected was exactly what happened.

When I went to the store to purchase the items I needed for my holiday innovation, my daughter saw a large box that contained those wrapped Christmas balls; you know the ones that are all the same size, shape, and color. These would not, simply would not, work with my idea. As I strolled around the craft store, my daughter kept going back to the box; I couldn't seem to focus her on my mission. Finally, she approached me with a forlorn look on her face. I knelt down in front of her, opened my arms, and said, "Come here honey. Tell Mama why you are so upset." Trying not to cry, she whimpered, "Those poor broken decorations are never going to be used by anyone; they will never decorate a tree or be admired and enjoyed. We have to take them, Mama, we just have to."

So vanity fought with compassion, and fortunately, you know which won; the enormous box of broken ornaments sat in the back seat of my car with my daughter joyously telling them how she planned to use them. The week before school broke for the holidays, our front yard was overly decorated and truly a sight that only a mother's loving eyes could appreciate. I swear I think I saw my neighbor swigging sherry each time she looked at our yard, and I mean morning, noon, and night.

One morning as we were waiting at the bus stop, we saw Maria drive by and wave frantically to us. I thought, "Oh no, she is going to be disappointed that we didn't use her holiday suggestions." But each time I grimaced when I looked at the decorations, I also smiled because the joy with which my daughter exhibited them held no bounds. When I got to school that day, Maria came running up to me with a big smile on her face. "Well that yard of yours is certainly the most beautiful one on the entire street. I swear I looked at each house and not one is as nicely decorated as yours." I was completely caught off guard and could not respond. Maria was too nice a person to have been saying this sarcastically, and she had way too much talent to think that our broken decorations were spectacular.

And then I realized what caused the mistaken identity. You see, we have to stand in my neighbor's driveway to catch the school bus.

It was there, in front of my neighbor's perfect house, that Maria had seen us that morning.

~Judith Fitzsimmons

A Fall from Grace

*A compromise is an agreement whereby both parties get what
neither of them wanted.*
~Author Unknown

I fell through the ceiling of my house today while attempting
to gather Christmas decorations from the attic. My husband
warned me not to go up there, claiming that most of the
flooring is thin plywood, but one rendition of "Jingle Bells" from my
three-year-old provoked me to perform my balance beam act.

I started out slowly, eyeing the surroundings of the attic from the
top step of the pull-down stairs. I looked down at my daughter, who
from the distance of a ten-foot ceiling seemed infinitely small. A sane,
less spirited person might have turned back at that point. Not me. I
felt excited, adventurous and yes, a little naughty.

I reached for the overhead light switch, foolishly expecting to
be greeted by an organized attic with plastic bins labeled and stacked
according to holiday. Instead it was evident that my husband, Richard,
who has laid claim to all attic territory, has been tossing items hap-
hazardly from the threshold. It is no wonder he did not want me up
there.

I pushed the family luggage aside and leapt to the first beam.
Not bad form, I thought. I grabbed an overhead truss and shimmied
forward until I noticed a stack of wreaths—bingo. I started launch-
ing lightweight decorations across the attic toward the opening.

My daughter squealed with delight as stockings, garland, and fake snowballs rained down on her.

In the midst of the excitement I lost my footing and stepped directly onto the plywood. Momentary panic subsided when I realized my husband was wrong, the wood could easily support a petite little flower like me. With renewed energy I began effortlessly moving boxes of ornaments, wreaths and Christmas lights, stopping only to hurl the occasional bag of tinsel at my giggling daughter.

I was finished, actually scooting back to the opening when I spotted the cowboy Santa Claus sticking out from under a pile of Easter baskets. He was a little outside what I felt was the safety zone, but I had to get him. Christmas wouldn't be the same without my cowboy Santa rocking his hips as he sang "Have a Holly Jolly Christmas."

I knelt on a beam and reached close enough to brush him with my fingertips. I remember saying, "I'm coming for ya, cowboy," right before I tumbled from the joist and crashed through the sheetrock with the right side of my body. I kept hold of the beam with my left arm and leg anticipating the complete ten-foot fall. I saw my daughter through the hole jumping wildly, clapping her hands with delight. This was just part of the show to her—another snowball on its way down.

"Honey," I whispered, fake smile intact, "go get the phone for Mommy."

As she skipped from the room I knew I had to make my move. If I could pull myself back through the hole, great; if not, well she had the phone and thankfully I had taught her how to dial 911. The thought of my child seeing this snowball sprawled out on the floor below gave me the strength I needed to pull myself back through the opening and get to the ground floor, by way of the attic stairs, safely.

When Richard came home and saw the hole in the ceiling he looked at me the way Ricky Ricardo would have looked at Lucy. I shrugged my shoulders and raised my eyebrows as if to say, "Well, someone had to get the rockin' Santa down." He shook his head, and just when I expected him to launch into his "I told you so" spiel, we were interrupted by our giggling daughter swinging her hips wildly from side to side as the voice of Alan Jackson belted out, "Have a Holly Jolly Christmas."

I looked at my smiling husband and realized we would compromise on this one; I would not blame his disorganization for my near death experience (or use terms like attempted manslaughter) if he forgave the fact that his petite little flower of a wife, in refusing to heed his warning, made a life-size hole in our ceiling.

~Kelli Mix

Under the Tree

What is a home without children? Quiet.
~Henny Youngman

We have a family tradition of decorating our Christmas tree as soon as Thanksgiving leftovers are whisked away. We are thankful, we truly are, but nothing excites us as much as Christmas. We simply want to enjoy the Christmas season as long as possible. So, with the aroma of turkey and pumpkin pie still lingering in the air, the Christmas tree decorating festivities begin.

My precious twin grandchildren, Heath and Hana, were coming to help one year, when they were four years old and in constant motion. I knew it would be double trouble or a double blessing, so with a deep breath and a quick prayer, I opened the door for the festivities to begin.

"Hey, Nana. We brought presents," they squealed in unison as they darted toward the tree, delivering the first gifts of Christmas.

"Wait," I pleaded. "Let's decorate the tree before we put gifts under it."

The look of disappointment spread over both faces. I guess I shouldn't have intervened. They had been so excited, and I had been a scrooge... an unintentional one, but a scrooge to them, nonetheless.

Their displeasure was short lived, however, as they scrambled toward the boxes of sparkling ornaments waiting nearby. And, the ritual began. One by one, Heath and Hana meticulously decorated the tree with ornament after ornament, trimming the bottom, while their mom, Dana, and I adorned the top.

At last, with the tree trimmed, and with unbridled enthusiasm, Heath and Hana raced toward the tree again with their gifts. And, once again, I had to cry, "Wait! Look," I explained, "the tree is leaning. Really. We can't put the presents under the tree until we fix it."

"Okay, Nana. We'll help you," complied Heath. So the search was now on. What could we put under the tree stand to correct the problem?

"Here is a book, Nana," Heath shouted gleefully. "Let's see if it will work." So, under the tree I crawled, with book in hand, to see if the perfect book had been found to adjust our leaning Christmas tree.

"Nope, too small," I yelled back to the twins. "See if you can find another one. I'll wait for you under here. Try to hurry, though. Okay?"

This time it was Hana who came running toward the tree with another book. It, too, was small, but with both books under one leg of the tree stand, our problem was solved.

Crawling out from under our now beautifully erect evergreen, their mom and I praised the twins for helping us solve the leaning Christmas tree dilemma. Heath and Hana's giddy laughter let us know that they, too, were pleased with themselves and with my next announcement. "You may now put your gifts under the tree!"

"Yea!!!" Heath and Hana both squealed as they ran toward the tree with their first gifts of Christmas, excited to finally be completing this long-awaited task of the evening. Then, as quietness surrounded us, I turned to watch as they gently placed their gifts under the tree. But, something wasn't quite right. Why was the tree leaning again? Why was it wobbling?

As Heath and Hana wriggled out from under the tree, we saw. Heath had placed his gift under the tree all right... under the tree stand, just like we had placed the books. In his mind, he had done exactly as I had instructed. He had proudly put his present under the tree.

His mom and I laughed quietly to ourselves, until his sister admonished him. I guess four-year-old sisters don't appreciate special moments like this as much as a mom and grandmother.

~Brenda Cook

The Christmas Chair

Do not quench your inspiration and your imagination;
do not become the slave of your model.
~Vincent van Gogh

To say that I love Christmas decorations is sort of like saying chocolate is tasty. It's not just an afterthought for me, it's something I start thinking about months in advance. Usually somewhere around March 15th.

In fact, when I was a little girl, I remember spending whole afternoons sitting next to our big family Christmas tree, just looking at all the ornaments and lights and softly (well, pretty loudly actually) singing Christmas carols.

We never had one of those cookie-cutter theme trees like you sometimes see in department stores. The ones with "themes" like "winter snow" or "red and gold ribbon." Ours was a hodgepodge of store-bought ceramic cartoon characters, pressed metal shapes with important dates and names ("First Anniversary 1977" or "Baby's First Christmas 1980"), and a mélange of homemade treasures: the ornaments my mom and grandmother frantically crocheted for my mom's first Christmas tree after leaving the nest; the school crafts featuring awkward photos of myself with various levels of embarrassing hair; the beaded ornaments my mom and I made together years later. They all formed this perfect harmony of past memories and beauty that seemed to perfectly capture our family's spirit during the holidays.

So, imagine my dismay when my fiancé and I realized during

our first Christmas living together that we just couldn't afford to buy a Christmas tree. It came down to either the tree or the trip home to see my family for the day itself. It was a no-brainer, but the decision didn't leave me filled with much holiday cheer.

He and I were struggling. He was working while I finished my last year of college. Plain rice topped with a deli slice of chicken was our idea of a "splurge" meal… the $80 Douglas fir I eyed at the local Christmas tree lot was out of the question.

Walter, my fiancé, knew I was disappointed. To cheer me up, he swiped a little tinsel from the decorations in his office for me.

Little did he know that I was determined to bring some Christmas cheer into our little apartment, no matter what.

In my mind, the tree is the pinnacle of all Christmas decorations. And I was going to find a way to get one.

I had a small box of ornaments that my mom had passed down to me, to get our decorating started. I had the tinsel. I just needed the tree itself.

I looked around the sparsely furnished apartment, full of hand-me-downs, textbooks and not much else.

And there it was… sitting in the corner, under a pile of laundry… a bright green armchair that the previous tenant hadn't bothered to take with him. Perhaps because it was so uncomfortable. And so, well… green.

I had my tree. A few hours later, I'd moved the "tree" to an exalted position by the living room window, pinned nearly every inch with my ornament collection and topped it with a generous helping of tinsel. I put my desk lamp on the floor beside it and aimed the beam at it to really make that tinsel sparkle.

When Walter walked in, he found me sitting next to the "tree" singing "O Holy Night" with a tear in my eye.

And, he burst out laughing.

"What on earth is that?" he exclaimed.

I looked at him, then looked at the "tree."

"It's our Christmas tree."

I had to laugh too. It was sort of ridiculous. "Okay," I said, "It's our Christmas chair... even better!"

He grinned and said, "Works for me! I love you. Merry Christmas."

We spent the rest of the night singing carols to our "Christmas chair."

Years later, we hang a peculiar little ornament on our "real" Christmas tree each year: A photo of a green armchair covered in Christmas spirit—and tinsel.

~Jennifer Lee Johnson

No Christmas for Me

The Lord said, "It is more blessed to give than to receive."
~Acts 20:35 (NIV)

Christmas is my very favorite time of year. It is that special time of year when you celebrate traditions of love and create memories of a lifetime. During vacations and holidays throughout the year I have always loved buying fun, unique gifts and storing them in a special closet. When November comes, it is always exciting for me to get them all out and see the lovely things I purchased throughout the year. The real fun for me, however, is piling them all on the floor and having a wrapping marathon. I love to wrap presents.

There is one rule I have about the holiday season though, one of my traditions. All the presents must be purchased by the end of November, preferably Thanksgiving. Then, the weekend of Thanksgiving, the Christmas tree is put up and decorated. Of course, you cannot have a decorated tree with no presents under it. So, the first week of December the presents must be wrapped and put under the tree. This way all the shopping and wrapping pressure is gone. Not only do you have a beautiful, decorated house during the entire month of December, but you can enjoy baking, holiday parties and all the wonderful things the season brings.

This year, however, there would be no Christmas for me. In August I had unexpectedly become a young widow at the age of forty-eight. There would be no holiday traditions this Christmas. I felt my children would understand, they were also dealing with the loss.

During this time I became reacquainted with a coworker from many years ago. He also had faced tragedy in his life during the past year and found himself alone with two children still at home. This would be his first Christmas alone as well.

One night while we were talking, he confided in me he didn't know how he was going to make it through Christmas. He had no tree and no decorations. In fact the prospect of the whole thing was overwhelming to him. My heart went out to him as I thought of his children.

Late one night while I was praying about how I could find the strength to make it through this holiday, an idea came to me. Deciding to pray about it over the next few days, I became excited. Wednesday night after church I invited my friend to have a cup of coffee. The plan was to present my idea to him.

"You may think I am crazy," I began, "but I have an idea. If it is too personal or too uncomfortable for you I will understand. However, it would really mean a lot to me."

Very puzzled, he looked at me having no idea what I was about to say. He could tell, however, it was very important to me.

"I have decided I am not going to have Christmas this year. However, I would like to help you with Christmas for your children. I would like to take you to get a Christmas tree and new decorations. I would also like to take you shopping to buy presents for your children and your family. Then I will take them all home and wrap them for you. Would you allow me to do that for you this year?" I asked, bracing myself for rejection.

Although the look on his face was one of surprise, it took him about two seconds to say "Sure!"

"Do you mean it?" I asked. "You can think about it if you want to."

"No, I am sure," he replied.

I was overwhelmed with excitement as I continued. "There is just one catch. We have to have all the shopping done by Thanksgiving and the tree up and decorated by the first weekend in December. That's my rule."

At first he laughed, and then he realized I was serious. Since this was the second week in November we had a lot of work to do, and not much time.

"It can't be done," he stated. He was clearly overwhelmed.

"Oh, but it can," I replied. "But we need to get busy! I can handle it all."

We made our plans the next day for shopping trips. Learning he had always wanted a real tree, just like when he was a kid, we made plans for that too.

The next Friday night we were on a marathon shopping trip at the mall. In three hours of shopping we purchased presents for his entire family, including the children. To my delight, there were sales everywhere and he even saved money. Needless to say, he was quite impressed.

Then, the big hurdle came. He had no decorations of any kind for a tree so we were starting from scratch. Luckily, Garden Ridge was having a forty-eight-hour sale on Christmas decorations. I explained to him that was where we needed to go and we could buy everything at once—and it was all on sale!

Again, he was overwhelmed. He had never stepped inside a place like Garden Ridge and really could not even imagine. After church Sunday, he went home to change. As he was leaving the house his daughter asked, "Are you going to play golf, Dad?" It was the perfect, sunny Sunday afternoon for golf.

"No, dear, I am going shopping," he replied.

"Shopping?" she exclaimed in shock. "You never go shopping!"

We spent the next three hours shopping with great success and walked away with everything we needed. The following Sunday we picked out his first real Christmas tree. To our delight, his children both had plans to be gone so we had the entire afternoon to decorate the tree and the house. The presents were wrapped and ready.

The look of indescribable joy on his children's faces that evening when they came home left us all without words.

Then he looked at me and said, "Now it's time to decorate your house for Christmas."

Yes, I had Christmas that year, too. He returned the favor by making sure my children and I enjoyed Christmas in our home.

The most special gift to me, however, was the Christmas he allowed me to give to them.

~Pam Wanzer

A King Kong Christmas Tradition

People seem to get nostalgic about a lot of things they weren't
so crazy about the first time around.
~Author Unknown

Many people have lovely angel ornaments that grace the tops of their Christmas trees. Not my family, though. We don't have an angel; we have King Kong.

Four years into our marriage, I finally let my husband talk me into getting a tree of our own. I'd had my reasons for resisting. We had three cats, we lived in a small apartment, and since I grew up in a Jewish family, I was not accustomed to having a tree in my living room. He wore me down, though, and when I relented at last, he dashed out the door promising he would bring home a beautiful tree and protect it with a cat-proof barrier that he would make himself.

"Not too big?" I pleaded, as he raced out.

"Right!" he answered, as excited as, well, a kid on Christmas morning.

"And ornaments?" I yelled after him.

"Sure thing!" he said.

Because my mother-in-law used to transform the family home into a jolly red and white winter wonderland, with Santas and reindeer on every possible horizontal surface, every December, I trusted that my husband would have the know-how to choose appropriate ornaments with which to decorate our first tree. I awaited his return, eager to begin a new tradition with special ornaments that we would hand down to the children we might have one day.

He came back some time later with a lovely, fragrant, and not-too-big tree, some lumber and hardware, and a few other things. But oh, those other things!

I'm still not sure why, but he'd decided to visit the local toy store and had returned home with a big bag full of the ugliest plastic animals I'd ever seen. I'm talking about dinosaurs and water buffalo and pigs and giraffes—each one more hideous than the last. Among these badly painted monstrosities was a rubber ape, with one arm raised menacingly over his head.

"What were you thinking, exactly?" I asked him when he proudly presented his sorry collection of would-be ornaments. I guess he might have thought something at the time, but wisely decided to keep it to himself. Instead, we put the bag of animals aside, and the two of us went to the store and bought a string of lights, bags of cranberries and popcorn and tinsel, and a few small ornaments. I spent a delightful afternoon stringing the popcorn and cranberries and placing the ornaments and strands of tinsel just so on the "not too big, is it?" tree. Those ugly animals disappeared somehow, but we kept the rubber ape and gave him the place of honor atop the tree. The cats kept a close eye on the whole process, tails and ears twitching.

The next year, we got a slightly bigger tree and added a few more ornaments. And we had our first baby. In the years that followed, we got more ornaments, had more babies, and bought bigger trees.

Once they got old enough to ask, "Where did King Kong come from?" we took each of our three children aside and explained the tradition. To their credit, they accepted the fact that their parents were a little goofy and let it go at that. They all helped decorate the tree every December as we hung their handmade ornaments, along with the ones we accumulated over the years. The big moment always came when Dad got up on the stepstool and placed King Kong at the very top.

When our house burned to the ground in October 1991, in the tragic Oakland Hills fire, we were left with the clothes on our backs and not much else. We packed up the few things we had taken with us when we evacuated, and moved into a rental house in a nearby town. Before we knew it, the holidays were upon us. My husband and I realized that there was no way to replace fifteen years' worth of acquired Christmas decorations and ornaments. Some were just plain irreplaceable, but others…

With fingers crossed, we drove back to that toy store to see if we could find a replacement for Old King Kong. What joy we felt when we spied the menacing little fellow in a bin full of other beasts! We purchased the new guy, along with a few reindeer, and brought them back to our temporary home, where we had a subdued Christmas in the still unfamiliar house.

It's funny how a little rubber animal helped turn our house into a home just by waving to us from his lofty perch. Even though our lives changed forever that year, the happy return of our faithful tree-topper made us feel as though we were somehow on the way back to normal.

In our family, it just wouldn't be Christmas without King Kong.

~Risa Nye

Let There Be Lights

That's not serious; it's just human.
~Jerry Kopke

W hen my wife asked me last week to hang Christmas lights on the house, I became dizzy with anticipation. Not Christmas spirit dizzy. More like impending disaster dizzy. The problem wasn't a lack of experience with hanging holiday lights, mind you. Through the years, I've successfully hung lights on a wide variety of items living and dead, including: Christmas trees, shrubs and hedges, a fake ficus tree, shelving and furniture, and an un-hung screen door that served as a surrogate tree the year my wife and I started dating.

What was so intimidating about this particular holiday project was that I'd never hung lights on the outside of a house before. Along with the risks and challenges of a guy with a fragile sense of balance standing high atop a low-budget ladder, there's the issue of how to attach the lights to the house in a fashion that will keep them hanging after you let go. Which, when you think about it, is really the most important part of light hanging.

I knew enough about hanging things outdoors to realize that Scotch tape wasn't a viable option. Too bad, considering how much stronger my qualifications were to operate a tape dispenser as compared to say, a staple gun. Actually, anything gun-like was beyond my capabilities, with the possible exception of a small, child-safe water pistol.

Then, in my hour of need, a solution appeared. While driving through the neighborhood the day before "the hanging," I spotted a homeowner in the process of putting up icicle lights. The ones he already had up were staying up and the ones he had left he was placing with great precision and ease onto plastic hooks positioned along his fascia trim under the roof.

Needless to say, I viewed this man with the awe one might confer on a great trapeze artist who juggles flaming torches while swinging high above the ground blindfolded. I needed to be him—a master of airborne electrical stunts. I needed to pay homage to him and reveal myself as a seeker of the sacred wisdom of the mystic lights. Mostly, I needed to get out of my car and say something before he finished and went inside for the night.

"Excuse me for being nosy," I said in my best "hey neighbor" voice. "But I'm hanging my lights tomorrow and I wondered what you're using to put them up."

He looked warily over his shoulder from his roost on the ladder. "I got a bunch of these plastic hooks," he said.

"Plastic hooks," I marveled. "No messy Scotch tape, no deadly staple gun mishaps."

"Right," he responded in the tentative way people agree with you when they're not sure if you're all there. "What can I do for you?"

"I'd like to buy your house, fully decorated for the holidays," I ventured.

"It's not for sale," he countered cunningly.

"In that case, may I ask where you got the hooks?"

"You can have these," he offered, extending a Ziploc bag full of the labor-saving wonders.

"I don't want to deplete your supply."

"Don't worry," he assured me, pointing to two other bags filled to the brim. "I overestimated how much I'd need."

Now you would think that with such a pivotal break in the dreaded light hanging project coming my way, I would be home free, a guaranteed success story—"Local Boy Lights Up the Season of Joy." You obviously don't know me very well.

The next day, after systematically affixing dozens of plastic hooks to the fascia trim of my home, I proceeded to hang fifty-five feet of General Electric commercial grade icicle lights. It was hard, methodical, tedious labor, but a couple of hours later, I stood back to admire my handiwork: A veritable festival of lights, perfectly proportioned and evenly distributed for maximum dazzle. I grinned elfishly.

All that was left to do was run the extension cord from the garage and plug it into the last strand of lights hanging near the garage door. My spirits soared as I poised to make the connection that would turn the magic on.

Unfortunately, the plug end of all the lights was on the other side of the house due to my having put them all up in the opposite sequence of what I needed to be able to connect them to the power source. Which leads me to a heartwarming little holiday riddle.

Question: How many Alan Williamsons does it take to hang icicle lights on a house?

Answer: Two. The cheerful, whistle-while-you-work AW who puts them up and the aggravated, despondent AW who takes them down and starts all over because of a bonehead mistake of colossal idiocy.

On the bright side, at least I didn't wound myself in a tragic staple gun mishap.

~Alan Williamson

My Nativities

"And she brought forth her firstborn son,
and wrapped him in swaddling clothes, and laid him in a manger;
because there was no room for them in the inn."

~Luke 2:7

The first person I knew who collected nativity scenes was Ruth Maldonado. I saw her collection during a couples Sunday School party in her home, and I was enthralled! Not long afterward, I was pleasantly surprised to discover that my mentor, Mavis, was also a nativity collector. I found out about her passion when Mavis hosted an open house to share her nativity collection with friends and neighbors.

The seed was planted! A tiny Guatemalan nativity, presented as a hostess gift from Steve Hanes, a pilot friend, and his wife, Nancy, launched my nativity collection.

I started in my home. My husband, Ed, and I each had nativities from our childhood. I had also inherited several nativities from deceased family members and friends. Over the years, I had accumulated an assortment of nativity Christmas ornaments. My collection was well on its way!

I began to seek out nativities as souvenirs during our travels. Friends and family added to my collection on special occasions.

Over the years, my collection has expanded to more than a hundred nativity sets with figures and animals, and another hundred or so nativity ornaments. My collection includes unusual items such as cookie jars, a tea set, a hot chocolate set, a mobile, a platter, candle-holders, an Advent wreath, and nativity jewelry. The nativity figures range in size from less than half an inch to over three feet tall.

There are nativities in almost every room of my home at Christmastime, including the bathrooms! I have nativity scenes from travels to Italy, France, Spain, England, Mexico, Africa, and parts in between. I have metal, glass, wooden, ceramic, and gourd nativities. I have nativities made by my children, and I have nativities made by well-known artists. All are special to me because of the memories they represent. Most importantly, my nativities are precious because they represent the birth of Jesus.

Several years ago, due to family issues, I "skimped" on holiday preparations, and didn't unpack all of my boxes of nativities for Christmas. I was simply too tired to spend additional hours unpacking, and then repacking, my entire collection. The thought of any more holiday decorating, in addition to all my other responsibilities, seemed overwhelming.

My "main" nativity scene, a large ceramic set, complete with stable, painted by my friend, Kaye, which always adorned the dining room buffet was conspicuously absent! I got comments and questions about the "missing" nativities. Christmas didn't seem quite the same without all of our nativities. However, the tradeoff of not being totally exhausted during the holidays seemed worthwhile to me at the time.

After Christmas, as I started packing away Christmas decorations, I wondered what it would be like not to have to put away the decorations each year. I found myself looking at curio shelves in my dining room that held the ceramic dog collection that I inherited from a long-deceased cousin.

I have fond memories of sitting on the floor playing with the dogs. Good memories, but I didn't have an extreme emotional connection to the collection. I suddenly realized that the dogs were taking up prime real estate in my dining room, which could be used to display my small nativities! I also realized a corner china cabinet in my dining room, and a painted bookshelf in my living room could house some of my larger sets. I went about the task of arranging most of my nativities into their new, year-round, homes. (By the way, I found a new home, in a guest bedroom, for my cousin's dog collection.)

I still have to unpack and repack a few of my largest nativities each Christmas as I decorate our home for the holidays, but unpacking the nativities is no longer the chore it once was! Seeing my nativity collection every day reminds me that we ought to celebrate our Savior's birth all year long, not just at Christmas.

~Jamie White Wyatt

Little Cabin in the Big Woods

Cookies are made of butter and love.
~Norwegian Proverb

Our newly purchased cabin was perfect, a small A-frame embraced by the arms of broad ponderosa pines, slender aspen, and towering spruce. An hour's ride from home, the drive wound through Rist Canyon, past Whale Rock, and up a narrow dirt road through Stratton Park. Each visit was an adventure.

Once, we forgot the key. No problem. We'd break in. Feeling oddly like burglars, we shattered a pane of glass in the door and reached through to turn the knob. Of course, repairs involved a trip down the mountain and the purchase of hand tools (no electricity marred the simplicity of our cabin). Another time, we opened the outhouse to discover that squirrels and chipmunks had hosted a TPing party. After that, we secured the toilet paper in a lidded coffee can.

Our children—ages ten, nine, seven, and four—anticipated weekends at the cabin. They raced to fill water buckets at the pump and spent hours leaping on the tire swing that swept across the ravine. When it rained, they sat on the porch plinking BB guns at the swinging target near the fire pit. They learned to build fires, heat water, and wash dishes—by hand. They learned to do without radio, TV, and electronics. The cabin was a place for the basics—acres to roam and plenty of time to do it.

We all looked forward to spending our first Christmas there.

"It will be just like *Little House on the Prairie!*" giggled our daughters.

After opening gifts a day early, we loaded our 1979 eight-passenger van with the necessities on my detailed list: enough food to feed eight for several days (Grandad and Grammy joined us), warm winter wear for everyone (it would be colder indoors, we had learned, than out), and a Christmas stocking for each person (Santa would find us, even though the cabin had a skinny stove pipe instead of a brick chimney).

"Looks like we'll have to chain up." My husband parked the van off the snow-packed road at the entrance to Stratton Park. He and Grandad pulled on gloves and jumped out. I kept a firm grip on Fiddler's collar so he wouldn't follow. Soon, he moseyed to the back of the van so the kids could shower him with attention. They adored Grandad's Standard Poodle.

With steel chain links slapping the ice, our Econoline made it up the steep road, slipping only occasionally—but to an excited audience that squealed and gasped. Several feet of snow clogged the lane, so we parked some distance away and piled our provisions on sleds that we pulled to the cabin door.

Before long, the warmth of a crackling fire began to thaw the room and our fingers.

"Is it time now? Can we chop down a Christmas tree?" one of the kids asked.

"Sure! Bundle up. And don't forget your mittens." I picked through the pile of coats and knitted caps. "And remember, make it a small one. This cabin can't hold a large tree."

An hour later, the crew stomped snow from their boots before dragging in a plump Douglas fir. Short and compact, it fit nicely on the low spool table someone brought from the fire pit.

"Let's get out the decorations." said the youngest.

Decorations?

Decorations!

I bit my lip to hold back a groan. Decorations hadn't made it to my list; I'd never given them a thought.

A wild-eyed look at my mother telegraphed my dismay.

"Don't take off your boots yet," she said. "You kids need to head back outdoors and gather some things."

"What things, Grammy?"

"Why, decorations. Stuff to give this cabin a good dose of holiday spirit."

"What kind of stuff?"

Grammy smiled. "You'll know when you see it. Now, scoot."

I peered out the window to watch the kids crisscross crunchy snow, giggling, tossing an occasional snowball, and shouting their discoveries to each other. Before long, they tromped back inside and heaped their bounty on the cabin floor.

Grammy and I nodded approval and showed them how to swag the doorway with pine boughs. We spread fir branches in the windowsills and layered them with glossy-leafed kinnikinnick whose red bearberries glistened. And in the center, we placed a fat candle to chase away the dusk that had arrived early.

"What about the tree?"

Ahhh. The tree. I was one step ahead.

I pulled out a big bowl of dough. "We're going to decorate the pioneer way—with gingerbread cookies."

"This really is like *Little House on the Prairie*." My daughters grinned their delight.

The kids loved rolling out the dough (a can of green beans made a handy rolling pin) and creating shapes with cookie cutters. They poked a hole in the top of each cookie (a clean nail from the storage shed did the job) and waited impatiently for them to bake.

Meanwhile, the kids sorted through the treasures they'd brought in and nestled them in the tree. Pine cones in every size. A delicate hummingbird nest. More sprigs of rubbery kinnikinnick.

The festive scent of cinnamon and ginger warmed our small cabin. Even Fiddler sniffed in appreciation while the sheets of cookies cooled. Supper was a simple affair, stew that had simmered for hours in the cast iron pot. When the dishes were washed and flannel pajamas donned, we set about the task of threading pieces of twine through each cookie.

Then, we settled, cross-legged, in the glow of candlelight to sing familiar carols, admiring the Douglas fir and the way the cookies swung from its branches.

"It's beautiful," breathed our older daughter. "The prettiest tree we ever had."

With stockings clipped by wooden clothespins to the twine stretched behind the stovepipe, we snuggled in our sleeping bags.

"We forgot to put out cookies for Santa," said our sleepy four-year-old.

I yawned and nestled deeper. "Don't worry. I'll take care of it in a minute."

But the last thing I heard was the dog thumping his tail until Grandad finally whispered through the dark for him to settle down.

Christmas morning arrived early, just like at home, with giggling children reaching for mysteriously lumpy stockings before the sun even rose.

"Santa made it down the stove pipe!" Excited kids pulled candy and small gifts from their stockings.

But, as the first light of dawn slipped through the frosted windows, someone gasped.

"The tree! What happened to the tree?"

Eight pairs of eyes darted to the Douglas fir. Eight pairs of eyes widened in disbelief.

Where tantalizing gingerbread cookies had swayed the night before, now rings of twine dangled, empty and limp. Only a smattering of cookies remained, scattered on the upper branches.

Our youngest wailed. "They're all gone! Burglars broke in and stole our decorations!"

"No," I soothed, "no one broke in. The cookies were just, well, they were…"

He brightened in sudden inspiration. "I know! It was Santa! He was really, really hungry after he came all the way to the cabin."

"That sounds plausible," I said, aiming a stern look at the older children.

Grandad and Grammy nodded. Even Fiddler thumped his tail in agreement… just before he gave a satisfied belch.

Loud.

And long.

~Carol McAdoo Rehme

O Christmas

Any mother could perform the jobs of several air traffic controllers with ease.
~Lisa Alther

The trouble with Christmas is that everyone wants to be a kid again. My daughters are young adults, one married with a small child and the other engaged. I noticed the disbelief in their eyes when I asked them to help with the food this year. After all, they prefer to be Christmased, not Christmas others. I understand. I feel the same way. But let's face it; Christmas is a mammoth job for the woman of the house.

Traditionally the holiday falls squarely on the shoulders of Mom. The bulk of Christmas carding, shopping, wrapping, cleaning, decorating, baking, cooking and Santa Clausing becomes hers by default.

By law, women are required to do these things because men do not understand the basic concept of equality. So what if Bob's gift costs $89 and Richard's only $7.50? It's Christmas! Who's counting? Mom (who understands inequality and wishes to prevent world wars and city-wide riots) rushes to the nearest discount store at 11 PM and sifts through mounds of mangled sweaters searching for a gift or two to even the score. Then she whips up a batch of homemade divinity to equalize the number as well as cost of presents under the tree. It's second nature to her. No wonder she ends up doing all the shopping. It's easier to do it right the first time rather than trying to fix it at the last minute.

My husband has no concept of what it takes to pull it all together.

Freely he invites extra people to join us for the holiday meal, not remembering or caring that our table only seats ten (and only if two people share each end) and that our dinnerware service is for twelve. "I'll help you," he promises. Sure. And this year I'm trying to cook for a vegetarian, another who won't eat pork and another who won't eat poultry. Try finding a menu to please all three!

O Magazine instructs me to keep my goals reachable and simplify my plans. It's good advice but shocking to the librarian who checked out my book the other day. "Have you finished your cleaning and baking for Christmas?" she asked.

"I'm doing neither this year," I said in my relaxed *O*-inspired voice.

"No baking? Or cleaning?" She nervously handed me my book and hurried away as if I had cooties.

I had crossed the line. The message was clear; if I planned to follow *O*'s advice, I'd best keep quiet about it.

This morning I got up early and began my solitary vigil of putting the turkey in the oven, preparing the family's favorite stuffing and finding a pan big enough to catch the ham drippings. The gifts are under the tree and the kids are home. The fridge is bulging with salad fixings, eggnog and pickled herring. I remember how I promised my son that I would make rosettes for Christmas. It won't take long to make a batch.

I consider the rest of the family sleeping in, waiting for me to conduct the extravaganza. How blessed we are to be healthy and employed. Our youngest just graduated from college and will marry soon. Our son has a permanent job after a year of temping. Our sweet grandchild lives near enough that we can be part of his life.

Christmas comes only once a year; it's a time to count our joys and put sorrows into perspective. The gifting and decorating are nice, but the real gift is being together.

The kids are sleeping in — I was the same way at their age. For years I let others do it all. And why not? Drudgery and responsibility come too soon; let them have one more Christmas without it.

After all doesn't the Bible say to Christmas others as you would have them Christmas you? Or something like that.

~Candace Simar

Dough
for All Seasons

Perhaps imagination is only intelligence having fun.
~George Scialabba

I offered to help my neighbor chaperone her daughter's birthday sleepover, because school was out for Christmas vacation, no one would sleep a wink and there'd be shenanigans aplenty. Besides, I enjoyed celebrating the joy, beauty and magic of the Christmas season through the eyes of children.

There was pizza for dinner and a chocolate fudge birthday cake for dessert. Afterwards, they watched a popular holiday movie the birthday girl had requested her mother rent for the occasion. As they enjoyed the movie in the den, the four ten-year-old girls whispered, giggled, chattered, danced, sang Christmas carols, and consumed two bags of microwave popcorn.

"I'm so glad they're having a good time," whispered my neighbor as we sat at the kitchen table sharing a piece of the left over birthday cake.

However, their contentment was short-lived. After the movie they joined us in the kitchen. "There's nothing to do," whined the four girls in unison. Before we could reply, they huddled together and shouted, "Let's bake Christmas cookies!" My neighbor's cheeks flushed red… there was no cookie baking on the birthday agenda.

Quickly, I suggested, "Instead of cookie dough, let's make clay dough. It's for crafting, not eating. I'll show you how to make ornaments, jewelry and other gifts for yourselves, family and friends." The girls screamed with glee and sat down at the kitchen table.

Only three ingredients are needed to prepare clay dough: cornstarch, baking soda and cold water. Since I had everything on hand for the project, I ran next door to gather what was needed.

As the girls watched, I cooked the dough on the stove until the mixture resembled dry mashed potatoes. Then I placed the dough on a plate, covered it with a damp cloth and let the dough cool enough to handle.

When the dough was ready, I taught the girls how to knead it until smooth on cutting boards sprinkled in cornstarch and how to roll out the dough with a cornstarch-dusted rolling pin to a 1/4- to 1/2-inch thickness.

Then the fun began. We cut out ornaments with cornstarch-dusted cookie cutters into the shapes of bells, trees, angels, wreaths, reindeers and Santas. We also formed by free-hand, initials of their first names and initials for those they planned to give as gifts. Next, we poked small holes with a toothpick at the top of each ornament and initial pendant and placed them on parchment paper-lined cookie sheets.

When finished, I placed the cookie sheets into a 350-degree preheated oven for one minute, and then turned off the oven to allow their handiwork to dry until the oven was cold.

In unison, the girls asked, "Can we stay up until they're dry?"

"No, it's way past bedtime," my neighbor said. Groans followed, but the girls merrily headed off to bed when we assured them their jewelry would be ready to decorate the next morning.

After an early breakfast, the girls began to put the finishing touches on their creations. They brushed their ornaments with thick white craft glue and sprinkled with red, gold and silver glitter. The initial pendants were painted with felt-tip markers and decorated by gluing on pieces of felt, sequins and tiny beads. Once they were completely dry, assorted ribbons or leather shoestrings were inserted through each hole.

By early evening, the pendants were dry. Each girl went home proudly wearing a pendant around her neck, and with a gift bag on her arm full of clay dough gifts wrapped in red and green tissue. The birthday party was a huge success.

There were many clay dough projects the following year and creativity ensued. Pendants and necklaces were also created for St. Patrick's Day, Valentine's Day, the Fourth of July and numerous other occasions. My Christmas clay dough recipe became known as the "Dough for all Seasons."

~Georgia A. Hubley

Chapter 5

The Gift of Christmas

It's a Wonderful Life

A Perfectly Imperfect Christmas

Striving for excellence motivates you; striving for perfection is demoralizing.
~Harriet Braiker

"Just look at this place," I wailed to my husband, Bruce. "I wanted everything to be perfect." We'd recently moved across town and figuring I'd be settled in time for our annual Christmas gathering, popped my invitations in the mail right after Thanksgiving.

What was I thinking?

I wasn't ready, or even totally unpacked, but at least the mammoth tree I'd chosen for our new home would be trimmed. After fluffing branches and rearranging some glass ornaments I stepped back for a final inspection. Hundreds of brilliant white lights twinkled from the full, fragrant boughs. Twelve magnificent feet of Douglas fir!

No matter what the event, I went overboard with preparations and then worried they weren't good enough. Quite simply, I was a deep-rooted perfectionist on a constant quest to get things, well... perfect. And those last few unpacked moving cartons in the corner trumpeted how miserably I'd failed.

"Tonight will be a total flop." I continued to carry on, my shoulders slumped in defeat. "I'm hosting this party in a half-finished house." The sight of my curtain-less windows, empty china cabinet and barren bookcase was too much to bear. Snatching up bundles of outdoor lights, I dumped them into Bruce's arms. "Can you hang these? At least the outside will look finished."

"Calm down, Sue. Everything always turns out fine, no matter what." He planted a kiss on my forehead and headed outside carrying the hundreds of feet of lights.

With a headache brewing, I headed into the kitchen to get a couple of aspirin. And there, lying open on the counter was Martha Stewart's magazine, mocking me. Sure! Her mantels were draped in garlands of fresh pine, and adorned with satin ribbons. She had an elegantly set table, which was of course, bathed in soft candlelight. Even her sideboard glimmered with magnificent silver and crystal. Why couldn't I be perfect like her?

I glanced at the clock over the sink and gasped. Three o'clock? My good china and holiday linens remained unaccounted for and I still needed to pick up some last-minute items for the buffet. I snatched the grocery list, threw a parka on right over my grungy sweats, and made a quick dash to the market.

Nabbing the last available cart, I wheeled into the store, where the wait at the deli counter seemed endless. And in the seafood department, I was certain the shrimp I needed were still in the ocean.

And then, the dreaded paper goods aisle. Gritting my teeth, I tried not to think about Grandma's embroidered linens still packed away, as I grabbed a red paper table cloth, green napkins, and some holly-trimmed dinner plates. How I hated using paper dishes while my pretty white china with the silver trim languished in some unpacked crate. I added paper cups and dessert plates to my cart and made my way to the checkout lines only to find each and every line was a mile long.

A moment later, a light flickered above the register by customer service. Yes! An express lane. Twenty items or less, and no waiting. Thank you, God.

"Looks like somebody is having a party," the cashier, with the nametag "Penny," chirped as she scanned my party goods.

"Mmm-hmm," I replied brusquely, quickly fanning open some plastic bags.

"Oh, I had mine the other night, right after work," she bubbled on.

I wished that she would just ring up my order.

"Everyone brought something to share," she added, "like a big potluck. We had a blast."

I stopped bagging and stared at her, slack-jawed. Potluck? Martha would never do potluck. I hurriedly wrote out a check and rushed out the door.

Back home I slid my soufflé into the oven and carefully arranged the shrimp on a platter. "A big potluck…" The cashier's words niggled as I added my punch bowl to the table. What's wrong with formal? I bristled. It's a good thing, as Martha would say.

There was just enough time for a quick shower and then I hurried to my room and slipped into my black velvet dress and matching pumps. After quickly applying mascara and lip gloss, I headed downstairs to light the candles, fastening my pearls as I went.

"Everyone brought something to share…" Why couldn't I get Potluck Penny off my mind?

When the doorbell rang I took a last look around. The perfect blend of woodsy pine and a hint of cinnamon hung in the air, but a spotlight seemed to hover over everything I hadn't accomplished. What will my company think of me? I tried to get into the holiday spirit as I passed hors d'oeuvres, but I couldn't stop criticizing myself for falling short.

"Sue, what a lovely home," a friend remarked, as I handed her a cup of eggnog.

I blinked. She didn't notice?

"Th-thanks…" Sheepishly, I replied. "Of course I still need to paint, and shop for curtains, and area rugs, and… well, you know, there's still a lot to do."

She arched an eyebrow, "What are you talking about? You haven't been here that long."

"Actually," another friend chimed in, "I wouldn't have taken on a party so soon after moving, but you did, and with your usual flair."

Flair? A weight seemed to lift from my shoulders. I exhaled quietly and then smiled. Grabbing a holly-trimmed paper plate, I sauntered along the buffet table, loading it generously. My guests moved into the dining room, and I joined them. As we ate and gabbed, I noticed that no one had anything to say about the paper plates, except to ask if I could put out some more. Carols played and laughter filled the room. Everyone was having a blast, including me. A blast...

A light, brilliant as a Christmas bulb blinked over my head. Just like Potluck Penny! She had a spur-of-the-moment get-together, while I ran myself ragged trying to make everything just-so. Did it matter? Her friends were probably as happy to see her as my friends were to see me, and she most likely received the same enthusiastic greetings and hugs from her guests. I was starting to see.

Later that night, after the last guest had left, I closed the door, and rested my back against it. I get it! It's about the season; festive, loving and joyful. No one noticed what was finished and what wasn't, they just enjoyed celebrating together.

I poured myself a cup of eggnog and plopped down on the sofa amidst the disarray.

"See?" Bruce fixed me with that smug, I-told-you-so look as he sat next to me. "Didn't I tell you everything would turn out fine? It was a huge success."

With a crooked smile and a soft nod, I agreed. As much as I adored Martha, it was time to create my own signature style. I rested my head on Bruce's shoulder and closed my eyes. He would never believe it, but I was already planning next year's perfectly imperfect potluck party.

~Susan A. Karas

The Night I Met My Grandmother

Other things may change us, but we start and end with the family.
~Anthony Brandt

Snow was falling softly outside. I remember watching each flake delicately floating to the ground and frosting the parking lot beneath a dimmed street light. Everything was quiet. I must have been ten years old at the time; but twenty years later, snapshots of the night still flicker through my memory like pieces of fool's gold dancing in a river bed. Among various pieces of meaningless sediment, I can still recall the beauty and intensity of that Christmas Eve.

We made our way into the small, empty Mexican restaurant and were greeted by a halo of Christmas cheer. The warmth of the lobby blanketed us from the cold Minnesota winter outside as "Feliz Navidad" played overhead. My grandmother was in town and had insisted on taking our family out for Christmas dinner.

Generally, we opened presents on Christmas Eve, so dinner was more an obstacle than an opportunity to enjoy the sentiments of the evening. At that point, I saw Grandma like a fairy godmother. I equated her with gifts, toys, and a never-ending supply of candy stockpiled in her Mary Poppins-sized purse. When she was in town, I knew it would be a Christmas, or at least a pile of Christmas presents, worth remembering.

Looking back though, I can't remember a single present I opened. Grandma sat across from me. The candle on the table dusted her soft, wrinkled cheeks, and she began to tell us a story. I don't remember how the conversation started. Perhaps something sparked memories of a Christmas years behind us, or maybe she felt the need to share herself with us before it was too late.

My dad says Grandma never talked much about herself before that night; in fact, she was a relatively private person. But, something changed that Christmas Eve. A wall cracked somewhere inside of her. I remember staring up at her deep, dark eyes and feeling compelled to walk with her through a piece of her history.

She talked about growing up during the Depression and losing both parents before she was sixteen. She recounted the wrath of the economy and remembered having to eat frogs for dinner so she could stay alive. She spoke about a doll she had made from rags and random bits because she had no other toys. She told us she had lied about her age so she could join the naval hospital corps as a scrub tech, and recounted meeting my grandfather after the war when she was in nursing school.

I was captivated by her. The room seemed to get smaller as the details of her life spilled into the air. We leaned in, wrapping ourselves tighter around the table. Hours passed in what seemed like minutes, dinner plates had been cleared, and opening Christmas presents was now a distant consideration.

Grandma was becoming real to me. She was materializing in front of my eyes, and creating a backdrop for the person I wanted to become. I felt like I was meeting her for the first time. She was radiant and raw. She was suddenly more than someone who showered us with goodies. She was a survivor, a hero, and an integral piece of who I was. She was a woman who fought to stay alive, persevered through tragedy, and appreciated simple things. She was stunning and strong, and I wanted to be just like her.

Grandma passed away only a few years later. Had I known how short her time with us was, I would have begged her to retell her stories every single day until she was gone. We never got to sit across the table from her again; but those intimate moments so many years ago created a legacy that still impacts me today.

That night, I found the importance of learning where I came from, celebrating the moments that stretch me, and remembering the people who love me.

I discovered the joy of significance, and experienced the real meaning of Christmas. I saw evidence of grace in my grandmother's stories, and encountered a longing for it in my own life. She showed me I could follow her footsteps in perseverance and could conquer life's challenges and fears head on. She taught me that everyone has a story worth telling, and gave me the confidence to write one of my own.

That night I learned a lot about life and what it means to love. I realized that the stories we create with our lives can impact generations to come, and saw the beauty of talking about the moments that make life worthwhile. I saw the importance of living a life that speaks of genuine substance, and understood what sacrifice and forgiveness looked like. Each year, on Christmas Eve, I am reminded of the night I truly met my grandmother. I am always amazed, and eternally grateful for the gift of legacy she gave me that Christmas.

~Kara L. Johnson

The Christmas Stocking

Every problem has a gift for you in its hands.
~Richard Bach

"A Christmas stocking is the least of your worries," I told myself. "Forget it. Do you think a five-month-old baby cares about whether he has a stocking hanging at the fireplace? Besides, you don't even have a fireplace. Or a Christmas tree. Or anything."

It did seem that my life was empty. I had a failed marriage and barely enough money to pay the bills. I sat alone in my little apartment, rocking my sleeping son. I'd chosen his name, Peter, for a reason. It meant rock. Solid, secure, unchanging. I wanted those qualities for him. His skin felt new and soft, his hair downy. He was beautiful. Still, I felt sad. I had nothing, but I wanted to give him everything.

As I rocked, I told him it was his first Christmas. "You're going to have your own special Christmas stocking," I promised.

Not just any old stocking would do, either.

When I was a child, my mother made mine. I still had it, red felt, lots of glitter and sequins. There was a little green Christmas tree, tiny red lights, an angel, and my name at the top. A stocking, it seemed, was a precious thing to keep. Something pretty, something special. Something that awakened excitement and anticipation.

I sat rocking, remembering my Christmas stocking, the smell of the apples, the oranges, almost tasting the nuts, the ribbons of Christmas candy that were there every single year. Usually there was a small toy in the toe, but that wasn't the most exciting part. It was the idea of going to bed with an empty stocking and waking up in the morning to find it filled to the brim.

A stocking represented, at least in a small way, hope.

After I put my baby into his crib that night, I saw the dirty dishes in the kitchen sink. There was still work to do, and then I had to get up early the next morning, rush out the door, drive to the babysitter, and get to my job. Life was about being practical. Why, in the name of good sense and responsibility, would I spend even a dollar on a silly Christmas stocking? Any old sock would do. The dutiful side of myself delivered its usual advice: "Your baby doesn't even know about Santa. He's too young for candy. His own fingers and toes are good enough toys for him."

Still I wanted him to have a Christmas stocking, a beautiful one. I wanted it this Christmas. His first.

"Wait for the sales after the holidays," I scolded myself. "Do you really think there is anything magical about the 25th? The exact day doesn't matter, does it?"

My heart said yes. Yes, it does matter.

In the following days, I discovered right away that department store stockings were out of the question. The fancy stockings were beautiful, but way too expensive. I tried the discount stores. Some of the stockings were cute, but they weren't beautiful or special. There were piles of them, all just alike. My baby was unique, one of a kind. His stocking had to be unique, too.

I tried the craft stores. These stores were full of possibility, but my pocket was not full of money. By the time I added up all the prettiest things I'd choose to put on the stocking, it was out of the question. I had enough for a plain felt stocking, with maybe one or two decorations glued on.

I'm stubborn. I don't give up easily.

The day before Christmas, I wandered into one of those expensive needlework shops, the kind that carries fine cashmere yarn, specialty fabrics, and designer kits with designer prices. It was fun looking because everything seemed exotic. Wonderful. The shop felt like Christmas. It was kind of like driving through the rich part of town as a child and seeing all the lights and decorations. Pretty to look at, but not for me.

I was just about to leave the store when I saw it.

A beautiful needlepoint stocking. The background color was blue, blue like winter ice, like the color of my little son's eyes. There was a bright red Santa, with fuzzy white trim, a rooftop, a chimney, sparkling silvery snowflakes, a big green Christmas tree with little fuzzy red balls and snowy branches. It was a work of art. Full of wonder. Full of beauty. Unique.

"It's handmade." The sales clerk approached me, smiling. My son was in his stroller looking up at her. He grinned that funny crooked grin and kicked delightedly. He was a happy little guy.

"It is so pretty," I told her.

"Yes, it is," she agreed. "It's one-of-a-kind, just a sample to show people what can be done with enough time."

"And money," I thought to myself.

"The thing is," she added, "it's been handled a good bit. See?" She pointed at the white on top. "The fur has gotten pretty dingy. Too many people touching it." I hadn't even noticed. To me, the stocking was magical.

"If you're interested, I can let you have it for a discount."

"Oh," I murmured. There was no price tag, but the woman had no idea the discount I would need. "I guess I'm just looking," I told her.

"How about five dollars?" she asked.

I wasn't sure I heard her correctly. She must have seen my face.

"That's including the tax," she told me.

It would be embarrassing to cry over a stocking. I swallowed. I had one bill in my jean's pocket. A five-dollar bill.

All the way home, I could barely contain my excitement. I hadn't felt so full of joy in months. Singing in the car is kind of crazy, but it was Christmas. I didn't care what anyone thought.

When I got back to the apartment and unloaded Peter from his car seat, I taped the stocking to the Formica counter top that separated my teeny kitchen from the living room sofa.

"You have your very own special Christmas stocking!" I sang. I made up some silly words, danced around like a child.

And then I had an idea. It's not that the stocking wasn't perfect. It was. Almost. The white on top did look a little worn, a bit dingy.

First I peaked underneath the fur to see if there was needlepoint behind it. I saw the edge of white stitches, then a bit of red yarn. The fur had been sewn on by hand, not so carefully. It was easy to pull the threads. In a moment it was off.

I could scarcely believe my eyes.

In bright red yarn, there was a beautiful script. It was a name. Peter.

~Martha Moore

Angel Tree

Memory is a way of holding onto the things you love, the things you are,
the things you never want to lose.
~From the television show The Wonder Years

I remember the year my son passed away at the age of twenty-eight, and the feelings of devastation that I had that very first Christmas without him. He fell asleep at the wheel in July of 1999, and shortly thereafter I joined a group of women who had all lost a child. I found the group on the Internet while searching for a place to talk about my loss. We exchanged e-mail messages every day in which we poured out our hearts as we faced the days and nights without our beloved children.

I think I found the group in August, and of course August led to September, and then came October and November. Soon thoughts of the holidays were upon us and we did not know how we would make it through. We knew we had each other to lean on, and we could share ideas on what might help while also talking about what things to avoid doing that might make us feel worse.

Since I always loved Christmas, I still wanted to decorate. One reason was because my son, Donnie, loved it so much. I remember how much I longed to call him, send him a special card, buy him gifts, and I dreamed of a visit from him. It was so difficult to adjust to the fact that he never again would spend Christmas with the family.

That first Christmas, with one of the moms as our "cheerleader," we all vowed we'd decorate like we've never decorated before, and do it all in memory of our children. One mom made a huge card with her son's picture on it for her front window. She inspired me to make a very large wooden, open Christmas card that read, "In Memory of our son, Don, Jr. ~ Happy Holidays!" I erected the sign in my front yard and surrounded it with white lights.

I remember that my other children did not quite understand or agree with us being so public with our grief. It upset them when they came home and saw the sign. It was too soon for them, and when I look back on it now, I think I made a mistake in not checking with them first. But I do know one thing for certain—each of us does what we have to do to cope with such a horrible tragedy as the sudden loss of a child. Even the best of grief experts will advise you to "do what you have to do to survive it."

My online friends and I wrote inspiring e-mails to lift each other up. Because I made scrapbooks of most of our e-mails, I still have them. One mom wrote: "Moms, the season is upon us. Now everybody listen to me: ATTENTION. Our kids are watching us. We need to decorate those trees and windows and the house. My son loved Christmas as all of our kids did. They don't want us to be sad. They are celebrating Christmas much better than we are. They are at Jesus' birthday party! If you cannot bring yourself to decorate, get someone to do it for you. If you have to cry, go ahead. Just look around at your family and loved ones and be so very glad that you have them and they have you. Let's make Christmas great for our loved ones."

Another mom expressed her feelings in this e-mail: "The holidays will come whether we are ready or not. I wish I felt 'normal' so that I could handle them. I wish the store clerks knew what we were going through. Maybe when we shopped, they would know that a simple smile and a 'Hello' would be more appropriate than an exuberant 'Merry Christmas! Are you ready for the holidays?' I want to tell them the truth, but polite society would frown on that. We know they don't really want to know the truth. We should have special lanes for the bereaved moms of the world to shop in. There should be 'generic' departments with merchandise marked 'Suitable for Any Elderly Aunt,' 'Gifts for Any Girl Ages 13-17,' or 'Sure to

Please That Special Neighbor' sections. Gifts already wrapped for us and gift cards attached. We could walk in these special sections to get our gifts wearing earplugs, and we would not have to hear 'Have a Holly Jolly Christmas' songs."

Then another of the moms in our group had a wonderful idea. She had a small tree, so she wanted to make it her "Angel Tree." When she told us about her idea, we decided to make it a group project. One of the moms with a laminating machine took small 3x3-inch pictures of each of our children on beautiful blue sky backgrounds and put them on cardboard and laminated them. She made enough for each mom in our group that Christmas. These "angel ornaments" were hung on our three- and four-foot trees in our individual homes. One of the moms even took her tree to the cemetery where her child rests in peace and put it there, anchoring it down with bent hangers so it would stand in the wind.

I put tiny white lights on my four-foot-tall tree, and added the pictures of all our angels. I also added small silver balls and tiny angel ornaments to fill it nicely. What a heavenly tree it was!

I'll never forget that Christmas and the mixed emotions I had to deal with, nor will I forget my beautiful angel tree that was a tribute to the children so dear to our hearts.

~Beverly F. Walker

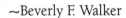

El Camino Angel

*The golden moments in the stream of life rush past us and we see nothing but
sand; the angels come to visit us, and we only know them when they are gone.*
~George Elliot

Deals are struck, swaps are made, souls are sold, paybacks are expected. That's how it's done. The finest FBI negotiators have nothing on young cops when it comes to finagling a holiday off and I'd successfully scored Christmas Eve.

Friday, December 24th, I finished the midnight shift at 7 AM and ran home to grab a couple hours of sleep before making the four-hour drive to Richmond, Virginia. By early afternoon I was at my parents' house adding brightly wrapped packages to the pile of presents already under the tree, stepping back and forth over my father who had stretched out on the floor to maximize his view of the loot. "O Holy Night" was coming from the radio as my stepmother leaned out of the kitchen to playfully scold him, "No shaking, squeezing or sniffing. No guessing. Get up from there!"

Not twenty-four hours later I was leaving. My brothers and sisters waved goodbye and turned back toward the house to spend the rest of the weekend with my parents. I wouldn't clear the city limits before they'd be playing cards and foraging for leftovers.

I should've been happy, grateful for what time I had. I knew it—but couldn't help feeling excluded and cheated. I was exhausted and depressed, dreading the return trip to Charlotte, where I would arrive just in time for Christmas night roll call and spend another eight hours driving a cruiser in the dark. My mood felt like the sky looked: gray and low. It could snow.

Straddling the Virginia/North Carolina border is about ninety miles of interstate... and that's all. Road and trees—that is it. There is an occasional overpass suspending a road that certainly goes somewhere but I can't imagine where and no matter how many times I pass, coming and going, I cannot recall a sign. Approaching one of these off-ramps is where my Datsun began to cough.

At first it was a polite little hiccup but it soon turned into a full-blown hack and I was able to roll two-thirds of the way to the top of the exit before it sputtered out completely. "Well what now?" I thought. It was 4:30 and getting dark in a hurry. I hit the emergency flashers, climbed out and raised the hood. Zipping up my coat, I hiked up the incline to the crossroad and mentally reviewed the situation. First things first, I needed to find a telephone.

Making a call was easier said than done in the mid-80s, back in the hard-to-remember days before cell phones, BlackBerrys and GPS. Then "mobiles" were about the size of a brick that only people on the cutting edge of technology carried around in bags strapped over their shoulders or lumped on the front seat of their cars, plugged into the lighters.

Once at the top of the ramp I could see a gas station on a service road that ran parallel to the highway on my same side. It was dark and obviously closed.

Across the bridge at the top of the northbound ramp, on the other side, was another gas station. Some small lights were on but I wasn't holding out much hope that someone would be there. I was only praying for a payphone that worked and that I had change for it.

Starting across the overpass, I knew I was an hour and a half south of Richmond. I was contemplating my father coming to get me—a three-hour round trip for him and me having to call my Sergeant long distance and explain why I couldn't get to work. He'd never believe me.

Just then I heard a car coming up from behind. There was virtually no traffic on I-85 so it must've come from somewhere on the unknown road. I turned my head and a blue El Camino slowed to a crawl in the other lane. I hadn't seen one of them in a long time. An older black man cranked down his window.

"Did you call?" he hollered over.

"Excuse me?"

"Did you call for a mechanic? Is that your car back there?"

"Yes it is, but I haven't called anyone. I was going to just now."

He said, "I have a garage down aways and someone called."

"It wasn't me," I said, "but I'm sure glad you're here."

We returned to my car and I explained what it had done. He nodded and picked a screwdriver off the front seat of his truck. In less than three minutes the man popped the distributor cap, opened the points, cleaned the contacts and said, "See if it starts." It did, ran like a champ. He slammed the hood and wiped his hands, "That was lucky. Merry Christmas." I thanked him repeatedly and tried to give him the $13 I had in my possession. He shook his head, waved and drove off.

I headed on home marveling at my incredible good fortune. As I drove I started to think: No more than six or seven minutes had passed from the time I left my car walking when the El Camino pulled up. Few cars passed on the highway underneath and there were definitely none up on the road with me, so who called? Where would they have called from? Even if they had called at the moment my car broke down it would've taken longer, until after dark, for someone to get there, and how would somebody know exactly where to call. Why would a person happen to be spending Christmas evening in his garage in Podunkville and just happen to answer the phone?

At that moment I realized that I had been the recipient of something pretty special. Maybe it was providence or incredible coincidence, who knows? It's just that when I was fuming and resentful, questioning my choices of having signed away life's ordinary pleasures—holidays with family, weekends with friends—I was presented with something most extraordinary. There have been similar occasions in the twenty-five years since then. It is like a trade I unknowingly made where I got something better than I gave and I learned not to question. After thirty years as a police officer, my life has been anything but ordinary. I didn't see many holidays off, but I did see a few miracles.

~Amy Brady

This Side of Heaven

You don't raise heroes, you raise sons. And if you treat them like sons,
they'll turn out to be heroes, even if it's just in your own eyes.
~Walter M. Schirra, Sr.

"I am deeply sorry. I just don't..." the roar in my ears prevented me from hearing my oncologist's words. I saw sadness in his averted eyes, sensed the warmth of his arms as he hugged me. "The cancer is back... we'll do all we can, but..." We'd beaten cancer five years ago. It looked like we would lose this round.

Mid-January, it was white winter outside. I was shaking my head in disbelief. My thoughts skittered out the doctor's office, away from painful tests, the sharp scent of disinfectant, the cacophony of employees at the end of a hectic day. I considered my Alaskan home, far from this busy Seattle medical office. Would I ever watch the swallows swoop and dip? What about my dear son, working the ski slopes in Park City? Was the recent Christmas to be our last one together on this earth?

Within a few days, I was submerged in a dramatic course of treatment including heavy radiation Monday through Friday, and on Wednesday, poisonous chemotherapy. Kind friends took weekly turns coming from faraway homes to care for me.

Most important, Michael packed up his black Labrador and his snowboard and drove from Utah to Seattle, to stay at my side every day for two months. Seeing his frightened smile, feeling the coolness of his cheek against my fevered face was soothing. I finally slept the night he arrived.

Soon my weakened body tried to reject the radiation, and the near-constant diarrhea was devastating. Recognizing toxins, with great valor my body attempted to purge the poisonous chemotherapy with protracted vomiting. Frequent hospital trips for IV fluids and then for IV nutrition became standard. I became weaker, sicker, and finally exhausted. I looked down at my protruding hip bones, not seen for ages, and shook my head at fate.

My light, my reason to wake up, was the focused love of my son. Some days we would speak little, he would encourage me to eat a little soup, then I'd fall asleep. Jerking awake, I would calm when I saw him, perhaps dozing in the easy chair or quietly watching a television show. On bad nights, he slept in an ancient cot beside me. He would waken at 4:00 AM to sleepily change my IV, carefully wiping the tubing with alcohol as he wiped sleep from his eyes. Some mornings my heart would break with love for this courageous young man.

I had always loved him, of course, had raised him alone. We had been through much. Signing up for school, me waiting at the bus for him—eager to hear about first grade. The fear we experienced when, at age five, he developed a high fever. The nurse tried to separate us because he was crying. She thought he would calm down without his mother. I whispered to him to hold his tears until we got home. Then I defied the nurse and held my son's hand for the frightening procedures he endured. Now I couldn't recall—did he cry when we got home? Was he still holding tears after these decades? Had I succeeded in my quest to be a good mother? Did my son know how deeply he was loved? My physical distress would interrupt the tumultuous thoughts. I would slowly make my way to the bathroom, once again.

One particularly difficult day, I woke from a troubled nap to find him sitting beside me, holding my hand. I smiled at him through cracked lips. We knew that the last Christmas was likely our final one. As tears leaked down my face, Michael said, "Stop crying, you need the fluids." His humor worked. I dried the tears, drew him closer to me.

And then, like everything else, the treatments came to an end. I went home to Alaska, to watch and to wait. My beloved son joined the military to serve his country.

Crucial surprise, once my body stopped being poisoned, I stopped vomiting. Over the months, my tattered body healed itself. And then it was December. All evidence pointed to the fact that we were going to have a Christmas. Together! I would not be "in heaven." We would be together. Somehow.

Upon leaving boot camp, Michael was sent to a small town in Alaska called Ketchikan. He was assigned to a ship, where he discovered seasickness. Miracle upon miracle, he was given Christmas day off, but with no time for travel.

With the unbelievable year behind us, this was no problem. I would fly to Ketchikan. Michael found a small bed and breakfast with a kitchenette. He reserved this for us, me for two days, him for one.

I flew into Ketchikan on December 24th. The short flight was exhausting and I took a long nap at our lovely B&B. A few hours later, Michael was knocking on the door. I flew into the arms of this tall confident young man. We held each other, frightening memories swirling around us. I made coffee and we caught up with each other. Then we wended our way to Ketchikan's one grocery store. Christmas Eve, it was jammed with harried shoppers pushing loaded carts. How would I make Grandma's special fruit salad without a single maraschino cherry? We purchased a roasting hen in lieu of turkey, bought two potatoes, bypassed the pumpkin pie.

Back in our little rented rooms, we enjoyed our traditional spinach dip, and chatted. It was hard for me to stop hugging this guy. He who had so richly given me a reason to live during my recent and dark hours. The strained memories of tough years of single parenthood evaporated in my gratitude for his strength.

To see this handsome, caring man brought tears to my eyes all over again. You cannot ever thank someone enough for something as profound as saving your life with love and courage.

Christmas morning I awoke with sparkles in my eyes to rival any child's. After a light snack and a walk, we made a semblance of our traditional holiday meal. Chuckling at our little chicken, making a mountain of stuffing and then shrugging (math and division is hard). We baked our potatoes—they don't have to be mashed and besides, we had no gravy. It was a simple meal, yet rich with meaning. Me gratefully growing stronger each day. Michael relieved to be off his ship and to not be nauseous. Both of us deeply elated to be together. Together on this side of heaven.

~Helen Eggers

The Letdown

Sadness flies on the wings of the morning and out of the heart of darkness comes the light.

~Jean Giraudoux

My mother always called the days following Christmas "the letdown." I had no idea what she meant. Whatever it was, it came after weeks of preparations, when the holiday wound to an end. We'd take the lights and ornaments off the Christmas tree, and Dad carried it outside, a few strands of tinsel still hanging from its branches. In a sad tone, Mom said, "Now the letdown comes."

Thirty-five years later, I finally understood. All the baking, decorating and shopping that led up to Christmas was suddenly over. The family gatherings and opening of presents had already turned into memories. My husband and I took down the tree and moved the couch back in front of the window. It was time to switch gears, but for some reason I couldn't get into a routine. I found myself gazing out the window and wishing the snow would melt. Instead, new flakes swirled down from the sky. Was winter ever going to end? I yearned for purple crocuses pushing out of the earth.

In the corner of the living room, a Christmas gift from my son and his wife still sat in its box. Knowing that I loved plants, Brian and Terrie had sent me a hydroponic herb garden. I picked up the instructions, page after page about adding nutrient tablets, pushing buttons and maintaining water levels. Too depressed to tackle the directions, I returned them to the box, feeling bad that my son and daughter-in-law had spent so much on this contraption.

One cold and cloudy Saturday in January, my husband asked, "Do you want me to set up your garden for you?"

"If you want to," I said, thinking that it would give his mechanical mind something to do.

It was like a new toy to him. In no time at all, he put the unit together, filled it with water and plugged it in next to the hutch in the dining room. The water pump hummed and the lights glowed.

That afternoon, darkness descended early, and instead of turning on a lamp, I sat near the garden to read the newspaper. The radiant light lifted my mood. The world seemed warmer and brighter. The next evening, I was again drawn to the garden, the brightest place in the house.

A week passed, and tiny green herbs sprouted—basil and dill and mint. I enjoyed watching them grow, inch by inch, day by day. As they flourished under the light, so did I. The herb garden turned out to be the perfect gift for me.

Perhaps what I'd really had, and what my mother suffered from years ago, was simply a case of the winter blues. All I needed to cure my "letdown" was a little light therapy and a gentle reminder that spring was on its way.

~Mary E. Laufer

My Christmas Homecoming

Where we love is home,
Home that our feet may leave, but not our hearts.
~Oliver Wendell Holmes

oving to a city 1,500 miles away after growing up in a little town, I was missing my family, friends and the small town feel I grew up with. The largeness of this city could be overwhelming, especially during the Christmas season. I thought about returning to the old familiar place that I knew so well, but decided to stay put for the approaching holidays. For months, I found myself driving around looking at the faces of people I didn't know and traveling on roads that seemed like they never ended. Coming from a close-knit family, I hadn't felt much connection to this city or the people in it.

The longing I felt for what I had left behind began to cloud my thoughts (to the point of almost jumping on a jet plane to return home for a visit), even though I was enjoying some things: the newness, warm weather, some events I recently attended, meeting new people and learning my way around. Shopping and setting up a fresh Christmas tree in my home while I put the presents under the tree, played music, and strung some lights, just as I used to do back in my family home, keeping me busy. Even baking a few cookies as I watched holiday specials started to give me that settled in feeling… but I was not feeling any true bonding yet.

As the weeks went by and the holiday season was upon us, I found myself still thinking about going home for a visit to experience the comfort of the family traditions I grew up with. But I had read somewhere about a sunrise service that was to be held on Christmas morning at the beach close to where I live. I made a mental note thinking, "This sounds neat; maybe I'll do this," while half-heartedly saying to myself, "I wouldn't be able to do that back home." I had visions of kids making snowmen in freezing temps back home as I frolicked in the sun and sand but I still had a deep rooted longing and homesickness that even the sun and ocean couldn't wash away.

Waking up that Christmas morning with a new sense of excitement, joy and playfulness I hadn't felt in awhile, I was looking forward to this day. Stopping to pick up some Dunkin' Donuts coffee, I headed to the beach, unsure of what to expect, carrying a heavy heart as I made my way out onto the sand. I was pleasantly surprised when I saw families arriving with children in tow. Coolers and blankets were soon spread out on the sand. Kids barefooted, scurrying to water's edge to plop down, playing with their sand buckets as young couples strolled past them feeling the water lap over their feet. Parents poured fresh orange juice and I looked about as everyone greeted each other with a nod saying "Merry Christmas."

Feeling the immediate warmth of these people I didn't know, I buried my toes deeper into the sand, feeling the cool mist from the sea. I felt grounded. I sipped my coffee seeing the sparkle in the eyes of smiling faces, hearing the delight of giggles from kids playing. Soft voices were heard whispering in the background while hands rubbed eyes, waking up, ready to welcome the glorious day ahead. The sun peeking out, casting its bright glow resembled an orange ball rising out of the ocean to greet us. At that exact moment, there was complete silence among the crowd, except for distant giggles of the kids. During the next few minutes, as I sat on the warm, soft sand taking in the sun rising from bluish-green waters against the early morning sky, for that moment we were all connected as one. The sea accommodated us with just a very fine ripple slowly coming towards the shore. Cameras clicking, kids running in and out of the water squealing while we drank our coffee, eyes fixed on what was now a soft yellow cast across the sky captured our total attention and lifted my spirits and flooded me with emotions.

I sat back, sipping my coffee and looking over the crowd; happy faces, bright eyes showing off the joy we all felt at that instant. I realized only then that it doesn't matter geographically where my physical being is. True, I was still physically far away from my hometown, but this was now my home. These people had been coming here to this beach for years for a sunrise service, to meet with family, meet new friends, pray and commune with nature. At that moment, I felt not only the warmth of the sun, but also the warmth of the people sitting here around me. After we all basked in the sun's welcome, we turned our beach chairs to face the stage. Music had been playing quietly but now the service was about to begin. As the children danced barefooted in the sun, we were ready.

And though few words were exchanged that morning, we were all connected through the sea and the music. We were a small community who had gathered there that morning to worship on this special holiday. As I looked around at the faces, still unknown to me, I felt a settled in feeling. And learning the true difference of what I thought I had settled for this year, was really settling into my new home to make new memories. This familiar feeling, deep inside of me was... a feeling of home, realizing this Christmas morning I had a special homecoming of my own.

~Paula Maugiri Tindall

Seven Ways to Survive the Holidays

Happiness is an attitude. We either make ourselves miserable,
or happy and strong. The amount of work is the same.
~Francesca Reigler

The day after Thanksgiving I was out in it, shopping. For the first time in my life, I stood in a line so long it snaked its way around the back of Best Buy in the pre-dawn darkness. The pre-Christmas sales had begun. And the crowds. The traffic. The overflowing parking lots. The long drives and, eventually, a conglomeration of relatives. Not to mention the possibility of a blizzard blasting across the plains at any time. Holidays are supposed to be filled with joy; however, like the "joys of parenthood," these happy times are also apt to be occasions when we get a lot of practice at, well, at practicing patience. And yet, I've found that happiness may be as close as a smile away, when I borrow a few tips from Santa.

Here are seven ways I give my sleighs a daily tune-up:

1. I CHOOSE TO BE HAPPY. As Santa would say, "Ho, ho, ho!" Rather than dwelling on my troubles, I bring to mind a happy memory, or imagine myself in a pleasant situation. I "practice joy," laughing at something, sometime every day. I'll read a hilarious book, watch a stupid movie, or talk with a

friend who always makes me feel good. If Norman Cousins could beat his "fatal" case of cancer through making laughter a daily part of his ongoing life, surely I can "ho-ho-ho" my way through the holidays.

2. I SMILE, AND ACT LIKE MY OWN BEST CHEERLEADER. Santa always makes it onto his own list, doesn't he? After rising in the morning, I smile at my reflection in the mirror. If I'm feeling stressed I recall some small success I've had, something I've done well—anything I can feel good about—and then I congratulate myself out loud. Like a slow but surely working miracle, I find that my self-esteem increases with each smile, each pat on the back, and I feel good.

3. I BREATHE. Hearty laughter like Santa's requires deep breathing. Besides a nightly regimen of deep breathing, often during the day I take time to breathe, really breathe: three slow, deep breaths, smiling all the while. The increased oxygen refreshes body and mind, and the restful pause raises spirits. Infinitely more beneficial than giving in to despair or temper, this practice works when I'm standing in the longest check-out line, relating to a weary spouse, or dealing with the volatile personality of a difficult relative.

4. I SHARE MYSELF. Santa is all about cheerfully giving (and receiving) gifts of love. Gifts need not be expensive; a smile, a compliment, a hug, a helping hand cost nothing but a moment of time. I make a point of addressing shop clerks by their first names, and speaking to the supervisors about the good job their staff has done. At home, I pet the dogs with a loving touch. On the road, I bless the reckless driver instead of uttering a thoughtless curse, for I know in my heart that the power of a kind word and the goodness of my intention reach farther than we can imagine.

5. CREATE. Santa and his elves keep busy all year long, happily involved in creative activities. Each day I try to write a poem, sing a song (not the blues), paint a picture or work a crossword puzzle. Sometimes I have the presence of mind to lovingly cook a meal. And every night I send out blessings, surrounding the mental image of the person being blessed with health, prosperity, love and light. This blessing activity is a lovely way to end the day.

6. I GO FOR A WALK. Or take a ride to see the lights, as Santa does. I see a lot of the natural world through the day, come blizzard, drought or rain shower, and this regular exposure to nature helps to ground me, to leach my troubles away and to reestablish my connection with Mother Earth. I have found that every season in the great Midwest holds some beauty: a flock of Canada geese flying overhead, a rose in bloom, a sugar maple wearing its colorful autumn attire, or ice-covered branches glistening in the welcome winter sunlight.

7. I PAMPER MYSELF. As happy as Santa is, he probably gives himself regular "down time." For a few moments every night, I give myself the present of peace (and a bite of chocolate). A warm bath. A time to meditate or pray. A moment when I'm not worrying about anything. If worries keep badgering me, I imagine giving those weedy thoughts a yank, pulling them out by their roots and tossing them onto a burning pile of leaves. Because our feelings radiate out in vibrations of differing frequencies and then attract other vibrations on the same level, worries beget new worries, fear creates new situations to fear, and peace engenders peace.

So, who cares if the tree tilts crazily, the turkey needs basting, the toys need assembling? Using these seven simple steps will help me feel happy enough to glide through the holidays with a Christmas carol in my heart.

~Michelle Langenberg

A Bear Hug for Mom

Death leaves a heartache no one can heal,
love leaves a memory no one can steal.
~From a headstone in Ireland

I shuffle into the garage. The Christmas boxes wait in their usual place lined up on the top two shelves. I remove one and dust the top. The pine scent from candles still lingers from the Christmas before. As I bring the boxes, one by one, into the house, the smell of buttery sugar cookies in the oven fills the air.

While melodic tunes of "Silent Night" play softly in the background, I begin the traditional Christmas routine. Pulling each item out, I arrange them in strategic places throughout the house: The red and green candles, the shiny, gold bells to hang on the front door, the musical boxes with winter scenes, bright red poinsettias, green garland spotted with burgundy velvet bows all transform our home into a lively winter wonderland. But the ceramic nativity scene placed in the center of the room illustrates the reason for the anticipated celebration.

Next, I retrieve three stockings to fill the marked places above the fireplace; each embroidered with our sons' names: Jason, Jeff, and Joe. Once Jason and Jeff's are hung, I collapse on the couch, clutch Joe's in my hand and hug it to my chest. I heave a familiar sigh. As I exhale, tears burn in my eyes. Like my heart, Joe's stocking would remain empty. Nothing could fill the void his absence had created. Three years ago, his lively personality, witty sense of humor and bright smile, like a Christmas tree, would light up a room.

But one tragic event robbed me from enjoying his charm ever again. On September 7, 2002, the phone rang around 2:30 AM. Our middle son, Jeff, raced into our bedroom shouting, "Joe's been hurt!"

We frantically pulled on our clothes and rushed out the door. When we arrived at the hospital, we were given only one small piece of information, "They're working on him."

Once in the emergency room, we received the heart-wrenching news. Joe had not survived the multiple stab wounds inflicted on his body.

This isn't happening to us! I thought with anguished disbelief. "These things don't happen to good boys," I wanted to shout.

I crumpled under the weight of Joe's death. My child was gone... I felt as if my own life had been taken.

Like a boat in a violent storm, I was buffeted by winds of unbearable pain. God's Word became my anchor. "Be still, and know that I am God." echoed in my heart over and over again. His word sounded loud and clear, "My grace is sufficient for you."

I made a decision—to surrender and believe in the sufficiency of His grace. And as I slipped my trembling hand into the comfort of His, I stepped forward holding on to it. I clung tight, not each day, or hour, but each moment. For I knew when left unguarded even for seconds, my sorrow could overwhelm me. I was diligent to fill my mind with reassuring verses from His word, from His firm promises and from His direct instructions.

With renewed strength, I gazed at the brighter horizon of my life as my tears dried one by one. My heart reviewed the seasons of Joe's life, memories precious to me. The spring of Joe's emerging vibrant personality; the summer of his warm hugs and those precious words, "I love you Mom"; and the fall of the remarkable changes as the teenager emerged from the small boy. Then came winter, bringing a Christmas that would never be the same.

Through daily prayer, God's grace brought a different light to our Christmas season. Unlike before when Joe's stocking held items bought just for him, it's now filled with treasures wrapped with golden threads of love just for me — the memories, the joy we shared, the moments we laughed together, the bear hugs he'd give me as he walked in from school and the pecks on my cheek while he rushed out the door. And even when he received my scolding, I smile thinking of his witty comments that erased any frown from my face.

Christmas now brings a reason for me to relish the gift God had given me in my son Joe. For nineteen years he filled my life with joy. And until I see him again, each Christmas becomes a joyful countdown till that day. It marks the anticipated event ushering the glorious moment when I'll receive the ultimate Christmas gift — wrapped in God's love, I'll delight in the biggest bear hug from my Joe.

~Janet Perez Eckles

The Gift of Christmas

A Few Good Elves

The Delivery

You may delay, but time will not.
~Benjamin Franklin

I t was early December and football season. My dad was an avid football fan and loved watching all the games leading up to the Super Bowl. I happened to drop in one day during one of the games and found him comfortably reclining in his chair and looking at the television through binoculars. "What are you doing, Dad?" I queried. "I can't see the details of the plays or the scores anymore," he replied. "So, I use binoculars."

The perfect Christmas present for my parents immediately came to mind. Mom and Dad had pretty much all they needed. It was hard to buy them gifts, so we usually tried to come up with one nice, big gift to cover all the gift-giving occasions for the entire year. This year it would be a big screen TV.

We decided that a great way to surprise them would be to deliver the television on the Sunday before Christmas while they were at church. Our church's Sunday service was a three-hour block of meetings: the worship service first, followed by Sunday school and then an hour of additional meetings for the men and women. We could all go to the worship service, our two sons-in-law, Brian and Ian, would leave immediately after that meeting in Brian's 4-wheel-drive truck and pick up the television from our house. They would have two hours to move the TV into place and get it hooked up before Mom and Dad would return home.

We were having a very snowy winter and there was a lot of snow piled up along the roads. That Sunday morning, it was starting to snow again. Mom called me early. "I don't think we'll go to church today. It's so cold and I really hate to drive in all this snow."

"I'll pick you up," I immediately insisted. "I don't mind driving at all and I don't want you to miss the Christmas Cantata." After a bit of convincing that it wouldn't inconvenience me, she agreed to let me drive them. As I picked up Mom and Dad, the snow started coming down harder and the roads were getting quite slick.

We met the rest of the family at the church and settled into the pews to enjoy the Christmas service. The Bishop stood at the pulpit to begin the meeting. He welcomed everyone and then announced, "The snow is coming down pretty hard and we're concerned about the safety of the roads. We've decided to go ahead with the Christmas Cantata and then cancel the remainder of the meetings for the day." I glanced back at my sons-in-law who were grimacing at the news. They immediately got up and quietly slipped out of the back door of the chapel. The rest of us exchanged nervous glances. Could we pull off the surprise in the shortened amount of time?

The meeting finished and I hurried out to the foyer and called Brian on my cell phone. "What's the status?" I whispered. "We're making progress but need more time," he said. "Don't bring them home yet!" I went back into the chapel where my parents were visiting with some friends. "I have to talk to some people," I stammered. "Just visit for a little while and then we'll head home." I proceeded to the hallway to try and stall for as long as possible. I could only delay for a short time as most of our friends were hurrying to get to their cars and head for home. I found Mom and Dad waiting by the door in their coats and boots. "Go get in the car and I'll be right out," I instructed. I again called Brian. "We're almost done but don't come yet!" he begged. "I'll call you when we leave the house."

Mom and Dad were waiting patiently in the car. I got in and we started toward home. The roads were very slick so I could convincingly drive very slowly. Luckily there wasn't much traffic, so it wasn't obvious that I was going about ten miles an hour slower than I really needed to go. Mom and Dad didn't seem at all suspicious of anything being out of the ordinary. I drove to about three blocks from their house and still hadn't gotten a call from Brian. I had to do something to further postpone our arrival.

"Something feels strange with the car," I alleged. "I'm going to stop and look at the tires." Mom looked a bit concerned.

"There is so much snow piled in the gutter, you could easily get stuck." Dad suggested. "We just have a couple of blocks to go, check when we get there."

"I think I better look now," I replied as I pulled to the side of the road. I could almost feel Dad rolling his eyes.

I got out of the car and pretended to check each tire. I had pulled toward a snow bank and could see that if I pulled forward I would get stuck in the mound. I had plenty of room to back up a couple of feet and then easily pull back into the road without getting trapped in the snow. I got back into the car. "There is some ice under the fender that is rubbing on the tires. I guess that was what I felt," I explained. Still there was no call from Brian. I made a spur-of-the-moment decision, shifted into drive and plowed into the deep snow. Mom sighed heavily and out of the corner of my eye I could see Dad slightly shaking his head. His mouth showed a bit of a smirk as he said, "Did I really teach you how to drive?"

I tried to look sheepish instead of triumphant as I suggested, "I'll call Brian. He has a 4-wheel-drive truck; he can come and get us out." I made the call and Brian answered, "We haven't left their house yet but we're just cleaning up." Luckily, Mom and Dad could only hear my side of the conversation. "We're stuck in the snow just a few blocks north of Grandma and Grandpa's house. Can you come and help us get out?" I pleaded. "Great plan, Mom!" Brian laughed. "We'll be there soon." We only had to wait a little while for Brian and Ian to come to our rescue and push us out of the snow bank. I drove the rest of the way to Mom and Dad's house and since I had no obvious reason to follow them in, I let them out and headed for home to await their astonished phone call.

It didn't take long for the call to arrive. Mom was overcome with emotion. "We can't believe it! Santa came while we were at church!" There was a slight pause. "How did you do it?"

I wonder if Santa ever had so much trouble delivering a Christmas present. Maybe we'll ask him to deliver our gift next year. We sure could have used his magic this time!

~Donna Milligan Meadows

Unexpected Joy

The manner of giving is worth more than the gift.
~Pierre Corneille, Le Menteur

On the first Sunday of Advent, snow started falling right after supper. By bedtime, the lawn and trees were awash in a silver glow. Around eleven, the doorbell rang. My husband and our grandchildren were sound asleep. My heart hammered in my chest; my imagination raced. I hoped it wasn't a neighbor, sick or hurt. Even more, I prayed it wasn't someone bearing bad news about a loved one.

My mind flashed back to almost two years earlier when late-night visitors delivered the heartbreaking news that our daughter Julie and her husband Mike had died in a motorcycle accident. Since then, my husband Walt and I had been raising our grandchildren, Cari and Michael.

I slipped out of bed and pulled my robe tight. Harley, our black Lab, followed me down the hall, barking all the way.

"Shhh," I said. "You'll wake everyone."

Switching on the porch light I held my breath. An engine came to life, followed by a car driving away—strange sounds so late on our quiet cul de sac.

I peered through the etched glass on the front door. With no one in sight, I exhaled a sigh of relief and poked my head outside.

Two sets of footprints were outlined on the snow-brushed porch.

The wind whistled, swirling flakes and rustling paper on a brightly-wrapped package sitting on the welcome mat.

I shook my head, wondering if it was a dream. Hearing Harley's bark, breathing in the crisp air, and exhaling frosty breaths made me realize it was real. I picked up the package and carried it inside. The gift had no note, no tag, only a bright red bow on top.

At the kitchen table I opened it and was delighted to find a make-your-own gingerbread house complete with directions, icing, decorations, and a sleeve of peppermint canes. It was a sweet Christmas treat my grandkids and I would have fun making, but there was no clue who left the goodies.

Back in bed, I tried to guess who did it. With a burst of insight I thought I'd solved the puzzle. Every October, one of our neighbors leaves Halloween treats on our porch, along with a picture of a ghost and a poem explaining how we'd been "booed." The ghostly note invites us to leave goodies for two more neighbors. Believing someone started a new secret Santa tradition, I fell asleep.

The next morning I showed the gingerbread kit to our family. They responded with a chorus of "Cool," "Awesome," and "Who did it?"

After explaining my suspicions, I said, "The note must've blown away."

For several days I was on a secret-Santa-seeking mission. Determined to know who left the package, I visited neighbors, phoned family, and asked friends. No one took credit, but everyone had a similar response: "What a great idea."

A week later the mystery remained unsolved. After turning in the next Sunday night I heard a car slow down, stop, then drive away. I hurried from bed and peeked outside. On this snowless night I found no footprints on the porch, but another package. This week's surprise was a homemade chocolate cake.

The next day I asked my family, "Who do you think is doing this?"

With wide eyes, eight-year-old Michael said, "Maybe Santa."

Twelve-year-old Cari shrugged. "Doubtful."

My pragmatic husband, Walt, asked, "Why do you have to know who left the gifts?"

I looked at him like he'd just cut up my credit cards. "Are you kidding? I need to tell them thanks."

"Maybe they don't want to be thanked," he said. "Why not just accept them and be happy?"

I mumbled, "No way."

Over the next week I hatched a plan. On the third Sunday in Advent, after everyone else was in bed, I turned out the lights and crouched in a living room chair, determined to catch our gift-givers in the act.

Monday morning I awoke with a stiff neck. I hurried to the door and opened it wide. Once again, a present graced the porch. Christmas cookies, but still no clue who left them.

The fourth Sunday of Advent came and went with no late-night visitors. The lack of a present puzzled me but worried me even more. What if our gift-givers were sick?

On Christmas Eve, I stayed up past midnight trying to catch a glimpse of our secret Santa. Christmas morning the front porch was empty.

New Year's Eve and New Year's Day came and went. No surprise gifts, and still no clues.

Resigned that the mystery would remain unsolved, I grudgingly agreed maybe Walt was right after all. I should be grateful for the gifts and not worry about saying thanks.

On January 6, the Feast of the Epiphany, a day which several Christian countries call "Three Kings Day" and the Irish call "Little Christmas," I was out running errands when we had another visit. Jim and Betsy, an Irish-American couple from our parish, along with their two youngest daughters, Brigid and Emma, stopped by our home.

Jim handed Walt a wrapped package with a silver bow on top, along with a folded piece of paper. The package contained a velvet box. Inside was an ornament with a hand-painted Nativity scene. The paper described the history of Advent, along with prayers for celebrating the birth of Christ.

Jim also told Walt about how, each year for more than a decade, one of their eight children took a turn selecting a family as their Advent friends. The first three weeks in Advent, they secretly visited the family and left gifts on their doorsteps. Then, on the Feast of the Epiphany, they delivered the final gift in person. That year, Brigid, a classmate of Cari's, picked our family.

What a lovely tradition and a special way to bring light and happiness into our lives at Christmas time!

Now, each Christmas season when I hang the special hand-painted Nativity ornament on our tree, I smile and remember our Advent friends. Even more than their lovely presents wrapped in shiny paper with fancy bows, I am grateful for the special gift they gave me. That year our Advent friends reminded me of the beauty of the Christmas season — a time of anticipation, mystery, love — and unexpected joy.

~Donna Duly Volkenannt

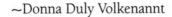

The Perfect Christmas Tree

I've seen and met angels wearing the disguise of ordinary people living ordinary lives.
~Tracy Chapman

When I first received my driver's license, I was willing to do anything to spend time alone behind the wheel—even if it was my mom's yellow station wagon with fake wood paneling! Some of those early desperation "get out of the house" excursions were to deliver hot meals through a program at our church to those who were shut in their homes due to age or declining health.

At first it was about completing the task as efficiently as possible in order to get back to driving. Knock on the door, deliver the food, and jump back in the driver's seat. One of the widows that a friend and I regularly took meals to was Mrs. Miller. Her bathrobe was the only attire I ever saw her wear and her Poodle yapped incessantly at us. After months of standing at her door and resisting her regular invitations to come in and talk, we overcame our initial hesitations and went in. Over time we developed an odd friendship with her. Her hospitality was always limited to a meager offering of cookies that were frozen as hard as rocks. The early stages of dementia that she was experiencing caused our conversations to consist mainly of volleying the same questions to her over and over again and receiving the same answers back every time. But somehow we became attached to her and looked forward to our visits.

A year or two later, my friend and I both left town to attend college. When we came home for the holidays, we just had to go visit Mrs. Miller. During one of our attempts at conversation, we asked, "Are you planning to have a Christmas tree this year?" She surprised us by answering "No." Unsure of whether she was fully aware of the question, we moved on to other topics. Later we asked her again, "Are you planning to have a Christmas tree this year?" Again, she surprised us by answering "No." We looked at each other and knew what had to be done. It was only two days until Christmas, so we sprang into action.

We made arrangements to drive to a friend's farm in the Tennessee countryside the next day, which was Christmas Eve, to cut down a Christmas tree for Mrs. Miller. It was a picturesque, postcard kind of morning with a light snow melting in the sunshine. We wandered up and down the hills looking for the perfect tree to cut down. We felt very masculine toting the small hatchet and some rope over our shoulders through the underbrush, surely in much the same way the rugged pioneers of the land would have done it!

After a few hours our initial adrenaline waned and we became irritated with each other. We were hungry and cold. We had argued over and over again what the perfect tree was for Mrs. Miller. Finally we compromised, made a selection and commenced with the hacking. It was no small feat for two college boys who had never used an axe before! However, once the mighty timber was felled, we dragged it through the woods and put it on top of the car (yes, I think it was the same yellow station wagon with the wood paneling). We drove back, two men on a mission—to give Mrs. Miller the perfect Christmas tree and to get away from each other!

We were still hungry but now we were not speaking to each other. We roared into the driveway, not sure how our great intentions had gone so wrong. We wrestled the tree and nearly each other in through her front door but we got the tree standing up. Finally, there we stood, admiring our handiwork and both supremely pleased with our efforts. Our hearts softening a little, we thought maybe all this work had been worth it. It was at this very moment we realized that we had failed to get any decorations for the Christmas tree. Our frustration had almost calmed, but now it flared again. With it now being late on Christmas Eve, we knew it would be impossible to get anything together in time.

We had failed to complete our task. We were not giving Mrs. Miller the Christmas tree we had planned and our friendship had been strained as well. What a great Christmas Eve this was turning out to be! As we plopped down exhausted onto the couch, still not speaking to each other, Mrs. Miller's face lit up and she pointed to the hallway closet. We shrugged our shoulders, wondering if she even understood what we had gone through or even what we had tried to do for her. Her eyes lit up and she walked over and opened the closet door. Not knowing what else to do, we both wandered over to look in and then could not believe our eyes.

More Christmas tree ornaments than you would believe! There were hundreds of ornaments—all hanging on the artificial Christmas tree that had been used the year before! I didn't know exactly how to feel but we both slowly reached for an ornament to pull off the tree in the closet. We both burst out laughing as we put them on our tree in the living room. It took hours to decorate the tree—not because it should have, but because we could not stop laughing. We joyfully chomped on frozen cookies, enjoyed the Poodle's yapping, and decorated Mrs. Miller's perfect Christmas tree!

~David H. Vaughn

Jake's Story

The world is hugged by the faithful arms of volunteers.
~Terri Guillemets

I entered my office on the afternoon of December 20th and turned on the "mood lighting." The Christmas lights that bordered the ceiling gave the room a soft glow. Since I was practically living in my cubicle, I'd gone ahead and made it cozy. As the Volunteer Coordinator for one of the largest lighted Christmas events in the state of Washington, I experience stress that makes even my shoulder blades burn, since I'm responsible for filling 2,500 volunteer positions in the month of December alone. This is much like packing a clown car with greased pigs.

Although it was still five days before Christmas, all holiday sentiment had long since left me. Since September, light-hanging crews had been decorating the grounds, dragging endless collections of brightly colored Santa displays and Titanic-sized Christmas trees out of storage. The crews spent endless hours draping the trees in lights as they hung suspended in cherry pickers like giraffes with heads stretched to the treetops. October brought a barrage of Christmas planning meetings where staff sang carols and ate candy cane-shaped cookies.

November brought sixty-hour workweeks. My job was to enter event data into my scheduling book ten hours a day as I sat alone in my dimly lit office, coming out only occasionally for snacks and naps. More decorating crews invaded campgrounds and took the interiors of every building by force, dousing them with garland and ribbon. By the time December 1st rolled around, every square inch of the grounds and the staff members' spirits were dripping with Christmas. If there had been an earthquake, Oregon would have experienced the Christmas splatter, and I would have been happy to have been sloshed out of Washington with it. By this time I had overdosed on Christmas and was mentally in the doldrums of January.

Every ring of the phone made my left eye twitch as I watched my evening volunteer schedule turn into a target at a gun range, as caller after caller took aim and destroyed my carefully devised planning. The call that came the afternoon of the 20th at first seemed no different. The voice on the other end introduced herself as Kimberly, and I could tell that her story was not going to be short. I sighed silently, thinking of the workload that was pressing in on me as the 5:00 opening hour drew closer.

Kimberly told me that she hadn't heard about the volunteer opportunities available until late in the game, and she was calling to see if there were still any positions available on the remaining nights. She added that her son Jake was developmentally challenged. She assured me the Jake was a very hard worker and excited about the prospect of coming to help.

"It just takes Jake a little longer to process things."

Kimberly also explained what a relief it would be for Jake to have something to do since she'd been diagnosed with cancer and her energy levels were low. She was unable to get out much, and Jake was going stir-crazy. By the end of the conversation my eye had ceased its twitching.

A few days later I made my way up to the lobby to meet Jake. In front of me stood the character of Lenny from *Of Mice and Men* personified. Jake was a giant of a man, strong, who loved horses and working on farms. After meeting him I regretted having to tell him I could offer him very little work. He'd volunteered so late in the season that my schedule was bursting at the seams. I watched Jake and his mother's faces slowly fall as the conversation progressed. They had hoped for more, but they understood.

Feeling a bit of a failure, I glanced away, only to discover that it was time for our staff debriefing before the gates opened. I had to go.

I sat down in my usual chair and stared at the table in front of me, mentally scanning my scheduling book looking for any openings. I'd become an expert at drowning out voices in any room while doing this. It took Mark, the supervisor of the pony rides, several attempts to get my attention. He looked at me with bloodshot eyes, straw stuck in his hair. Then he bent over, placing his elbows on the table in front of me and put his head in his arms. I heard his muffled voice say, "If I have to lift one more kid on one more horse, I may die."

While I had gotten Mark plenty of volunteers, they were all under 5'2" and 120 pounds. So Mark had single-handedly become responsible for lifting children up to sixty pounds onto horses for five hours a night. And he'd be doing it for the remaining six nights the event was open.

"I just need someone with a strong back, Jessica, even if it's just for a couple hours."

A smile lit up my face.

"I think I know a guy."

A phone call later Jake was scheduled to help Mark each night through the end of the event. I later came to find out that Mark had grown up with an autistic brother. He and Jake were the perfect fit for each other.

The next day I pretended to work in my office until the gates opened and then eagerly made my way toward the pony rides. It was a slow night, and Jake sat with his back to me on the platform that the children stood on to be lifted onto the horses. Another volunteer waved at me, and Jake turned around. A moment later he recognized me. A giant smile lit up his face.

"JESSICA!" his voice boomed. Realizing how loud he was, he lowered his volume and covered his smile. I heard my name again through his hand. "Thank you so much for getting me this job. Mark says I'm doin' a good job, and he gave me a hug, and guess what? My mom is so proud of me!"

And then Jake hugged me with his big bear arms. My muffled, cracked voice came from the inside of the elbow of his winter coat.

"I'm proud of you too, Jake."

As I walked back to my office, tears streamed down my face, and I smiled. Little did Jake know that with one hug and his selfless spirit he had given me back my Christmas.

~Jessica Beach

Christmas Tree Need

Isn't it funny that at Christmas something in you gets so lonely for—
I don't know what exactly, but it's something that you
don't mind so much not having at other times.
~Kate L. Bosher

I can't say that I was sad, but maybe disappointed or apprehensive. This was my first Christmas married. A year ago, I hit the early morning sales after Christmas and bought a few ornaments and decorations for the magnificent tree we would have our first Christmas, like the trees we always had at home.

It's an understatement to say that sometimes what we dream isn't necessarily the way it turns out, and this was one of those times. First off, it wasn't my home but ours. I guess I was a little carried away with the "me" part of my dreaming. Marriage the first year or so is not only a marriage of two people but two ways of doing things, two ways of understanding, and lots and lots of adjusting.

We were adjusting all right. The second thing is, we were getting used to the fact that right after our first anniversary it would no longer be the two of us but three. That little adjustment to our lives caused other changes. Since I was pregnant, I would not be doing the last term of classes and my student teaching. (Pregnant women weren't allowed to teach back then.) I was also temporarily out of a job. When we married, we knew finances would be tight but we were okay with that. When he got a small raise, we accepted that we could afford to have a baby. Only, more changes occur when you find out that everything costs more than you planned.

Now it was a week before Christmas. Over the weekend we had gone out to the forest and cut some pine. I had planned on making wreaths with candy attached for my young brothers and sisters-in-law, and wreaths or door swags for our parents. It wasn't much but it was something we could afford. On my way home after my last classes before the holiday break, I stopped and, by careful calculations, bought small gifts for the brothers and sisters on both sides of the family and something for both sets of parents. Of course wrapping paper, ribbons, and tags cost money, too! Things I took for granted when I lived at home were adding up as I worked out how to accomplish what I envisioned as Christmas in my adult life. I knew I could squeeze the Christmas baking out of the household larder if I stuck to just a few cookies. We would be going to Mass with his family at midnight and would travel to my parents' for gifts and dinner on Christmas Day. It was all working out… but… but it wasn't how I wanted it, the way I dreamed it would be.

Reality was as cold as the days of the approaching winter. It didn't bother my husband. He said we didn't have to do anything for Christmas. We didn't have to have decorations. We didn't need gifts. I loved him and he loved me and although I knew we didn't need those things, couldn't he understand that I wanted them? Of course we didn't need a tree but I wanted one. There were just no more dollars to stretch. I gave up on the tree. Even a little one was out of the question… besides, a little one just wouldn't do. The decorations I had bought last year would stay in the closet.

As I turned into the drive I told myself I needed an attitude adjustment. It was almost dark. The baby made me tired more, but I had a couple of trips to make to the upstairs apartment to carry up my books and my purchases. It seems I always counted steps when I climbed that stairway. I should have been counting my blessings, not the steps. After all, I was happily married. I was expecting a baby. Although the apartment was small, it was clean and nice and we could afford it. I was almost finished with classes for a while and the holiday break would give me a rest. I was able to buy gifts for everybody, even if they were small. I could finish the wreaths and could bake tomorrow or Sunday. That is a lot of blessings, but why didn't I feel blessed? That gray cloud of disappointment (or was it immaturity?) hung over me.

I stacked my purchases in the closet to take care of later. Although I really wanted to put my feet up, maybe nap, there wasn't time. After picking up the debris from my shopping expedition and straightening up the pile of pine stacked on newspaper on the kitchen table, I grabbed the broom and started to sweep. The pine needles seemed to have traveled all over the apartment, but it didn't take long to have things tidied up.

I made a salad and put it back in the fridge. There were fixings for sandwiches. That would do. Since I had the car, I had to go downtown and pick up my husband from work.

I always loved picking up my husband at night. Friday nights with no work for the weekends were even better! I was glad I didn't have to wait too long for him to come out. It was getting cold! I moved over and he drove. We didn't talk about much on the way home. We were comfortable even with the Christmas thing hanging over us. Maybe the cloud was lifting but that longing was still there. It felt good when he put his arm around me protectively as we walked up the stairs of the house. Once in, he turned on the hallway light and I preceded him up the narrow steps. When I had made my trips up and down the stairway I hadn't bothered with the light. It was dark but the light from the landlady's apartment spilled out so I hadn't needed it. Now with the light on I saw I should have cleaned the stairway. I was embarrassed to see so much mess from my wreath project. Being the kind of wife I thought I should be was harder than I expected it to be. I'd borrow the landlady's vacuum and get the stairway tomorrow.

As I opened the door to the apartment I thought the fresh pine smell was even more fragrant than it had been earlier. I reached in to switch on the light and… SURPRISE!

The apartment was full of people! Where had they all parked?

There was food and drink! There were packages and there in that little living room was a tree from the floor to the ceiling. Oh, my! In a little over an hour friends had maneuvered a huge tree up the stairs and had gathered at this late hour. The landlady had agreed to let them in. My father had made dozens of ornaments. Friends had brought some and I could pull my boxes out of the storage closet! I just couldn't believe my eyes. Never in all of my imagining would I have conjured up their outpouring of love to make my Christmas dream come true. While it was true that I hadn't needed a tree, I needed those signs of love.

~Nancy D. Vilims

Cal's Place

Nobody can do everything, but everyone can do something.
~Author Unknown

The closest I'd ever gotten to Callie McCallister was the moment I stepped between her and Charlie Johnson. Apparently, she had taken all the mouthing she could stand, and her toes teetered on the threshold of an all out knock-down, drag-out fight. She already had her fist drawn, and Charlie's mouth was still in motion.

I positioned my five-foot frame so I could slide in between them. Honestly, looking back, I don't know what I was thinking. She was a big girl with broad shoulders, built from the hard manual labor most kids today will never know.

She was a frequent offender on the school discipline report, and her reputation preceded her. From what I heard, she had enough power behind her punch to knock out anybody who stepped in her way. Unfortunately, I feared the victim would be me by proxy.

Charlie, on the other hand, was six feet tall and solid. He was a nice looking kid and book smart. He had everything he needed to succeed in life, except a good dose of common sense. He was, after all, taunting Cal McCallister.

I didn't have a plan, and I recognized my shortsightedness when Cal looked down into my eyes. All I could do was quietly whisper, "Please, don't." She withdrew her fist but not without giving Charlie a final dirty look. But from that moment on, she and I developed a bond.

It wasn't easy being on the good side of Callie McCallister. She usually slept through her other classes, but she never slept through mine. No, she paid close attention, asking questions and making comments that kept the class in stitches. For once, her classmates were laughing with her and not at her.

As Cal became more comfortable with me, I invited her to join several youth fellowship activities with the teens at my church. My husband served as the youth minister there, and every week we always had a houseful of kids.

One October evening we held a fellowship at our home, inviting the students to drop by, to play games, to eat ice cream and just to hang out. I had invited Cal, but I doubted she would actually show up. You can imagine my surprise when I opened the door and saw her face. She was our first guest.

At first our interactions were awkward and uncomfortable. She didn't know what to say, and neither did I. I excused myself from our living room and popped into the kitchen to check on the final preparations for the evening.

Every so often I poked my head into the living room to make sure she hadn't snuck out and that she was still comfortable. When she wasn't watching me, I watched her. She seemed to take in every little detail of our home—our comfy, lived-in furniture, the family photos hanging on the wall and the mounted scripture hanging above the fireplace.

Then the doorbell rang, and the remaining guests filed into our home. Oh, to have had a video camera back then! The looks on their faces were priceless! When they saw Callie McCallister sitting on our sofa, their jaws literally dropped. Callie exuded coolness, but I knew the truth. She was terrified. She wasn't used to hanging out with kids who were quiet and well-mannered, with parents who cared about their whereabouts and activities.

I wasn't able persuade her to join in the board games with the other kids, but it was just as well. While the other kids laughed and played, she and I had a chance to talk. Only then did she seem to relax and to feel at ease. She actually seemed to enjoy herself. She felt safe.

She opened up quite a bit that night. I learned she had actually moved out and was living in a truck stop on the edge of town. The victim of abuse for many years, she shared that she never really knew what it felt like to be loved. She had never been in a home like mine.

As the school year grew closer to Christmas break, I noticed that Cal's attendance grew more infrequent. I took her aside one day and asked her why she wasn't coming to school anymore. She seemed embarrassed, but she opened the door to her life a little wider.

Apparently, due to the previous abuse she had suffered, she was undergoing some medical situations that required frequent doctor visits. She was too embarrassed to go into more details, and I didn't push.

December rolled around, and I couldn't get Cal off my mind. All I could think about was her separation from her family at Christmastime. All she had were her coworkers at the truck stop. I shared my concerns with the small group of girls who attended my Sunday school class, and they came up with the wonderful idea to shower Callie with gifts on Christmas Eve.

I didn't take the other girls with me because I didn't want to invade Cal's privacy, so I went alone. I must admit I was a little afraid that I might not make it back. I gathered my courage and drove out to the truck stop and was greeted by a friendly waitress who told me Cal was in the back.

I didn't have to wait long before she walked into the diner. It was as if she couldn't believe her eyes. What was her teacher doing at a truck stop on Christmas Eve? Careful not to embarrass her, I whispered she had several friends who wanted to make sure that this was her best Christmas ever. I asked her to walk out to my car with me, and she helped me carry in the bags.

By now she had overcome her embarrassment and was excited. She invited me to the back to see "her room." I've worked with hundreds of teenagers over the twenty-plus years I've taught high school, but to this day, I can't recall ever feeling the way I did when I saw Cal's place. The room she was so proud to show off consisted of a stained mattress lying on a cold concrete floor in the center of a very small room that stored shelves of canned goods. When I watched Cal open gift after gift, I knew that at that moment I would have traded every material thing I owned just to give Callie McCallister the gift of love at Christmas.

Then she did something I never expected. She reached out and wrapped her two big, beefy arms around me. To be truthful, I wasn't sure if she wanted to hug me or smother me. She and I were the only two in the back room. There weren't any other witnesses. But when I saw her face and saw those big tears rolling down her cheeks, I knew Cal had just given me the best gift I would receive that Christmas.

She gave me the gift of her heart.

~Teresa Lockhart

No Christmas Presents

The true meaning of life is to plant trees,
under whose shade you do not expect to sit.
~Nelson Henderson

As the most special day of the year—besides my birthday—came closer, something happened that would change the way I looked at Christmas for the rest of my life. I grew up in a family of seven children. We learned, pretty early, not to wait around for seconds at the dinner table. They used to tell us, "Eat everything on your plate. There are kids in other countries who don't have as much as you."

To which I'd fire back, "Fine with me. They can have all my liver and onions!"

We also knew that when it came to Christmas presents, an only child was going to do a whole lot better than we were. We could never expect to get everything on our lists, but each Christmas we submitted one to our parents anyway, hoping for something big that year.

The Christmas I'm going to tell you about happened over fifty years ago. That special day was less than three weeks away, and our lists were in. I had requested a wrecker truck, a rodeo set, and a cowboy outfit, complete with two guns on a leather belt, along with a few other things I never expected to get.

Because there were so many children in our family, my parents began saving Christmas money months in advance. Much of my father's income came from freelance writing and a few books he had written.

A special missionary speaker came to our church. He owned a big ship that he used to reach out to Eskimo villages. "Many of these people have nothing, especially the children," he reported.

It was not unusual, because of my father's writing, and his work in film production, for many people to visit our home. This included a few who were famous, other authors, pastors, and lots of missionaries. My parents had dreamed of going into the mission field themselves, but their life took a different direction.

They invited the Eskimos' missionary to our house for dinner. This man had all kinds of wild stories about his ship, storms he had weathered, and the people he wanted to reach. We laughed as he and our dad told jokes like the one cannibal inviting the other cannibal to his hut saying, "I'd like to have you for dinner."

"The needs are great," he reminded us later, "especially the children. Many of them will have nothing for Christmas."

I looked at the large family sitting around the table and thought our needs were pretty great too. Besides, Christmas was coming. I'd already handed in my list, and now dreaming about what I'd get was all I could think about. When it came to Christmas and presents, it's fair to say that I was, more or less, just as selfish and self-centered as the next boy under ten years of age.

The missionary went on his way, and life returned to normal for the next few days... or so I thought.

Then, something more dramatic than any of my dad's films happened, and I'll never forget it. Dad called out in his loudest voice, "Family meeting! Family meeting!" Anyone growing up in our house knew that "family meeting" always meant that something big, really big, was about to happen to us. We'd have a family meeting when it was time to buy a new car, our first TV, when my dad received a big royalty check, or we were going on vacation. When we heard "family meeting" we nearly broke our necks running to the living room.

"Get out of the way!" my older brother shouted as he raced past me in the hallway.

When I slid into my place on the floor I wondered if this was the year I would get everything on my list.

But I noticed my parents had serious looks on their faces. Sometimes in family meeting, we had to discuss a difficult subject. Those times were called Family Council.

"Mom and I have something important to discuss with you," my father began, "and your vote will help us decide what to do."

I swallowed hard. Not sure I liked the sound of that.

"You remember when the captain was here," he continued, "and he told us about the needs in the villages?"

I looked around to my brothers and sisters. Most were staring down at the floor.

"Well," my mother added, "we were wondering if our family shouldn't do something to help?"

"Like what?" my older sister asked.

My father smiled. "We thought about taking the money we'd set aside for presents this Christmas, and sending that to him for the children he told us about."

My voice barely squeaked, "All of it?"

They both nodded. It felt like my throat had just squeezed shut, and a sick feeling took over my stomach. But this is Christmas, I thought, our Christmas.

"So, what do you think?" my father asked.

I was sure they didn't want to know what was really going through my head at that moment. But we began to talk about it as a family. And the missionary's words came back to my mind, "The needs are great, especially the children. Many of them will have nothing for Christmas."

It didn't help that we lived in Michigan, where a white Christmas was never in doubt. The smell of our Christmas tree, already sitting over in the corner of the very room where we would cast our votes, had no presents under it yet.

No Christmas presents! Then, one by one, hands began going

up to vote yes on mailing our happy Christmas away to some Eskimo kids we'd never meet. I could hardly believe it, as I watched my own hand go up too. The vote was unanimous. That money was Christmas as far as the Anderson children were concerned.

Then, something happened on Christmas Eve day that we still talk about today. Again we heard, "Family meeting!" That had never happened a second time so soon. When we raced to the living room this time, our parents had broad smiles on their faces.

"We have the most wonderful news," my dad said. He held up an envelope. "I received a check in the mail today, for a story I had long forgotten about."

My mother's eyes glistened, her voice cracked with emotion as she said, "And it is exactly the same amount as we sent for the Eskimo children!"

Well, you have never seen such an excited bunch of people in your life. My parents rushed out to do their Christmas shopping. And they were gone for a long, long time.

Our family had Christmas that year after all. Of course, it would have been Christmas anyway, but the presents just made it that much better. Around the tree that night, our parents told us that, because they waited to shop until the night before Christmas, everything was fifty percent off or more. We got twice as much that year as any Christmas before or since.

~Max Elliot Anderson

The Christmas Miracle Bowl

How beautiful a day can be
When kindness touches it!
~George Elliston

Christmas 1980 threatened to be my bleakest, loneliest Christmas ever. I was about 1,000 miles from home, my two bubbly roommates had just gotten married, and I now lived alone in my top-floor apartment in one of Salt Lake City's scarier neighborhoods. As a fledgling Special Education teacher in a tough west side elementary school, I was learning that Christmas for many families was not all festivities filled with visions of sugar plum fairies and dreams of outrageously toy-laden trees. For many of my students, Christmas break would mean more time on the streets in gang warfare and too many nights going to bed with empty bellies.

Because I had recently graduated from Brigham Young University, one of the few bright moments I anticipated was the upcoming December 19th Holiday Bowl Game pitting my beloved BYU Cougars against the Southern Methodist University Mustangs. BYU had never won a bowl game, and had just lost the previous two Holiday Bowls. I could hope, couldn't I?

One snowy evening, two weeks before this much-anticipated game, I trudged to the local laundromat over ice-encrusted sidewalks. As I crammed my laundry into washing machines, I thought about the ever-present dilemma of how to entice minds struggling with hunger, abuse, or gang wars with the magic of fractions and decoding. Suddenly, my dryer-inspired swish-swirl reverie was shattered by the entrance of a mom and four small children weighed down by bags of the family's laundry. I dreaded the soon-to-erupt chaos, "Mom, he's shoving me!" or "Mom, it's my turn to put in the quarters!"

Instead, I was greeted with eerie silence. The flushed faces and frigid red fingers of the children revealed that they, too, had made the trek to the laundromat on foot. But where were their gloves and snow boots? Two of the children wore frayed sweaters instead of winter coats, and one little boy had on several pairs of well-used socks instead of shoes. The mom stuffed all the laundry in the fewest possible number of machines, and the family sat down in the welcome warmth of the laundromat.

Two decades of extreme shyness waged battle against my growing sense of urgency that this family desperately needed help. My gently probing questions revealed there would be no Christmas this year for the little family, not even a tree. By the final spin of my dryer, I had gleaned the ages and sizes of each child and the family's address.

The phone calls to my friends started as soon as I crossed the threshold of my apartment.

"Hey, have you ever wanted to be an elf?"

"So, what are you doing for the next two weeks?"

"Finals? No biggie! Have I ever got a project for you!"

My cronies at Church rejoiced at the chance to be Santa's elves. My apartment became a North Pole outpost and soon overflowed with brightly wrapped toys, coats, shoes, food and even a fully decorated Christmas tree that the corner tree lot owner donated when he learned of our Secret Santa project. By December 19th, we were ready! About two dozen of us knocked on the door of the bare little apartment and started hauling in large bags and boxes of goodies and the glorious tree. Santa himself could not have been greeted with happier tears or more wide-eyed amazement. The cold, dreary room soon glowed with twinkling lights and our impromptu chorus only slightly butchered "Here Comes Santa Claus," "Jingle Bells," and "Silent Night."

As we started out the door to the strains of "We Wish You a Merry Christmas," the children had hugs for everyone, and the mother clung to me and did not want to let go.

"How can I ever thank you?" she whispered.

"Thank me?" I thought in amazement. If only I could thank her! If only she knew the impact that helping her sweet little family had on all of us that Christmas season. Especially me! When I remembered how forlorn, depressed, and mired in self-pity I had been that night at the laundromat, and how on fire with true Christmas joy I was now that I had learned the true meaning of Christmas....

Needless to say, we were all dancing and hugging and laughing and singing by the time we got back to my apartment to share hot chocolate and rejoice over our best Christmas ever. We were barely through the door when one of the guys cried out, "Oh, no! We missed the Holiday Bowl!"

At least half of us were BYU grads and raced to my tiny television set. There were four minutes left in the game. SMU was thrashing BYU 45-25. All our Christmas exuberance fizzled fast. Then, almost as if angels smiled on our little band of Santa's elves and decided to reward us then and there for our act of Christmas kindness, BYU scored 21 points in the last 2 minutes and 33 seconds to win the 1980 Holiday Bowl 46-45. The touchdown in the last second of the game, according to Wikipedia, "is one of the most miraculous touchdowns in college football history."

The exquisite joy of both remarkable miracles that chilly December night has fueled twenty-nine annual Christmas projects since, gradually increasing over the years to include as many as sixty-five families as we recruit more and more elves and times grow more challenging. Christmas 2010 is already in full swing as my Idaho Santa's outreach workshop (a.k.a. our three-car garage) is bursting at the seams in anticipation of more Christmas miracles to come.

~Randy Joan Mills

You Are Loved

Be an angel to someone else whenever you can, as a way of thanking God for the help your angel has given you.
~The Angels' Little Instruction Book *by Eileen Elias Freeman*

She sat huddled in the doorway, trying to fight off the biting December wind. With a thin coat and her leg in a cast, she seemed small and vulnerable, but I knew she must be tough—much stronger than I, or most people I knew. She was the only homeless person on the streets of San Francisco who didn't ask us for money. Never, not once.

My husband and I were on a weekend getaway, to a city we both loved. (He for the sourdough bread and I for the shopping.) As we got out of our cab in front of the hotel, we saw her for the first time. I liked her right off because she wasn't drinking from a mysterious brown paper bag and she wasn't aggressively asking for money as so many other homeless people were. She was reading. Hunched over her book, trying to capture the last of the winter daylight, she struggled to both keep warm and lose herself in its pages. I wondered about her the rest of the night. I wondered what got her to this place of desolation and cold, of hunger and loneliness. I tossed and turned in our warm and clean hotel bed, knowing she was outside somewhere with nothing more than one blanket and one book.

Every time we left the hotel, we would see her in a different doorway, always keeping to herself and always reading her book. She never responded to my cheerful "Hi!" and I knew she just wanted to be left alone. She had long dark hair, deep brown eyes and looked small and frail huddled deep in the doorways that were her shelter from the world.

On our second night, as we headed back to the hotel, my husband and I talked about the quiet homeless woman. We both wanted to do something for her, but didn't know how she would react, since she never asked for anything and seemed to want to only rely on herself. But deep in my heart, I knew I couldn't leave without at least doing something. Christmas was looming in only a couple of weeks and my heart ached for a woman who would spend it in solitude and cold, without family, without gifts.

I said a quick prayer in my heart, asking God to help me know what we could do. Before returning to our hotel, we found a department store and wandered through, looking for exactly the right gifts for our friend who had no idea who we were. We kept looking at each other and laughing at our own excitement. Warm gloves were my husband's first suggestion. We found perfect red, thick wool gloves and grinned, knowing her hands would now be warm. Being an avid nighttime reader myself, I knew the next "must" on our list was a good flashlight and extra batteries. She could read at night and chase the demons away when the dark got to be too much for a woman sleeping in a doorway in Union Square. We added a few small treats—it was Christmas after all, and then went in search of the last gift I knew I must give her. We headed for the nearest bookstore and I said another quick prayer for guidance. Buying a book for someone is really difficult, especially if you have no idea what they like to read. Almost immediately I walked right up to exactly the right book. I felt a delicious thrill as I read the author—my favorite, Maya Angelou. Her stories and poetry told of hard times, but of deep determination and strength within. A woman of great strength, I knew her words would reach this woman's soul and hoped they would bring her comfort during the bitter winter she was facing.

We hurried back to the hotel to put it all together and happily spotted her just outside, once again reading her book, her leg in its cast resting on her thin blanket. I tried my "Hi!" one more time and once again she ignored me. I somehow knew this would be more a gift for me than for her.

We returned to our room and quickly filled a Christmas bag with our gifts. I wrote inside the cover of the book "Merry Christmas! You are loved." And said a quick prayer that she would accept our gifts and they would, in some small way, be of use to her.

Hand in hand, we walked outside again, buttoning up against the wind and half-ran to her spot in the doorway.

It was empty.

We looked around and could see her nowhere. With tears in my eyes, I realized we were too late. She had found better shelter or left the area entirely. We walked the streets off Union Square until it was very late, her bag clutched in my hands and a constant prayer that we would find her in my heart. We ended up back at our hotel, the bag still with us and the woman nowhere to be found. I couldn't stop the tears. Where was she? Was she hurt or freezing or scared? I couldn't stand the thought of anyone so alone and so lost in such a big city. Now all I could do for her was pray.

The rest of the weekend my husband and I searched for her. We looked in every cubbyhole, doorway and bench that she might have gone to, but we never found her. My husband had to fly to another state for business, and I stayed on to visit with friends living nearby.

Finally, I had only a couple of hours left in the city and my determination to find her strengthened. My friend Joe picked me up and we spent our morning looking for her yet again.

"Sooz, I think she's gone." Joe was always the realist.

"One more time around the block," I pleaded. "We'll just give it one last shot and then I'll quit." I prayed very fast and very hard.

And there she was.

For the first time, I saw her talking to other people, her back to me. Her long black hair cascading down her back and her leg in its cast confirmed I had finally found her. There was nowhere to park and Joe quickly circled the block again. Spotting her and not wanting to lose her again, I jumped out of the car and sprinted over to the group. Suddenly I was embarrassed and feeling stupid. Well, I was here and I couldn't turn back now.

I tapped her on the shoulder and as she turned around I grinned like a kid, held out her bag and finally got to say my "Merry Christmas!" to the woman I had agonized over and prayed about for three days.

I wasn't sure how she would react, since she seemed not interested in making friends, but what she did next brought tears and made my heart swell.

"Oh, THANK you!" She snatched the Christmas bag and without hesitation peered inside. She stared hard and when she looked back up at me, her eyes too were filled with tears. "A Christmas present." She sounded as if she hadn't had a gift in a very long time. "Thank you!" she said again and my teary words are now a blur, but I reached out and hugged her tight. I then found myself saying something I had not planned on.

"I just want you to know... you are loved." She looked as surprised as I was, but I saw the tears and knew I had delivered my message, given the gift I was meant to. With trembling legs, I walked away, to my friend's car and away from her forever.

I'll never forget that incredible woman who braved the hardest thing I can imagine with quiet dignity and courage. I hope she is somewhere warm and safe and I hope she knows she is loved. She never asked for a thing, but what she gave me will stay with me a lifetime.

~Susan Farr-Fahncke

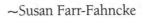

Last Minute Elves

Christmas is the season for kindling the fire of hospitality in the hall,
the genial flame of charity in the heart.
~Washington Irving

"Oh, no. A blizzard on delivery day!" cried my daughter. The heavy falling snow and blowing drifts threatened to give us the most treacherous driving conditions we had ever faced trying to get our annual Santa project's bags of gift-wrapped toys, clothes, and food baskets to struggling families in our local community.

"That's what we get for waiting till the last minute," my son said.

Unforeseen catastrophes had forced us to plan our last deliveries on Christmas Eve, and I was determined that "neither rain, nor sleet, nor dead of night" or blizzard would make any of our assigned families wake up to a bare tree Christmas morning. The fact that we also had Christmas dinner and essential groceries for some of the most desperate families did not escape me.

Just as dusk was settling, only one family remained—a Spanish-speaking family whose address I was unable to confirm. Finally, a dear woman who could understand a little Spanish was able to contact them and wrote down an address and some garbled directions. We loaded her car with toys, bags of groceries, and clothes, and waved from the porch as we watched her taillights disappear into the white-out.

"Oh, no!" I cried out in disbelief. "We forgot the Christmas dinner!"

A huge ham, fruit, dairy goods, and bags of veggies had been stored in the makeshift refrigerator of my front porch. My friend had no cell phone, and I could not leave my home base in case any of the other drivers called in with an emergency.

"I'll catch her!" my son offered.

"Not a chance," I quickly replied. We were still reeling from back-to-back accidents the last time he got behind the wheel. And that was on dry roads!

As I stared at the bags in despair, a car emerged from the swirling snow. A construction company owner who had called hours earlier about a snowboard my son was selling had decided on a whim to drive about thirty miles in the blizzard on Christmas Eve to check it out. As he described where he and his wife lived, I realized they would drive home right past the address my friend had gleaned from the Spanish family.

"Have you ever harbored a secret desire to be an elf?" I queried these poor unsuspecting strangers.

They looked more than a little leery and hesitant to respond, so I explained my Santa crisis and asked if they would consider dropping the ham and other food off to the family on their way home. They were overjoyed to be enlisted as last-minute elves, bought the snowboard, loaded the food, and disappeared back into the deepening drifts. It seemed that prayers I had not even had time to ask had already been answered in a most bizarre and miraculous way. I sighed and went back to my post by the phone.

The panicked call that came through was from these last impromptu recruits.

"We've driven back and forth a dozen times past the area of the address you gave us and I promise you there is absolutely no sign of that house number. In fact, there are no numbers even close to that one," the wife reported. "What do you want us to do next?"

The unrelenting snow and gloom of night compounded the risks of any further searching and made driving all the way back to my house to return the food virtually impossible. I had to give up.

"Thank you so much for trying so hard," I said. "Please, head on home to Nampa. Perhaps, on your way, you will find a needy family to share it with."

Their final phone call to my Santa's outpost was one of pure joy and awe-filled excitement.

"Once we hit Nampa," the husband explained, "a very clear image of one of the workers on my summer construction crew popped into my mind. I wasn't sure of his exact address, but I had a vague idea of the part of town he lived in. When we drove up to this one apartment complex and checked out tenants on the mailboxes, I knew we had found him. We gathered up all the food and knocked on the door."

Now his wife grabbed the phone.

"When the door opened, all we could see was a mattress on the floor in the dark. Javier told us he had run out of money, and the power had been turned off. He and his wife had been huddling together on the mattress in the dark trying to keep warm. They admitted there was no food left in the apartment for any kind of meal, let alone Christmas dinner. They saw the ham and goodies, and we got the hugest hugs ever!"

The couple begged me to keep their phone number and call them to help with more deliveries next year. On that most blustery of Christmas Eves, these Christmas angels closed with the words, "Best Christmas ever!"

~Randy Joan Mills

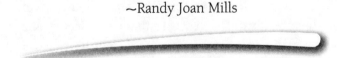

The Christmas Angels

Anyone can be an angel.
~Author Unknown

It was December 23rd. My children and I lived in a teeny house. Being a single mom, going to college, and supporting my children completely alone, Christmas was looking bleak. I looked around me, realization dawning like a slow, twisting pain. We were poor.

Our tiny house had two bedrooms, both off the living room. They were so small that my baby daughter's crib barely fit into one room, and my son's twin bed and dresser into the other. There was no way they could share a room, so I made my bed every night on the living room floor. The three of us shared the only closet in the house. We were snug, always only a few feet from each other — day and night. With no doors on the children's rooms, I could see and hear them at all times. It made them feel secure and made me feel close to them — a blessing I would not have had in other circumstances.

It was late, almost eleven. The snow was falling softly, silently. I was wrapped in a blanket, sitting at the window to watch the powdery flakes flutter in the moonlight, when my front door vibrated with a pounding fist.

Alarmed, I wondered who would be at my home so late on this

snowy winter night. I opened the door to find several strangers grinning from ear to ear, their arms laden with boxes and bags.

Confused, but finding their joyous spirit contagious, I grinned right back.

"Are you Susan?" The man stepped forward as he sort of pushed a box at me.

Nodding stupidly, unable to find my voice, I was sure they thought I was mentally deficient.

"These are for you." The woman thrust another box at me with a huge, beaming smile. The porch light and the snow falling behind her cast a glow on her dark hair, lending her an angelic appearance.

I looked down into her box. It was filled to the top with treats, a fat turkey, and all the makings of a traditional Christmas dinner. My eyes filled with tears as the realization of what they were there for washed over me.

Finally coming to my senses, I found my voice and invited them in. Following the husband were two children, staggering with the weight of their packages. The family introduced themselves, and told me their packages were all gifts for my little family. This wonderful, beautiful family, who were total strangers to me, somehow knew exactly what we needed. They brought wrapped gifts for each of us, a full buffet for me to make on Christmas Day, and many "extras" that I could never afford. Visions of a beautiful, "normal" Christmas literally danced in my head. Somehow my secret wish for Christmas was materializing right in front of me. The desperate prayers of a mother alone were heard, and I knew right then that He had sent His angels my way.

My mysterious angels then handed me a white envelope, gave me another round of grins, and each of them hugged me. They wished me a Merry Christmas and disappeared into the night as suddenly as they had appeared. What felt like slow-motion time was over in probably less than a couple of minutes.

Amazed and deeply touched, I looked around at the boxes and gifts strewn at my feet and felt the ache of depression suddenly being transformed into a childlike joy. I began to cry. I cried hard, sobbing tears of the deepest gratitude. A great sense of peace filled me. The knowledge of God's love reaching into my tiny corner of the world enveloped me like a warm quilt. My heart was full. I hit my knees amid all the boxes and offered a heartfelt prayer of thanks.

Getting to my feet, I wrapped myself in my blanket and sat once again to gaze out the window at the gently falling snow. Suddenly I remembered the envelope. Like a child I ripped it open and gasped at what I saw. A shower of bills flitted to the floor. Gathering them up, I began to count the five-, ten-, and twenty-dollar bills. My vision blurred with tears, I counted the money, then counted it again to make sure I had it right. Sobbing again, I said it out loud. "One hundred dollars."

Even though my "angels" had showered me with gifts, they had somehow understood how desperately money was needed. There was no way they could have known it, but I had just received a disconnect notice from the gas company. I simply didn't have the money needed and feared my family would be without heat by Christmas. The envelope of cash would give us warmth and a tree for Christmas. Suddenly, we had all we needed and more.

I looked at my children sleeping soundly, and through my tears I smiled the first happy, free-of-worry smile in a long, long time. My smile turned into a grin as I thought about tomorrow. Christmas Eve. One visit from complete strangers had magically turned a painful day into a special one that we would always remember. With happiness.

It is now several years since our Christmas angels visited. I have since remarried, and we are happy and richly blessed. Every year since that Christmas in 1993, we choose a family less blessed than we are. We bring them carefully selected gifts, food and treats, and as much money as we can spare. It's our way of passing on what was given to us. It is the "Ripple Effect" in motion. We hope that the cycle continues and that some day, the families that we share with will also pass it on.

Wherever my angels are, I thank you. And so do many other families. Without knowing it, you have touched many lives.

God bless you and all the Christmas Angels out there.

~Susan Farr-Fahncke

Chapter
7

The Gift of Christmas

I'll Be Home for Christmas

Bones for Christmas

Dogs are miracles with paws.
~Attributed to Susan Ariel Rainbow Kennedy

For many of us, Christmas is about families, gift giving, and celebrations. My Christmas of 2002 was about saving Bones.

"I'm telling you this dog must go... I don't care if it's Christmas Eve... can you just come and get him?" The man on the phone was irate.

I slowly counted down to ten before even attempting a response. 10, 9, 8, 7...

"Hello? Are you there? Are you listening to me?"

6, 5, 4, 3, 2, 1. "Sir," I answered, "I understand that this stray dog has happened upon you at an inconvenient time, but, I'm due to fly to St. Louis tomorrow morning. Is there any way I could come look at him — say — Friday? That's only four days away."

"Nope — I'm taking him to the pound — which is what I should have done in the first place — skinny mutt."

At that point my rescuer's instincts kicked in. His intentions weren't a visit to the pound — they wouldn't be open Christmas Eve. I had no choice.

I was the founder of a Labrador Retriever rescue. I had given my word that if God would help me get this venture off the ground, I'd make every attempt I could to save these animals. That was two years and almost nine hundred Labs ago—and I didn't plan on breaking my promise that Christmas Eve.

"Okay," I said, "I'll come and get him. Please give me detailed directions because it will be close to dark when I arrive, and I don't see too well at night."

The man gave me the directions, I placed a call to my family, and I loaded up what basic necessities I figured I would need. I added a few extra Milk-Bones to the pile... it sounded like this would be a welcomed treat.

We've all heard the saying "it's best to make lemonade out of lemons"—and that is what I intended to do. The trip to Cartersville was going to take me close to three hours... I had a lot of lemonade to make.

When I arrived at the dilapidated farmhouse, I was one hundred percent certain of my decision. No Christmas lights or decorations welcomed me and gloominess hung over the place like a thick fog. I had come alone for this rescue, and I admit that at that particular moment, I was questioning my sanity.

The doorbell light was on its last leg but I proceeded to press it anyway. No answer. I decided I might have better luck knocking on the door. As I opened the storm door to get a good pounding in—I noticed a small note tucked between the crevice of the door and the frame. It simply said, "He's around back."

"Great," I mumbled to myself. "What a way to spend Christmas Eve. It's freezing, I'm all alone and goodness knows what I am about to find at the back of this house... but here goes." Talking to myself like that, out loud, had a soothing effect and made me feel not so alone.

I carefully crept my way through the darkness—calling out to a nameless Lab who was hungry, scared, and cold. As I started to call out the second time, I heard a rustling in the undergrowth... coming straight toward me. Then came a loud and deep-throated bark and I just knew I was a goner. Out of nowhere he appeared before me. A beautiful black Lab who should have weighed at least ninety pounds, but appeared to weigh closer to sixty. Poor guy. But talk about friendly! There wasn't an ounce of shyness in his bones. It was as if we were long lost friends reuniting for the holidays.

"My goodness—you are nothing but skin and bones!" I cried as I gave his ears a good scratching. "Bones... that's it... that's your name!" He must have liked it because he began to waggle like only a Lab can do. The front part of his body was twisting in one direction while the other end was completely moving in the opposite direction. The whole time his tail was wagging and his body was wiggling.

The trip back home was quite enjoyable. I learned a good bit about Bones (he liked to smack his jaws together making a funny sound) and he about me. If you've ever owned a Lab, you know they are better than any therapist you could pay for.

Finally we were home. Bones began to get very excited and that smacking sound got a little louder and louder. He knew he was in a safe place and that I was going to take good care of him. We were both pooped. I wasn't sure where he was going to sleep, but he knew. As soon as we headed inside, he jumped on the couch, did a couple of 360's and settled in like he owned the place. This was turning out to be a pretty good Christmas Eve after all.

The next morning—Christmas—I rushed downstairs to visit my new bundle of love. I looked on the couch... but he wasn't there. I rushed into the kitchen; this is usually a favorite place for Labs, but no luck there either. There was only one room left, my office. As I rounded the corner I wasn't sure I was seeing what I thought I was seeing. Bones was all curled up in a ball as snug as could be underneath my Christmas tree, one single Milk-Bone resting by his head. What a precious gift lay before me!

We all know that Christmas is about giving and not receiving, but that Christmas... I think Bones and I were even.

~Lisa Morris-Abrams

Take My Turkey... Please

The most remarkable thing about my mother is that for thirty years she served the family nothing but leftovers. The original meal has never been found.

~Calvin Trillin

Could I offer you a hot turkey sandwich, a bowl of home-made turkey soup, some turkey pot pie? Have mercy on the overstocked. I'm a simple person. I don't ask for much. I specifically didn't ask for much turkey this Christmas.

"Just get a small one, honey," I said. "There are only four of us, two of us are very tiny and one of us has a teeny appetite for leftovers."

"Where's your spirit?" he grinned. "It's Christmas; you never know who might drop in."

He bought a twenty-five-pounder.

The fictional Whos who supposedly crave leftover turkey didn't show. We had Whos who dropped in for a peek at the tree, Whos who dropped in to extend Season's Greetings, Whos who dropped in for one small drink, but they were all pre-stuffed.

"Couldn't fit in one more bite," they swore.

"Just came from Mother's, had to loosen my belt a couple of notches, can't even look at food."

Tell me about it. I've taken that bird from roast pan to soup pot, to frying pan and microwave, and I swear it's gained weight.

Not surprising, it happens to everyone else this time of year. I've done Canadian, English, American, Italian, Chinese and Indian but I haven't seen the last of it. I dream that one morning I will open my fridge and see space. I long to sit down to a meal of fish or beef. I don't mean to be wasteful. I know there are thousands starving in Africa. I know it's good wholesome food. But no matter how I disguise it, my stomach rebels... not turkey again!

Every year it's the same. Hubby gets visions of Christmas tables only a Walton would recognize. Uncles, aunts, grandparents, cousins, neighbours, all around a table that stretches forever. The problem is that's not our table. Our relatives are few and far away. Our neighbours and friends have their own tables. It's four of us against the bird—but he forgets.

I can't knock the man for being generous. Besides, it will be all over by New Year's Day. He's already begun preparation for that. He's been huddled with a magazine all morning and he's got me curious. Something about the look in his eye as he left the house has me wondering. I pick up the magazine and it falls open to a colourful page. "Olden Days Feast" the caption reads. There in the centre of a ten-foot table sits a whole roast pig with a rosy apple stuffed in its mouth.

I really have to run. I've got to get to the butcher shop fast. If there's one thing I don't wish for in the New Year it is 365 days of leftover pork.

~Donna D'Amour

A Home for the Holiday

Scratch a dog and you'll find a permanent job.
~Franklin P. Jones

"We want a dog for Christmas." When spoken by my children, these words used to squelch my Christmas cheer faster than scorching the turkey with my mother-in-law, fork in hand, perched at the holiday table. As my daughter named her fantasy dog and my son pointed to his dog's future sleeping quarters at the foot of his bed, panic set in and I began a frenetic search for gifts that would trump any adorable, barking ball of fluff.

Each day before Christmas, I'd say, "I've been thinking. Instead of a dog, how about a... (insert the newest, coolest toy on the market)?" praying to change the children's minds before Christmas Eve. After all, no mother wants to witness her child's disappointment as the last gift under the tree happens to be flannel pajamas, cozy and fluffy, but lacking the excitement of a Golden Retriever.

I feared the dog would follow at my heels, begging for attention as the children played the new video game they had received from Santa instead of playing ball with the new pooch. My husband would offer no help and merely toss me the I-told-you-so look. Experts repeatedly warned about the dogs dumped into shelters after the novelty of the holiday wore off and the reality of dog ownership set in.

As a result of having read magazine articles on the dangers of dogs sickened by a poinsettia, an overindulgence of turkey, or tinsel from the Christmas tree, I vowed to my husband that any dog brought home in the month of December would have stuffing and glass eyes glued to its head. My downfall was failing to stay away from the local pet supply store where, during a meet and greet for the local Greyhound rescue group, we saw dogs dressed in Santa hats and reindeer antlers.

No, we don't need a dog, especially at Christmastime, I reminded myself as I tried to sneak past the table with the flyers outlining the number of retired racers that needed homes. The thin, lanky dogs looked majestic, yet pitiful with their protruding ribs. Their muscular legs and sleek build were a reminder of their extreme athleticism, a trait which allowed people to take advantage of their natural gifts.

My son Holden said, "Doggies!" and pointed toward the table.

"They're just big couch potatoes," the woman said, holding the leash attached to the red-brindled Greyhound. "They don't need much. Just someone willing to give them a second chance."

"Second chance"—the words snagged my heart like a wayward fishing lure. Wasn't Christmas a time to give to those less fortunate? I'd have to be Scrooge not to offer a neglected dog a second chance. My hand slid down the dog's head and ran across her smooth, bony back. She didn't respond with a tail wag, a lick of my hand, or a rub against me. I looked into the dog's eyes for any emotion. It took time, the woman warned, for a retired racer to respond to a human's touch since the dog had never experienced loving hands.

The woman talked of the Greyhound's heart problem that prevented her from winning races, so she was no longer deemed worthy of continued care when not earning her keep. She cost the owners money—not exactly good business.

The rescue group had spared the dog's life and would provide her foster care until adopted by someone willing to give the Greyhound a loving home. Would I be that someone, the woman's gaze asked?

The foster family had taught the dog how to maneuver up and down stairs, to walk across the linoleum in the kitchen without being skittish, to avoid darting through glass doors when spotting a rabbit outside, and to adjust to everyday sounds such as the microwave and the television, so the dog would be ready for her new home. The Greyhound had a temporary name—Eleanor—a little more personable than the racing number tattooed in her ear.

As the woman continued to tell me of the rewards of owning a Greyhound, my mind wandered to my unfulfilled Christmas gift list, untrimmed tree, and pending holiday meal preparations. Perhaps she noticed I was drifting when she said, "Unfortunately, we can't save them all. These are the lucky ones."

I glanced at the Greyhound and at my son who now had his head buried in the nape of Eleanor's neck, gently stroking her. We'd give her the gift of a second chance and a permanent home for the holiday.

We had a quiet Christmas as our Greyhound adjusted to her new home and her new name. We turned down party invitations and cancelled out-of-town travel in favor of feeding, walking, and grooming our new family member. Since it was Christmas, and she was red, we thought the name Holly was fitting: Holly Berry on the days she was a good girl and Holly Peño on days she was a bit naughty. We remained patient as she settled into family life, and we eventually joined the rescue group to help raise awareness of the need for adoptions. Several foster dogs spent time in our home before finding their adoptive families. Holly donned reindeer antlers for the next seven Christmases, blessing us with her loyalty and love.

"Mom, I want a dog for Christmas," my daughter Piper said this past year.

This time, I didn't panic or attempt to sneak past an adoption table. Instead, I asked, "What kind of dog do you think we should adopt?"

We sat on her bed and looked through a dog book, carefully studying each breed's temperament and basic care requirements.

"A Pembroke Welsh Corgi," Piper said confidently.

I contacted the local Corgi rescue group and completed the adoption process in time to adopt Penny for the holiday. Although we spent Christmas day coaxing our frightened and trembling dog from the corners of the house with tasty treats and kind words, we couldn't imagine a more fulfilling Christmas than offering a second chance to a dog who needed a loving, permanent home—a true gift for us all.

We are currently blessed with three dogs, so it will be a while before we can adopt another Christmas rescue. But that doesn't stop our family tradition of visiting the animal shelter bearing gifts of blankets, treats, and toys for the dogs. We are always a bit saddened that we can't take the dogs home with us. As we leave the shelter, our Christmas wish is for each dog to be given a second chance and a loving home for the holiday.

~Cathi LaMarche

A Christmas to Think About

Attitude is a little thing that makes a big difference.
~Winston Churchill

I think a lot of us have heard the statement that the best way out of a problem is to change one's thinking. I know I've heard it. However as we all know, hearing is the easy part. It's the doing where things get a little tricky, and that's exactly what I discovered when my twenty-nine-year-old son and only child Tim called and announced that he would be spending Christmas Day with his fiancée Julie and her family and not with me.

We were a small family anyway, just the two of us. So translated, what this meant was I had to be alone Christmas Day. I felt rejected and replaced but most of all, I was devastated.

With Tim getting married I knew life between the two of us would shift and change. I would have to share him now. Intellectually I realized this, but emotionally I didn't, and that was the problem.

For me, things were pretty bleak. I had been rejected by my own son!

I even complained to my friend Marilyn over lunch one afternoon "that I just wished I could take a pill and not wake up until Christmas was over."

Perhaps it was her reply of total silence or maybe it was my own self-pity but for some reason I called Gil, my seventy-eight-year-old friend with Lou Gehrig's disease and invited him for Christmas dinner. Confined to a nursing home, he jumped at the chance. When I asked if Tom, his nurse who often drove him places, could bring him, Gil surprised me. Not only could Tom bring him, but due to a divorce, Tom's nine-year-old daughter, Christina, was visiting him for the holiday break and Gil was certain they both would be thrilled to join us, otherwise they too would be alone.

That same afternoon I happened to see Bill in the post office. Divorced after a brief marriage and now struggling with cancer, I figured he too would be alone. "What are you doing for Christmas, Bill?" I inquired. "Why don't you come over and have dinner with me? I've got friends coming and you would sure be welcome."

His quick answer and smile surprised me. "I'd love to."

Next, while coming out of The Save-A-Lot, I saw Sharon. She too was spending Christmas alone. I knew things were hard for Sharon since her auto accident. However, after fourteen surgeries and a shunt in her head, she still managed to smile and be upbeat. "That would be fun!" She beamed, then added, "Now I get to wear my new Christmas sweater."

On the Wednesday before Christmas I saw Kelly. Kelly is handicapped and homeless and we met at the soup kitchen where I volunteer. While visiting with him, I blurted out my next invitation to this "spur-of-the-moment Christmas dinner" and asked if he would consider having Christmas dinner with us.

"You sure you want me there with all your friends?" he asked.

"None of us has a place to go this Christmas, so we're all in the same boat. I'll pick you up at one at the Drop In Center. Alright?"

"Great. In that case I'll be waiting for you," he assured me.

Now with Christmas being only three days away I had to swing into full gear. I planned the menu, shopped, cooked and put up the Christmas tree. (I decided we needed one.)

So by the time Christmas morning rolled around, I was finally done. My old dumpy house actually looked beautiful. Even the tree fit nicely into the corner, with no need to prop it up with a book either.

I spent the morning making dinner preparations. Finished at last, I looked at the set table and giving it all a final nod, put the ham in the oven and left to pick up Kelly.

Shortly after our return the rest of my special dinner guests arrived and that's when things slowly began to go downhill. Since no one knew each other I figured it might be awkward and it was. Painfully awkward in fact. From the kitchen I strained to hear an occasional word but there was none. It was obvious everyone was uncomfortable.

About that time Bill asked where the television was because they wanted to watch the Bears and the Vikings game.

I answered with a weak, "I haven't got a TV."

"What?" they were shocked. "No TV?"

Another painful silence and this time it was dear, sweet Gil who broke the spell. "I guess we're going to have to do something unusual now... talk." But even that didn't work. More silence.

Finally dinner was ready and to get something going, I asked Bill to carve the ham and Sharon to pour the water and Christina to carry out a dish and announce to the others that dinner was being served.

"Think I could sit in this dining room chair today, Tom?" It was Gil. He hadn't sat in a dining room chair in eight years. So with the help of Bill, they were able to get him comfortably seated in a real dining room chair, and we all clapped!

The rest took their places around the table and holding hands we said The Lord's Prayer, together, while stumbling over the trespasses and debtor part.

I'll never know what changed the mood of things. Maybe it was saying The Lord's Prayer or maybe it was sharing Gil's special moment or maybe they didn't feel quite so alone anymore, but somehow everyone began talking to one another.

Then one by one, each began to tell their story, cautiously at first but building as they shared life with people who had hours ago been strangers. They talked about challenges they overcame, wrong choices they hoped to right, relationships they hoped to keep or mend, and like a tailor sewing up a garment one stitch at a time, they helped bind up one another's wounds.

"I'm thinkin' in a new way," Sharon reminded us. "It ain't a cure all, but it sure helps!"

Hours later our special gathering drew to a close and my guests prepared to leave. No longer strangers, they hugged one another and wept openly. Humanity was at its finest!

Everyone finally left.

Tom even took Kelly home.

I did dishes, straightened the house and collapsed in a delicious heap. It was then that I realized I hadn't once thought of being alone or rejected! It was contagious! I had changed my thinking too. We all had.

I thought about my situation. Had it not been for Tim's shift in our Christmas plans, I would have missed this wonderful experience and the opportunity to change my way of thinking.

And like Sharon said, "It ain't a cure all but it sure helps!"

~Linda LaRocque

A Minnesota Christmas

When you look at your life, the greatest happinesses are family happinesses.
~Joyce Brothers

White suddenly enveloped our rental car. We had been lucky on the three-hour drive from the airport in Minneapolis to my hometown in rural Minnesota—it was December 23rd and the weather had been perfect in a place where brutal winter storms were the norm. Now we were only thirteen miles from our destination and a Christmas celebration with my family, and we could no longer see the road. Not daring to stop for fear of being rear-ended, we slowed to a crawl.

"Ralph, there's a curve in the road somewhere near here," I cautioned my husband.

"Well, I can't see a thing." Ralph was used to driving in snow country, having been raised in Colorado. But nothing there really compared to a blizzard in Minnesota, where no hills broke the wind and the heavy snow fell sideways and tumbled over the flat fields in a solid swirling wall of white.

"Keep going really slow. I'll open the door and look for the edge of the road so we can follow it." My early training kicked in. My high school girlfriends and I had traveled to many an out-of-town basketball game this way, in a full blizzard, one of us hanging out the passenger door watching the edge of the road.

As we inched along, red lights appeared faintly out of the white swirl on our right—one the rotating beacon of a tow truck and the other two angling up. Someone had already gone off the road into the steep ditch. Finally, we came upon a pair of pale taillights moving slowly ahead, and cautiously followed them around the one wide curve in the road and for the several miles remaining until the ghostly outline of the buildings of town came into view.

Snow continued to fall as we checked into our hotel on the edge of town. I called my mom, now in her eighties and in assisted living a mile away, to let her know we had arrived safely. Then I called my brother Jim, who lived in a little town an hour away, and laughingly expressed the hope that my brother and his family would be able to make it through the snow to Mom's for Christmas Eve tomorrow since we had made it all the way from California where the sun was probably shining on the palm trees this very moment. He said they'd be there if they had to drive the snowmobiles over.

It stopped snowing sometime during the night. When I woke in the morning, I looked out the window on a world covered with a thick white blanket. In the parking lot below there were bumps where cars had been and the sticks of winter trees were festooned with flocking.

"How beautiful!" I said to Ralph, who was just opening an eye. "Come over here and see… it's a white Christmas."

"Yeah, I'll bet it's pretty," he murmured as he turned over in the bed and stretched out. "How deep do you think it is? I'll probably have to dig the car out."

"No doubt. The snow on the trees is at least a foot thick, and the cars are buried. I hope the hotel has shovels."

"Hey, this is Minnesota. They'll have shovels."

Ralph got up, put on jeans and a ski jacket, grabbed the car keys and went out to shovel. It was eight in the morning and we wanted to get to my mom's early to help her get ready for Christmas Eve. I got in the shower.

By the time I finished getting ready and had unpacked the gifts we would wrap at Mom's, an hour had passed, but Ralph hadn't returned. I looked down from the window to the parking lot. There he was, shovel in hand. Several men were standing around him. The car was running, I could see the exhaust in the cold air, but its snow blanket was only partly shoveled away. I pulled on my coat and snow boots and went out to help.

Ralph looked perplexed as I waded through deep white to get to him. "What's up?" I ventured.

"The car locked," he said. "I started it to warm it up, and it locked on me while I was shoveling. Now it's running and I can't get the doors open."

"You're kidding." I was incredulous. "Why would it just lock?" Of course, we had only one key since it was a rental car.

"These guys say it's a safety feature on these new cars. All the doors lock a few minutes after you start the car." A couple of the men nodded. "I never even thought of it. We'd better call someone to get the car open. Do they have Triple-A here?"

One of the men spoke up. "Yeah, sure. Jack Johnson will get it open, but he'll be busy on account of this storm. He's the only one."

We trudged back to the room and I called Jack Johnson. His voicemail said, "Leave a message, I'll get it," so I did. A woman called back in half an hour and said Jack had a lot of calls and he would get to us as soon as he could. We should stay there, or we would lose our turn. Ralph found a bright spot. "I'll get to watch the basketball game," he teased as he switched on the TV. "That's more than I'd get at your mom's. Her TV only gets soap operas." He settled in on the bed. "Anyway, he'll probably get here in an hour or so." It was nearly ten when I called my mom to tell her we'd be late.

Eleven o'clock came, and then noon. Ralph's game was over. In the parking lot below, the car was still running and Jack Johnson hadn't come. By now I was worried. This was a quick trip; we planned to leave to drive back to Minneapolis in the morning. We had come to spend Christmas Eve especially with my mom and now we couldn't even get to her. In frustration I waded through the knee-high snow to a nearby Hallmark store to buy wrapping paper and ribbon. At least I could get the presents wrapped, I thought, as I labored back to the hotel.

At 1:30, my brother called. They had arrived at Mom's.

"I'm coming over," he said. "I have some skills from my criminal youth; maybe I can break into that car." He was laughing. "Mom's about to have a cat over here waiting for you."

He showed up ten minutes later in his four-wheel-drive truck with my niece Kristen in the passenger seat. He and Ralph went down to the car and got right to work, but no luck.

"What a piece of crap," Jim growled. "If it was mine I'd sure disconnect that thing before I even drove it out of the lot." He rubbed his beard. "I bet it'll be six or later before that guy shows up. There are cars in the ditch all over the place and a lot of people in worse shape than you are. We'd better bring everything over here, and Mom too."

Oh great, Christmas Eve in a motel room in my own hometown. But what could we do, someone had to stay there in case help arrived and no one wanted to leave Ralph to wait alone on Christmas Eve. So Jim shuttled the rest of the family over to us. In they came bearing smiles and gaily wrapped gifts and Tupperware containers of food, and last of all Mom's miniature electric Christmas tree.

The little tree twinkled merrily in the fading afternoon light. With Mom in the seat of honor, the motel room's easy chair, and the rest of the family lounging on the two queen beds, we sang carols and toasted each other with drinks sent up from the hotel bar as we opened our gifts and told our stories. In the parking lot the car continued to run. At six o'clock Jack Johnson finally came and got the car open, but the glow of our family celebration lingered. On that cold and snowy Christmas Eve in a little country motel room, we were reminded that it's the people, not the place or the circumstances, that define the joy of Christmas.

~Dana Hill

A Home for Christmas

Each day of our lives we make deposits in the memory banks of our children.
~Charles R. Swindoll, The Strong Family

In the summer of 1957, my mother made the most loving and courageous decision any mother can make: She gave me up for adoption. The decision to give up an hours-old infant is agonizing enough, but I was not a newborn baby; I was seven years old.

This is much too complex a story to tell in its entirety here, of course, so I'll condense it to this: My parents divorced soon after I was born and my mother had custody of me until I was three years old, at which time she was forced for financial reasons to give me up to my father. I lived with him and my grandmother until I was five, when he remarried and moved us from our home in Boston to live in Oregon with his new wife.

My life for the next year became hell on earth; the new wife was a bitter, violent alcoholic whose jealous rages against me escalated until my father, in fear for my life, finally sent me back to my mother.

My mother by this time had remarried and had given birth to two more children. She was completely unprepared to deal with an emotionally wounded and distraught six-year-old child, especially one who didn't want to be there. And in truth, she had not spent more than a few days with me since I was three—we were mother and child, but strangers. Her husband was a merchant marine who was gone most of the time and the stress of being, for the most part, a single mother, was overwhelming to her. I couldn't have come at a worse time. She begged my father to take me back. He, of course, couldn't. Both of my parents were at an impasse.

But something amazing happened during that traumatic year. In circumstances that could only be described as miraculous, my father learned of a couple in Portland who were heart-hungry for a child and because they were an older couple, wanted a child of three years or more. He met with them and immediately recognized the love, comfort and financial stability these tender-hearted people had to offer his little girl.

After seeing only a small, black and white photograph of me, and hearing my story, they agreed to take me as their own. My father called my mother, told her about them and asked her to sign the adoption papers that would be coming in the mail.

The decision to give me up was a hellish one for my mother. To relinquish her child to complete strangers was inconceivable; she struggled with guilt and self-condemnation. But she also knew that her own emotional state at the time was not best for my welfare. Finally, after weeks of agonizing, she agreed, and one day in early June, she put me on a plane and sent me across the United States to my new family.

My adoptive parents were the most patient, caring people any little girl could wish for. Bringing an emotionally scarred child into your home is heartbreaking much of the time and frustrating most of the time. I was angry, and scared and lonely; I did not fall in love with them overnight. But as the months went by, their patience and love healed my wounded spirit; I looked forward more and backward less. I was becoming their little girl.

As December approached, my new parents began to talk with excitement about Christmas. I didn't share their exuberance; the last Christmas that stood out in my mind was the dark and miserable one

I had spent with my stepmother. Christmas had been just another day to survive.

But my new mother and father's enthusiasm finally became irresistible; there was an excursion to visit Santa, a drive through Candy Cane Lane to see the beautiful Christmas lights, caroling with my new friends and neighbors, a visit to the mall to see the Cinnamon Bear and of course, shopping for presents for my new parents with the allowance they gave me. My mother filled the house with scents of baking holiday cookies and whipped soap flakes into a fragrant, fluffy snow to cover cedar boughs for the fireplace mantle. And the tree! There may have been a tree that last Christmas I didn't like to think about, but I didn't remember it, so this one was glorious to behold; its sparkling lights and heady pine scent were a healing balm.

Christmas Eve brought new family members: aunts, uncles and cousins for a luscious dinner that outshone even Thanksgiving. An air of affection and joy in the gathering filled me with a sense of belonging that was both new and wonderful. It wasn't easy to fall asleep that night… Santa was on his way! The cookies and milk were on a table by the hearth and I had no doubts anymore that he would come. I finally nodded off, wrapped in a cocoon of my new family's love.

"Wake up, sweetheart. It's Christmas!" My new mother's grin made her look younger than I'd ever seen her. My new father waited, smiling, in the doorway.

When I walked out into the living room and looked around, I was awestruck. The entire corner of the room was filled with presents! It looked like Disneyland!

There were gifts of every size and shape and color, most of them with tags reading, TO TINA FROM SANTA. As I walked closer, I saw more gifts, these tagged for me from Mom and Dad, with little hearts next to the signatures.

"Are these all for me?" I breathed.

My father scooped me up in his arms, stood up to his full 6'4" height and hugged me. "You betcha," he said. "Looks like Santa thinks you've been a real good girl." He set me back down and my mother nudged me forward. "Go ahead and open them, honey."

I was speechless. It took me over an hour to open every gift. My new parents weren't rich by any means, but they had bought every present I had mentioned wanting over the previous months. There were toys, Barbie dolls and baby dolls, new clothes, Nancy Drew mystery books, coloring books, stuffed animals and candies. They had wrapped every little thing separately so that there would be more packages for me to open. It was a labor of time and money that even now I'm overcome with love thinking about.

That first Christmas, something had melted in my child's soul; something that had been walled off for protection came into the light; something that had been empty, had been filled. I had been heart-homeless for a long time. But thanks to the tender care of my wonderful new parents and to the courage and sacrifice of my birth mother, in spite of the guilt she lived with for most of her life, I finally had a home.

~Tina Marie

Tinsel, Terror, and Toenails

Fire takes no holiday.
~Author Unknown

In many ways, Christmas 2004 was typical. We had a tree decorated with clumps of tinsel, an overabundance of Christmas cookies, and a pile of presents for the kids to open. But also, as we gathered with loved ones around our table, we had a funny story to share.

On Christmas Eve morning, thanks to the wood-burning stove in the basement, our house felt cozy and warm. My husband, Jory, and I were tidying up in preparation for our guests. He vacuumed the basement and I made the beds, while Leah and Chloe, our four-year-old twins, ran around half-naked, giggling and dancing to "Jingle Bell Rock."

When I came out of the bedroom, I saw smoke in the kitchen. That's strange, I thought. Was something burning? But then I reminded myself that I hadn't even turned on the oven yet. Still more curious than alarmed, I called down to Jory. At the same time, I opened the door to the garage to find out where the smoke was coming from. And there it was: a room full of hazy, white smoke.

"Jory, there's a fire!" I screamed. He came pounding up the stairs.

"What do we do?" he shouted.

I panicked. Then the films I'd seen in high school health class came back to me.

"I'll call 911."

My voice shook as I gave the dispatcher our name and address.

"They'll be right there," she promised.

After hanging up, I ran to the girls' bedroom and pulled open a drawer. Chloe should at least be wearing underpants before we left the house. I pulled out a pair, thrust her legs into the openings, and then wrapped her, mummy-style, in a comforter I'd wrenched off the bed. As I slung her over my shoulder, Jory snatched up Leah, who cried, "But what about our presents?"

We left the girls at a neighbor's house and returned, full of adrenaline, to pace the sidewalk outside the house. With the garage door open to the driveway, the smoke seemed to have cleared, and we saw no flames. In spite of this, I remained outside, clad in my dad's old pajama bottoms and a Winnie the Pooh robe under my parka. Within minutes the sheriff pulled up in a squad car, and he and Jory went into the garage to find the source of the fire. Soon after, three fire engines clanged up the hill, sirens blaring, and fifteen or so firefighters jumped out in full dress—fireproof jackets, suspenders, pants, boots and hats. After speaking with the sheriff, only four of them came into the house. But they couldn't find the fire.

The commotion drew our neighbors outside. I saw friends across the street and ran over to fill them in on the situation. Other neighbors waved and asked if we needed help. Finally, I returned to my position outside the garage. As I chatted with the sheriff—still no fire—I glimpsed the vacuum canister on the back wall of the garage, the repository for our whole-house vacuum system.

"Did you check that?" I asked the sheriff, pointing at the canister. "My husband was vacuuming around the time I noticed the smoke."

Jory immediately mounted a ladder and peeked inside. As smoke drifted out, he started calling himself all kinds of names. Apparently, while vacuuming, he had sucked some live ashes from the stove hearth. That was the extent of our "fire."

The firefighters were nice about it. They helped Jory remove the canister and dump its smoldering contents in the snow by the curb. Then they ran a high-powered fan to blow the smoke out of the house and began packing up. As they waited for the final all-clear, Jory and I stood in the entryway with a few of them.

These were big, strong country guys—men who looked like they'd be at home on a football field or downing a beer in a single gulp. We soon ran out of small talk, and, as people do when they're standing in a circle with nothing to say, I looked at the floor. I studied the firemen's heavy boots, my beat-up shoes, and a small stain in the carpet. Then I noticed something else: my husband's toenails.

They were bright pink, having been painted a few days previously with strawberry-scented nail polish. Chloe had received it in a gift exchange at preschool, and after painting her own toes with it, her good-natured daddy had let her paint his, too.

Christmas Eve night. After opening our presents, we nibbled cookies and laughed again over those toenails. And I'll bet that as our firefighter friends gathered around their own Christmas tables, some of them had a funny story to share, too!

~Sara Matson

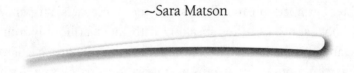

A Gift Not Wrapped

Christmas is not as much about opening our presents as opening our hearts.
~Janice Maeditere

Organized chaos... that's what it was going to be! For more than two years we had been planning to bring our entire family together for Christmas in Wisconsin. My mom's sister was coming with her family of four grown kids and two grandchildren. They were joining the rest of us, who had never moved away from the place we called home since birth. Grandpa Buz was more excited than anyone because it meant that all of his grandchildren would be celebrating the holiday with him. He didn't care about the presents or the food; he just liked having his family around. And that was the plan... until I got the phone call at work eight days before Christmas in 1996.

"You need to come to the University Hospital. Grandpa's had a stroke."

Grandpa had driven six miles with a mailbox dragging underneath his truck when a police officer stopped him and asked him what had happened. Grandpa didn't know, but obviously something was very wrong. It didn't take long to recognize the signs of a stroke, and soon the medical helicopter was whisking Grandpa away to the University Hospital in Madison. That was the last second of normalcy for our holiday.

One by one, the family started to trickle into the airport, with boxes and bags in tow—each overstuffed with presents for loved ones. But rather than quickly deliver those presents to the closest Christmas tree, each person instead journeyed to the hospital to spend some time with the cornerstone of our family.

It was too sterile—too impersonal—even by hospital standards. His room smelled of cleaning supplies and alcohol wipes, while at home cinnamon and pine candles would have filled the air. The white sheets draped over his frail body lacked the warmth of the green plaid blanket that would have been covering his feet while he reclined in his favorite chair, his grandchildren sitting by his side. There was no tree. There were no presents. There was no holiday food... just an occasional bowl of chicken broth and red Jell-O. Hardly a Christmas feast.

We tried to keep some sense of custom by still attending Christmas Eve on my husband's side, but before we made that short one-hour trek to their house, we stopped by the hospital to see Grandpa. His bed was slightly elevated now. His hair had been washed. His arms lay limp at his side. His face was devoid of expression. The sounds of leg compressors and a whimper from the man in the next room were all I heard. The scene was far from what we had been dreaming about, but he was still alive. Enough said!

I sat next to him and told him about the day... that it was snowing outside and cold... and that he was lucky to be wrapped up in such warm blankets on such a gloomy winter day. The entire time, I tried hard to convince myself, but in fact he wasn't lucky at all. He was getting cheated out of time with his family while he lay there with hoses and machines protruding from every part of his body. I was angry, but I didn't let my voice or my face show my emotion. I continued to stroke his aging hand, tell him stories, and quietly pray that God wasn't ready for him yet.

Not this Christmas, God. Please don't let a funeral be the real reason we're all together!

One by one and for days on end, children and grandchildren gathered at Grandpa Buz's bedside while holiday parties and gift exchanges continued around us. Christmas Day had come and gone and the presents still remained under the tree in Mom's living room. Nobody—even the grandchildren—seemed to care that one of the greatest traditions of the holiday was being missed. But after several days of taking turns driving back and forth on ice-covered, snowy roads to the hospital, someone finally remembered that we had missed Christmas... and that the presents were still under the tree.

Lacking some of our usual spirit, we opened them. A blanket here. A couple of sweatshirts there. Tokens of our love for each other had been wrapped in perfect little packages. But the best gift of all would have been for Grandpa Buz to be in the middle of it all—enjoying it with us. As I continued to watch the lackluster gift opening, an extra layer of sadness fell over me. This was the worst Christmas ever!

Grandpa's condition continued to improve and my out-of-state family returned to their respective homes. I continued to visit him each day, though. And each day, I reflected on the "Christmas that never was." Sitting by his bedside watching him sleep one afternoon, I was struck by a new thought. Maybe this Christmas wasn't so pitiful after all. In fact, maybe—without knowing it—we had just experienced the most wonderful Christmas of all.

Grandpa didn't get cheated out of time with his family; in fact, he had more time than he would have if we would have all gathered in his living room to open gifts and eat dinner. Being hard of hearing, the hustle and bustle of our normally not-so-quiet family would have been disturbing to him. He would have turned off his hearing aids so he wouldn't have to deal with all the unnecessary chatter. Grandpa loved to be the center of attention with his repetitive stories. Gathering our entire family in a few small rooms over Christmas would have stolen his thunder. He wouldn't have gotten a word in, even if he tried. Instead, lying in a hospital bed with each child and grandchild keeping vigil for a few hours at a time gave Grandpa just what he needed. We talked to him. We loved him. We prayed for him. We spent uninterrupted time with him.

Grandpa got a great present that year—time with his family without all the usual chaos.

~Heidi J. Krumenauer

Seasoning's Greetings

Cooking is like love. It should be entered into with abandon or not at all.

~Harriet van Horne

"You remember that story you always tell about how your dad lost the Band-Aid off his finger while he was stuffing the Christmas turkey?" asked my friend Anna Marie during this year's holiday dinner at her house.

I paused with my fork halfway to my mouth. We'd never found that particular missing Band-Aid. What, exactly, was she trying to tell me here?

"Well," Anna Marie continued, "I know for a fact that I started off with two paper seasoning packets in the dressing mix, but now I can only account for one."

Everyone at the table exhaled at the same time, resulting in the need to relight the centerpiece candles. Lost seasoning packet? No problem! Dad's Band-Aid, however, was a whole other story....

I smiled at the memory. "It's something we'll laugh about later," Dad had told me. Dad had been right. We've laughed about it for over thirty years now, and each year there are new faces at the Christmas dinner table who haven't heard the story told, and so it is repeated, once again, for posterity.

Every family has their share of semi-disastrous culinary experiences. Accidentally using baking powder instead of baking soda; substituting semisweet baking chocolate for Nestle morsels; leaving an apple pie to cool on the back porch and later discovering the neighbor's Standard Poodle has made short work of it.

Good thing Mom had placed her legendary "Chocolate Surprise Pie" on the rack above the refrigerator to set that Christmas. She always made a big deal out of her chocolate pudding pie, and handled it with utmost care.

Early on the morning of the feast (she waited till the last minute so the crust would stay flaky), Mom mixed up the pie dough. It was usually my job to keep stirring the pudding in the double boiler, making sure it didn't stick to the bottom of the pan. There'd be all heck to pay if the pudding scorched, and I made darn sure it didn't happen on MY watch!

Mom rolled out the crust to a uniform thickness, deftly crimped the edges around the glass pie plate, and poked numerous small holes in the dough with a fork so it wouldn't bubble up while baking. Then she stood guard at the oven door, watching the crust turn a light golden amber.

"Don't look," she'd tell me, as if I didn't know what she was up to. "I'm going to put a surprise in the bottom of the pie."

Mom's "surprise" was always a layer of thinly-sliced bananas, which was carefully concealed beneath her expert signature swirling pattern on the top of the pudding.

"Okay, who wants chocolate pie?" Mom joyfully asked after dinner the year the sixty-plus-pound Poodle absconded with any choice in the matter of dessert.

"Ooooh," said my slightly-more-sarcastic-than-droll brother John, "is it…," he paused for effect, "could it possibly be…." His eyes got bigger as he exaggerated his excitement. "Did you have time to make us a CHOCOLATE SURPRISE PIE?"

Mother shot him a look. "Do you want some pie or not?"

John assented, and Mom gave him the first piece. Without examination, he took a big bite. Mother hovered just close enough to his chair to arouse my suspicions.

"HEY!" exclaimed John with his mouth still full. "What'd you put in the bottom of this pie?"

"SURPRISE!" shouted Mom, gleefully clapping her hands. "I gotcha!" She looked proud as a strutting peacock. "I put mini-marshmallows in the bottom this year! I gotcha, fair and square!"

Good friends, good food, good stories. What would the holidays be without them?

"I just feel so foolish," said Anna Marie a few weeks ago. "I mean, what kind of mother am I? I don't often manage to pull off a big sit-down dinner for my family and friends, and when I do, I have to admit that not only did I not make the dressing totally from scratch, but I misplaced one of the packets of seasoning." She sighed and shook her head.

"Don't feel bad, Mom," said Anna Marie's son little Ricky (who frequently reminds me that he's thirteen now, and I simply MUST stop calling him little Ricky). "You may never be Martha Stewart, but you can always be a Spice Girl."

Now THERE'S a kid imbued with the spirit of the seasonings!

~Jan Bono

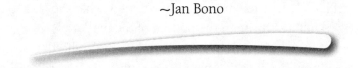

**The
Gift of
Christmas**

Toy Story

Christmas
with Melissa

You give but little when you give of your possessions. It is when you give of
yourself that you truly give.
~*Kahlil Gibran*, The Prophet

I hopped off the bus and ran all the way home. It was officially Christmas vacation. Opening the door, a wave of warm air and smells of pine, oranges, and cinnamon enveloped me. I smiled, removing my coat and bag—Christmas was just about here!

As I tugged at my heavy boots, I heard an excited voice. "You're home! Come play with me!" Melissa, my baby sister by three years, knelt on the living room floor, surrounded by an army of Barbies. She looked at me eagerly, her little fingers wrapped around a half-clothed Barbie, waiting for my response.

I was going to be in high school in just a couple years. Too old, I felt, for Barbies and other childish things. I hesitated, trying to think of an excuse that wouldn't make her cry or whine to our mom, when a sudden sinister thought came to my mind. "I'll play with you," I said, "if you let me play with the red car." The red car was a toy convertible for the Barbies and it was the crown jewel of Melissa's expansive toy collection.

Melissa quickly grabbed the car. "No!" she shrieked. She never let anyone else play with the convertible. Ever.

"Well," I said, pleased with my cleverness, "guess I can't play today."

As I started walking to my room, Melissa called out to me, "Have you got my Christmas present yet?"

"Not yet, but I will," I said.

"I've got what I'm giving you," said Melissa. She smiled and added, "It's going to be the best present ever!"

"I'm sure it will," I said flatly. I still remembered the handful of pennies and old lollipop she'd wrapped and given me the year before.

The days leading up to Christmas went by in a flash. The whole family spent Christmas morning "oohing" and "ahhing" over the gifts exchanged. I had bought Melissa a ceramic figurine of a cat at the local dollar store. When she opened it, I was pleased that she liked it. All of us kids were wearing the flannel pajamas we'd opened Christmas Eve and I could smell the Christmas ham baking. I leaned back into the couch and sighed. It had been a good holiday.

"We need a dump truck for all of this wrapping paper," Dad joked, sweeping up big armfuls of colorful scraps.

"Wait, Daddy!" said Melissa. "There's one more." She wriggled underneath the Christmas tree, to the very back of the stump, where she had hidden one last gift. It was about the size of a shoebox and it was clear she had wrapped it herself. It had at least four layers of paper, was sagging in spots, and pieces of tape were coming loose. With glowing eyes and a smile she tried to resist, she handed the haphazard package to me. "For you," she said, with more excitement than she had shown all morning.

Curious, I peeled back the paper. Stunned by the contents, I stammered, "Lissa, I can't... this is..."

"What is it?" asked Mom.

I pulled back the rest of the paper to reveal the gift to the rest of the family—one red Barbie convertible—Melissa's car. I couldn't speak. I looked back and forth between the gift she'd given me and the cheap figurine I'd given her. Melissa loved that car more than all her other toys. Why was she giving it to me?

Realizing Melissa was giving her favorite toy away, Mom spoke up, "Honey, you don't really have to give her your car. I'll take you shopping for something else later."

Melissa's face squared, "No, Mom. I want her to have it."

I pushed through the confusion I was feeling to say, "Lissa, really, you don't have to. This is nice of you, but you should keep it."

Fiddling with the edge of her pajamas, she whispered, "I loved that car… but I want you to have it." Then she bounced up and gave me a quick hug.

And there it was. In that moment I knew. Melissa wasn't giving me a toy; she was giving me her heart—even if it came in the form of a little red plastic car. Christmas wasn't about parties or presents or getting things. Christmas was about love. And I would never be too old for that.

~Amanda Yardley Luzzader

A Child's
Christmas Faith

Every tomorrow has two handles. We can take hold of it by the handle of anxiety, or by the handle of faith.
~Author Unknown

As a new mother, I tried to protect my young son and daughter from all the sad and scary things in their world—from bad dreams, loud noises and creepy shadows to broken toys, cancelled play dates and other childhood disappointments. But, I never imagined having to protect them from something like cancer.

Nevertheless, just six weeks before Christmas, I was diagnosed with a rare and aggressive form of sinus cancer. The surgery and radiation treatments left me weak, and I had little energy to participate in holiday preparations. Still, I didn't want my poor health to frighten the children or spoil their Christmas.

"Isn't it funny how mommy looks like Rudolph the Red Nosed Reindeer?" I joked, pointing at my irradiated nose.

Their laughter convinced me that I had shielded them well, and that their holiday experience would remain intact. Still, the Christmas spirit eluded me personally. I wasn't only physically fatigued, I was emotionally and spiritually drained as well. I continued to wrestle with the question "Why me?" Why a thirty-seven-year-old woman who had never smoked? A wife. A mother. A person who clearly still had much to do on earth. Was I going to die?

Despite the turbulence of my own thoughts, the calendar pages continued to march steadily onward, getting closer and closer to December 25th. With the help of family and friends, lights were strung, ornaments hung and cookies baked. Shopping lists were dutifully fulfilled, gifts wrapped and food delivered. Soon our home began to smell like cinnamon and pine needles. My son and daughter scampered about, curiously shook boxes under the Christmas tree, and asked their dad to hang the stockings just a little bit lower so that Santa would be sure to reach them.

As the big day grew close, their faces beamed brightly with anticipation. My son reminded me of the gifts he hoped Santa would leave under the tree. One of those items was particularly problematic. As an avid Thomas the Train fan, my son dreamed about the engine coming to life just like in the movie.

"I want a life-size Thomas train," he would say. "And I want to drive Thomas around the neighborhood."

He was only four at the time, but already I found myself in the uncomfortable but inevitable position of being a "dream-crusher."

"Ben," I said softly. "Some wishes are really tough ones. They can't all come true. I don't want you to be disappointed when there's not a life-size Thomas waiting for you on Christmas morning."

His lip quivered a bit. He nodded and seemed to accept my words. But, as he turned to walk away, I saw a glint in his eyes, just a flicker of hope that perhaps I was wrong. Maybe the train would be there after all.

I envied him for that, for having the ability to cling to hope. I wanted so badly to harness the true spirit of the season myself, to be a faithful believer, and to hope with a child's heart just like my son. But instead, I felt empty. Lost. Alone.

On Christmas Eve, we attended early mass. The red poinsettias around the altar looked vibrant and festive and the choir sung with that special holiday fervor. The sights and sounds made it easy to fall back into memories of Christmas Past from my own childhood.

I remembered walking home as a teenager after midnight mass one frigid year. The sky loomed infinitely black and I could see my breath in front of me like vapor. Although the night cold could have easily swallowed me whole, something made me stop along the way. I listened to the distant church bells ring and studied the perfection of new fallen snow. And in the sweet stillness of that moment I remembered feeling closer to God than ever before. How could I have forgotten about that?

The memory was still with me like a hand on my shoulder when we returned to my parents' home for dinner. After a wonderful meal, we cleared dishes, making room for the card games and coffee that would inevitably follow. A large candle burned in the middle of a holiday centerpiece. My son leaned over to blow it out.

"Make a wish," his grandfather joked playfully. Ben furrowed his brow and concentrated fiercely on extinguishing the flame in a single blow. I waited for the predictable words to follow, a wish for the life-size Thomas train under the tree. But instead, Ben said something quite unexpected.

"I wish," he glanced at me hesitantly. "I wish that my mommy would get better. I don't want her to die."

The room suddenly hushed. Then, Ben turned to me and asked, "Is that a tough one, Mommy? Do you think that one will come true?"

I swallowed hard and held back tears. Then I felt the answer rush out of me as sudden and unexpected as a gust of winter wind.

"Yes, Ben! That one will come true!" And in that instant, I knew it was so.

In the weeks and months that followed that particular Christmas, my faith grew stronger. I prayed for resilience and the ability to overcome my health challenges rather than for the answers about why I had to face them. In time, I came to feel at peace about my situation, to accept it even if I didn't understand it.

Since then, I have celebrated eight more Christmas seasons without a single cancer reoccurrence. I have seen my children lose teeth and grow inches, ride bikes with no hands, skin knees, climb trees, flip cartwheels, dance and sing and swim in the Gulf of Mexico. I've watched them become caring, vibrant young people who believe in God and optimism and faith. And I'm thankful each and every day to be a part of that.

So, when I think about the true spirit of Christmas, I remember the stillness of a winter night, the sound of church bells in the distance, and a feeling of utter completeness. And I remember that Christmas day is a gift, a time to renew faith, and a chance to believe again… like a child.

~Madeleine M. Kuderick

The Year of the Rat

*There can never be enough said of the virtues, dangers,
the power of a shared laugh.*

~Françoise Sagan

Childhood memories are basted together with traditions. The years blend together, and what I remember is the rituals that followed us from year to year. The one exception was the episode that was forever after known in our family annals as "The Year of the Rat."

My dad was the neighbourhood pharmacist, and owned his own store. Christmas Eve meant working a full day, and then rushing home in time for the family to participate in the Christmas Eve candlelight service. I remember the magic of lighted candles in a darkened room, and the hushed tones of "Silent Night." On the way home, snowflakes peppered the sky, and I bounced between my parents with barely suppressed excitement.

Daddy often brought home last-minute treats to put under the tree. He had an aversion to gift wrap, and would place his treasures, unwrapped, among the other presents. It had been a busy night, and he forgot to tell Mom about his addition to the gifts.

Christmas morning began with my stocking on the end of my bed. I was always amazed that Santa filled it without waking me, and the contents kept me amused for a precious few minutes while my parents slept. The toe always held a clementine orange, which I thought was sufficient breakfast, but my mother had other ideas.

Before presents could be opened, we had to eat, even if it was a bowl of cereal or a piece of toast. Later in the day we would have an elaborate brunch, which usually included someone who had been bereaved in the previous year. For now, Mom wanted something in our stomachs before the excitement of opening gifts.

Next, we all waited in the kitchen while Mom marched to the basement to turn on the lights (including those on the tree) and light the fire that had been carefully laid in the fireplace the night before. Suddenly, the peace was shattered by a terrified scream. Startled, we watched my mother race up the stairs and burst into the kitchen.

"Rat!"

Rat?

"There's a huge rat among the Christmas gifts!"

Frowning, my dad descended the stairs, and then burst into laughter. The gift he had placed among the presents was a pink, stuffed beaver. In the half light of the basement, my mother had seen a rat.

There is a veil drawn over my memories of the rest of that Christmas morning. Inevitable tension reigned, as my dad kept laughing and my mom was having difficulty forgiving him. Only the blurring gift of time allowed her to see the humour.

I kept that beaver long after I was past the stage of playing with stuffed animals. It guarded my bed, and inevitably brought a smile to my face as I remembered the Christmas that Mom saw a rat.

~Ann Peachman

My Buddy

A characteristic of the normal child is he doesn't act that way very often.
~Author Unknown

It was 1986, my brother was three and all he wanted for Christmas was a "My Buddy" doll. He would see a commercial for it and go into hysterics to express his immense desire for the toy. For months leading up to Christmas, it was all he could think about. He told our mother, our father, our grandparents, even random people in the grocery store, that he just had to have the doll. It was the one toy he really wanted that year.

Unfortunately, it was the one toy every child wanted that year. My mother searched the stores, hoping to locate the one possession that her child just had to have, only to find the shelves, where "My Buddy" should be, empty.

At the time, her parents were living in California and planned on coming to Georgia for Christmas that year. After hearing my brother beg for the toy, my grandmother went on a search of her own, scouring the shelves in search of My Buddy. There was no stopping my grandmother; she searched every store she could find until she located the last remaining My Buddy doll.

She proudly announced her find to my mother and they kept the secret of my brother's surprise gift until Christmas Day. Christmas arrived and after we played with all that Santa brought us, we gathered around to open our gifts from the family. My grandmother and mother shared a knowing smile as my brother was handed a large package to unwrap.

They watched him with joy as his little hands tore through the wrapping paper, revealing the one toy he'd just had to have. When my brother made eye contact with his prize, he jumped up from the floor, holding his My Buddy and screaming. He ran towards our back door, flinging it open with a crash. Still screaming, he threw My Buddy down the concrete steps and began to cry. He turned around and ran back into the living room, still screaming in fright.

My grandmother went outside and got the doll, confused as to why it has provoked such a reaction in my brother. She brought it back to him and attempted to hand it back to him, reminding him that this was My Buddy, the doll he'd been telling people about for months!

It was to no avail. My brother was deathly afraid of My Buddy and wouldn't have a thing to do with it. He snatched it from my grandmother's hands, chubby little legs carrying him back to the door, where he promptly tossed the offensive present outside again.

My mother was in fits of laughter, and was incapable of trying to soothe him. She giggled uncontrollably as my grandmother tried to figure out what went wrong, my brother continued to scream for his life, and I tried to "fix" my brother.

My Buddy didn't make it back inside that day, or any other if I remember correctly, but the story of that doll will follow my brother for the remainder of his life. In fact, I think I'll go get on eBay and see if I can find a My Buddy to give him this year for Christmas....

~Shannon Scott

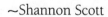

What Giving Truly Means

Act as if what you do makes a difference. It does.
~William James

There have been so many gifts that I have received over the span of my life. However, the gift that I remember most vividly is the one I gave away. Many people remember their first date or first kiss, but I recall the first time I understood what giving really was. It was the first Christmas after our family had opened our own business. Up until that time, we had struggled financially, but now the blessings were being poured upon us in ways that we had never known. We had a new house, a new vehicle, and this was sure to be our best Christmas ever.

About a week before Christmas my mom packed all six children into our minivan and drove us to a department store. I can still remember the excitement in the air, the Christmas music on the radio, and the warmth of the heater as it circulated in the van. As we pulled into the parking lot, my mother gave us specific instructions that we were to pick one thing in the store that we wanted for Christmas more than anything else. I was so excited. My three sisters and two brothers seemed to be upset to have to pick only one item, but one gift was all I needed.

For months I had been seeing advertisements for this one doll. She was a beautiful doll with long blond hair and her own make-up kit. I was so excited that I ran straight to the aisle where I thought I would find her, grabbed her from the shelf and held on to her with both arms. I walked over to my mother and stood as if to say, "Okay, we can go now." It took what seemed to be a lifetime for my brothers and sisters to agree on their one item, and then we were off to the checkout.

As we walked toward the front of the store, I was deciding what name I would give my newest friend. My mom took the doll from my arms and handed her to the clerk. I remember her asking the clerk to wrap the doll in Christmas wrap, along with all the other toys that my siblings had chosen. All of the toys were wrapped in the most beautiful Christmas paper I had ever seen and placed in a large bag.

Once my siblings and I were back in the van, we began to drill my mother about when we would get to play with our new presents. My mother simply replied, "I asked you to pick out one thing that you wanted. I did not tell you that you would get to play with it." That answer was not enough to satisfy any of us, but we also knew better than to question our mother more than once. We sat there puzzled, assuming that we would have to wait to open the gifts.

For a moment, my mind drifted away from my new doll and I realized that we were not taking our normal route home. The road that my mother had turned down was unfamiliar. She drove to the end of the road and pulled up in front of a small wooden house. I still vividly recall the shaky steps that led up to the screen door and the half-starved dog from the yard next door that would not quit yelping.

My mom turned around in her driver's seat and peered into the back seat of the van; she began to speak. "Kids," she started, "your dad and I have never really had enough money to help other people out. But over the years, there have been many times when other people have helped us out. This year we have some extra money, so we decided that we should help someone out. Today when I asked you to pick out one thing that you really wanted for Christmas, it was not for you to keep, but for you to give away to someone else."

She continued, "There is a family who lives in this house. They have children in their house that are close to the same age as each of you, so I wanted you to pick something special out that I knew these children would like. You all are going to help me bring this stuff in to give to them. Do you understand?"

I was young, but I understood. My heart just dropped. I understood enough to know that I was about to have to hand over the one thing that I really wanted for Christmas to someone I did not even know. I felt a lump form in my throat. As my mom passed out all of the presents, I took my shiny box from the bag. I was trying to hold back the tears. I knew what we were doing was important, and I wanted the little girl in the house to have a doll—just not my doll. "It will be okay," I thought to myself. "Santa will bring me another one." But then panic broke in. "But what if he doesn't? I may never get another one!"

We walked up the rickety steps and into a dank, dimly lit living area. My mother talked with a woman and handed her a bag of groceries and then my siblings began handing over the wrapped presents to the children who stood around. One by one, children reached up and grabbed the gifts with grateful smiles and tearful eyes. Then, it was my turn. I slowly looked up and my eyes met those of a young girl who was not more than a year younger than me. She smiled so brightly that I felt guilty for thinking that I should keep the present for myself. I held the box out to her. She took the box from me and immediately set it on the floor and ran out of the room. I looked up at my mother. Before my mom could speak, the little girl returned. She held out her own hands and inside was a small ragdoll. She held it out to me and insisted that I take it.

My mother finally told me that it was all right to take the doll, and we walked back to the van and drove away. When we pulled away from the house, I was no longer feeling angry or sad for giving up my doll. I looked down at the dirty little rag doll and smiled.

On Christmas morning I was delighted to see that Santa had brought me a doll like the one I had given away, but what I received was no longer the most important thing to me. At a very young age, my mother and a sweet little girl had taught me what giving truly means, and I understood that is the best gift that anyone can ever receive.

~Courtney Rusk

Special D
on the Special Day

Some things have to be believed to be seen.
~Ralph Hodgson, The Skylark and Other Poems

"The Shredder action figure!" emphatically stated Robbie.

Santa Claus nodded knowingly, as this request was obviously not his first, and asked, "Anything else?"

"Well," said Robbie, "I already have Raphael, Donatello, Michelangelo, Leonardo, and Master Splinter, but I really need The Shredder for combat. Yes, I would also like to have Bebop and Rocksteady. Then I have five good guys and three bad guys—enough for plenty of fighting."

"I'll see what I can do," said Santa as he looked at me, standing close by and hearing the interchange that I had certainly expected.

"But the thing is," continued Robbie, "I won't be at my home in Kennesaw, Georgia, for Christmas. I'll be at Momma's and Grampa's on Hilton Head, near the big lighthouse on the golf course. Here is where I'll be on Hilton Head."

Robbie handed Santa a folded piece of paper on which he had spent some time that morning copying his grandparents' address in his newly acquired first grader's scrawl.

"Just in case you're not sure you have the right chimney, my stocking with 'Robbie' on it will be hung from the mantelpiece."

"I'm sure I'll be able to find the right house," affirmed Santa, "and I'll take care of that Special D."

"What's Special D?" asked Robbie.

"Oh, that's short for Special Delivery because you have given me a special request."

"Thanks, Santa. And I'll leave you the usual oatmeal cookies and milk, just like in Kennesaw," said Robbie as he slipped from the chair on which he had been perched—"I'm too big now to sit in Santa's lap!" I had been told—and stood with an elf who would escort him to the exit.

"That'll be fine, Robbie! Merry Christmas!"

Robbie rejoined me with a very satisfied look on his face and said, "Okay, Dad, I think the situation is under control," the very words I would frequently use when I was pleased with a result.

As we left Rich's downtown Atlanta department store on that Saturday morning, 1989, Robbie was in a great mood, a much different frame of mind from when he had returned home from school on Friday afternoon, the beginning of Christmas vacation. He told his mother and me that one of the boys—"He's naughty most of the time and not nice"—didn't think Christmas was such a big deal and was spreading rumors. "I'm not going to tell you what he said, Dad, but he was not very kind."

The crisis seemed to have passed, but I called another father whose son Tommy was in the same first-grade class with Robbie. Yes, Tommy had been upset, too, but his father had a suggestion. I listened and agreed with him.

Several days later we packed the car and left Kennesaw for Hilton Head Island. As we neared our destination in Sea Pines and Robbie saw the huge lighthouse that has become the symbol of Harbour Town Golf Links, he exclaimed, "I bet Santa can use the lighthouse to guide him to the house. I'm sure he'll find it now."

Christmas Eve soon arrived, and a very excited Robbie set the plate of oatmeal cookies and the glass of milk on the tray table right beside his stocking by the mantelpiece. The four Teenage Mutant Ninja Turtles and Master Splinter action figures were arranged on the mantelpiece, ever vigilant as they awaited their archnemesis and his street gang. Then Robbie went to bed, probably not getting much sleep, but greatly anticipating the magic of the season.

When he awoke the next morning, he discovered a vast array of presents beneath the tree, a stocking filled to the brim with goodies, and an empty cookie plate and glass. After he devoured the goodies in his stocking but barely ate his breakfast, Robbie was ready for the presents under the tree.

Among the usual clothes, books, and school supplies, Robbie ripped open two boxes bearing the inscriptions "To Robbie, From Santa" to discover the villains, Bebop and Rocksteady. When all the presents had vanished from beneath the tree, however, The Shredder was missing, too.

Robbie was beset with disappointment but tried to hide it. I said to him, "I thought Santa would bring you The Shredder. He practically said he would. Let's assume he did. What could have happened that would have prevented the gift from getting under the tree?"

Robbie thought quietly for a moment and then exclaimed, "Perhaps it fell out of Santa's bag. He has an awful lot of presents to keep track of. Maybe it's on the roof."

Robbie, Momma, Grampa, Mother, and Dad all trooped out the door and headed toward the back of the house.

"There it is," yelled Robbie, "right beside the chimney!"

Sure enough, a brightly wrapped package lay upon a shingle. I quickly found a ladder, placed it under the roof, and retrieved the object.

"To Robbie, From Santa," read Robbie. As the wrapping paper disappeared, samurai armor and a cape and blade-covered extremities soon appeared.

"I guess that really was Special D," I said to Robbie.

Holding the skilled master of Ninjutsu at arm's length as he admired him, Robbie replied, "I think the situation is under control."

~Leigh B. MacKay

A Magic Memory

*Family faces are magic mirrors. Looking at people who belong to us,
we see the past, present, and future.*

~Gail Lumet Buckley

Christmas Eve was the one night my brother and I couldn't
wait to go to bed. We placed cookies on a plate and
poured a glass of milk for Santa. Then, we slipped under
the covers and dreamed of the magic ahead.

Sometimes, I woke up early, hoping Santa had already arrived.
Heart pounding, I tiptoed down our creaky stairs to look at the tree
twinkling in the night. The floor around it was bare. The house was
dark and still. Not yet. I wondered what part of the world Santa was
in and how long before he made it to Pittsburgh. I crept back to my
bed.

This time, I slid into a warm, deep sleep until I felt a shake
on my shoulder and heard a rallying cry. "Kelly, Kelly, wake up, it's
Christmas."

When I rubbed my eyes and saw the blurry image of my smiling
brother, I knew this was it.

I bolted up and without even grabbing my glasses, flew down
the stairs so we could take in the marvel together.

Our eyes widened at the sight of the tree encircled by brightly-
colored presents. Kevin and I tore into our packages at the same time.
We stopped just for small bursts of sharing.

"What's that?"

"Cool!"

"Look at this!"

Thrilled, we held our favorite gift in our hands and sat cheesing amidst the red-and-green wrapping paper and bows as Mom snapped photos. Then, we scrambled to get the gifts we made for her and watched in excitement as she opened them. Gone was the brother-sister bickering that marked some of our days. On Christmas, we were one.

Last year, I was reminded of those enchanting moments when my daughter woke up early and ran to her brother's room.

"It's Christmas! It's Christmas! Wake up!"

A toddler, he didn't fully understand the fuss. But if big sister said this morning was special, it must be so. She ran down the steps and he slid on his belly, feet-first, behind her.

She tore into her presents and helped him rip open his. They had that same look of wonder as they clutched a favorite book or toy, and that same spirit of joy when my daughter handed us gifts to open. My husband and I beamed at the sweet scene. Then, it struck me. There was someone else I had to share this moment with too.

Later that day, I called Kevin. And I laughed when I heard his morning had been about the same. His children opened their gifts in a happy rush as he and his wife looked on.

Though Kevin and I live miles apart, we're connected every Christmas by a special bond. It's a memory filled with twinkling lights, holiday magic and love.

~Kelly Starling Lyons

Happy Holidays
to FBS
from SLH

*It is one of man's curious idiosyncrasies to create difficulties
for the pleasure of resolving them.*
~Joseph de Maistre

I freely admit it: I'm a sucker for big, tinselly, gold foil-wrapped Christmases. I love everything about the season, from the first cup of eggnog to all the holiday commercials and Christmas specials. I especially enjoy the ads that portray cozy fireplace-lit living rooms complete with a twinkling Christmas tree in one corner and gaily wrapped presents spilling out underneath in every possible direction. That living room, I've always felt, looks the way Christmas is supposed to look. A little bit like a furniture showroom, and a whole lot like Santa's Workshop.

When our boys were younger, it was fairly easy to come up with a reasonable facsimile of a holiday toy commercial in our own house. Small children's toys are often quite large and usually not astronomically expensive. For years and years we were able to satisfy my desire for the Santa's Workshop look without going too deeply into debt.

Our younger son, Hank, helped immensely during the long phase he went through when he had to wrap at least one present per day and then put it under the tree. His "presents" ranged from things like fake mice the cat had discarded, to hastily drawn scribbles on paper that Hank had made and then wrapped up with a red or green ribbon. Like his mother, Hank enjoyed seeing a large pile of gifts under our tree.

As every parent on the planet knows, time flies far too swiftly between the days of buying plastic racecars to put under the tree to that inevitable moment when every single item on your child's wish list is small, uses electricity, and is unbelievably expensive.

The first year our boys morphed from Thomas the Tank Engine fanatics to tweens who suddenly desired things like CDs and video games, I found myself in a state somewhat close to shock. Sure, shopping took a lot less effort and wrapping gifts was completed in under fifteen minutes. But as I stood back and surveyed our Christmas tree, with its two small stacks of presents underneath, I felt as bereft as the Whos down in Whoville ought to have felt after waking up on Christmas morning and seeing what the Grinch had left for them.

It simply wasn't going to work. There had to be some way to inject a little of that glittering, over the top holiday sparkle back into our living room. But, without breaking our bank account... how? How could I make the presents we were giving the boys more mysterious? How could I turn the process of counting down to December 25th more thrilling? How could we work some under-the-tree magic so that the few gifts we had weren't opened in less than five minutes Christmas morning, not giving my husband and me time to finish even one cup of coffee? Hiding the presents in the front hall closet, I was determined to figure out a solution.

The answer came to me during a casual conversation with a ten-year-old girl I know. Anna was telling me how her mom was driving her "crazy" that Christmas season. "There's a huge package under the Christmas tree, a teeny one next to it and an even smaller one next to that one," she said.

"And how is that making you crazy?" I questioned.

"Well, my brothers and I don't know who's getting what. My mom didn't put ordinary tags on anything."

"But how can she tell them apart?" I asked, knowing my own

tendency to forget the contents of any package moments after wrapping it.

"She put initials on them that don't stand for our names!" Anna rolled her eyes. "She made up fake initials. That isn't fair!"

The proverbial light bulb went off over my head. I could do that. I could put tags on the presents under our tree with just initials on them, "fake" ones, like Anna suggested, that only I knew the meaning of. Then all I had to do was sit back and watch while Joe and Hank went a little crazy themselves while waiting for Christmas to come. "Thanks, Anna," I told her. "You've just given me a great idea."

To make things even more interesting, I repackaged the presents we'd bought in different sized boxes we had around the house, taping DVDs inside empty cereal boxes, Legos to five hundred piece puzzle boxes, and CDs in the largest containers I could find.

I was also careful to initial each gift as soon as it was wrapped and then jot down on a list what those initials stood for. FBS was First Born Son.

BIM meant Birthday In March. FLD? Future Lego Designer. Thinking up the initials turned out to be more fun than shopping that year.

At first, Joe and Hank didn't seem all too keen on the idea of initials replacing the more traditional name tags they remembered from every other Christmas. I knew their doubts had faded away when I overheard Hank asking Joe, "Do you think you're YPITH or I am?" (Hank won that honor as the Youngest Person In The House). Another bonus of labeling presents in code: it virtually eliminated the boys making stacks of "my presents" and "your presents" and then counting who had more. I liked that a whole lot.

The stack of presents under our tree might have been smaller that Christmas, just as it probably will continue to be in all the Christmases to come, but we're happy to have figured out a way to keep things exciting. Not to mention a method that allowed my husband and me ample time to finish our coffee while our sons tried to figure out who SLH might be. I'd almost forgotten that one myself—a pair of cozy red socks from Santa's Little Helper to Santa's Little Helper, AKA Mom.

They fit perfectly.

~Nell Musolf

High-Thread-Count Christmas

We worry about what a child will become tomorrow,
yet we forget that he is someone today.
~Stacia Tauscher

Chase, my niece's son, is a cute little guy with red chubby cheeks and white hair. He only needs pointy shoes and a funny green hat to fit right in among Santa's elves. After Chase started kindergarten last year, my niece Laura decided it was time for him to stay in his own bed.

"But Mommy," he said. "Your bed feels nicer than mine."

"What do you mean?"

"Your sheets are smoother."

They examined the beds and sure enough, Laura's sheets were smooth while Chase's racecar set felt rough to the touch.

"Why do your sheets feel better?"

Laura explained the difference between high-thread-count sheets and ordinary polyblend sets. He continued to complain about it, but began staying in his own bed all night without trouble. Laura was surprised at Christmas to see "high-thread-count sheets" at the top of his Santa list, above the usual requests for a new bike and a skateboard.

"I want smooth sheets just like yours, Mommy."

It seemed so ridiculous, a little boy worrying about thread count.

There were no racecar sheets to be found in the higher thread count variety and so Laura reluctantly purchased ordinary blue sheets without benefit of cartoons or super heroes. Chase was thrilled.

This year, as they snuggled in the rocking chair, Laura asked him what he wanted for Christmas.

"A Hickory Farm meat and cheese gift basket," was his instant reply.

"Of course," Laura said. "Why didn't I think of that?"

~Candace Simar

Name that Deer!

Every child comes with the message that God is not yet discouraged of man.
~Rabindranath Tagore

lthough I was an elementary teacher, I never had children of my own. I often joked that I got my "kid fix" at work, but I was happy to occasionally cover for my friends who needed a babysitter on short notice.

Babysitting three-and-a-half-year-old Kendra was a true joy. She was an only child, the apple of her mother's eye, and quite articulate for her age. I must admit, I spoiled her rotten, taking her presents and playing games with her long past her usual bedtime. I don't know which one of us ended up having the most fun, but we always had a great time.

One Saturday in early December, her mother called and asked me to come over "for a play date with Kendra" while she did her Christmas shopping "unassisted," and I was only too happy to comply. "But you don't need to bring her any more toys," she said.

Kendra met me at the door.

"Aunt Jannie!" she exclaimed, hopping up and down excitedly. She stopped hopping and gave me a big hug. "What did you bring me?" she asked, in typical not-quite-four-year-old fashion.

"Kendra!" admonished her mother. "That's not polite!" She turned to me and smiled. "So what did you bring her?"

I sheepishly removed a new coloring book about animals from my tote bag, "I promise, it's educational!"

So before allowing a single mark in the book, I read the entire text to my young friend, pausing to comment and ask questions about the animals on each page.

Beneath the picture of several deer were the words, "Here are the deer. The largest deer is the American Moose." I asked her if she'd ever seen a live moose.

"I've seen Bullwinkle on TV," she replied without hesitation.

On the next page was a picture of a deer with a red nose and a holly wreath wrapped around its neck. The words below it asked, "Can you name a special deer that is popular during the winter holidays?"

I looked at Kendra, raised my eyebrows and asked, "Can you name that deer?"

"Yes," said my small friend, nodding sagely, "I can name her Josephine."

~Jan Bono

Santa's
Silver Tea Pot

*Unselfish and noble actions are the most radiant pages
in the biography of souls.*
~David Thomas

It had been a long day and I was tired. I'd just finished getting my four children out of the tub, into their pajamas and into bed. I was tucking seven-year-old Troy into bed when he said, "Oh, I forgot to tell you, I'm supposed to take a king costume to school tomorrow. I'm one of the three kings in the Christmas program on Friday."

"You need it tomorrow? Why didn't Mrs. White tell you sooner?" I asked.

"Oh, she sent a note home last week but I forgot to give it to you."

I gave him a kiss and sighed. I wouldn't be going to bed early tonight. I had to make a king costume. Luckily, I had saved an old red velvet bedspread that had gold fringe on it. Two hours later, the costume was finished and I finally fell into bed.

I didn't have much Christmas spirit this year. My income had dropped drastically and I was struggling to pay my bills and support my family.

The next day, I took the children to school and carried the

king's robe into the gym where all the children were rehearsing the Christmas program.

Troy's teacher, Mrs. White greeted me and asked if I could bring some cookies for the Christmas party at the school.

Luckily, it is a small school. There were only 145 students from kindergarten through the sixth grade. I could easily bake cookies; I already had all the supplies I needed.

"I'll be happy to bring cookies. How many do you need?" I asked.

"Well, I haven't asked any of the other mothers to help yet, so do you think you could bake about twenty dozen? That would come out to roughly 240 cookies, and that would be two cookies per child plus some for the teachers and parents who come to the party. Maybe to be on the safe side you should bake about twenty-five dozen," Mrs. White smiled.

"All right," I said. "No problem." I tried not to think about the amount of time it was going to take to bake and frost and decorate 300 cookies.

"Did you hear about Jimmy Baker's family?" she whispered.

"No, what happened?" I asked.

"There was a fire at their house. The house didn't burn down completely but it was heavily damaged. Mrs. Baker said they didn't know how to tell Jimmy that Santa just couldn't bring as many toys this year." She looked sad.

"Oh, I'm so sorry. Please tell Mrs. Baker not to worry, I'll buy some gifts for Jimmy and bring them to the school. I'll put tags on them saying they are from Santa and Mrs. Baker can pick them up after the Christmas party," I whispered. "I don't want any child to go without a gift from Santa."

"Oh! That's so generous of you!" Mrs. White got tears in her eyes and I felt embarrassed by her reaction. After all, I wasn't doing that much.

Now I know for a fact that I'd said I'd bake cookies and that I'd bring a few toys for Jimmy and give them to his mother but what happened next left me speechless.

Mrs. White marched out into the center of the gym and clapped her hands to get everyone's attention.

"I have an announcement!" she said, "Mrs. Knight is furnishing the refreshments for our Christmas program and she is bringing toys for ALL the children in the school!"

I would have fainted or run for the exit but the children were cheering and the principal and teachers were clapping for me.

I just smiled weakly and staggered to my car.

I had four children of my own and was already very close to the limit of my budget. I had only offered to buy a few toys for Jimmy. I know I did not say I was bringing toys for all the children in the school!

My Christmas list had gone from four children to 149 children!

I'd thought I was baking a few cookies but now apparently I was baking twenty-five dozen cookies and furnishing snacks and punch for the party.

I didn't have the money for that many gifts. Christmas was only a week away and I felt desperate.

"Help!" I whispered. I couldn't bear to disappoint the children. I needed a Christmas miracle!

As I sat at the kitchen table my gaze fell on the silver tea set sitting on top of the cupboard. I'd inherited it from my Aunt Kathleen. It was a precious family heirloom but the only time I used it was for Christmas dinner. The rest of the year it sat on the top shelf and gathered dust. I remembered how much my aunt enjoyed helping others and I knew what I had to do. I took the ten-piece set off the shelf and polished it until it looked like new and I drove to an antique store and sold it.

An hour later I had $750 in my purse and I was pushing three carts down the aisle of a store that sold everything for a dollar or less. Every child would get a stocking filled with candy, two books and two toys. I went to another store and bought Jimmy some cars and action figures and a big plush teddy bear. I placed the remaining cash in a card for the Baker family.

The party at school was special as only children can make it. The smiles on the children's faces when they received their gifts made me feel as if my heart was going to explode with happiness. Mrs. White didn't know it, but her mistake made it possible for me to get back my Christmas spirit.

On Christmas day, we invited Jimmy and his family to join us for a turkey dinner.

As we all sat around the table, the children told each other what Santa brought them and Jimmy was thrilled with the toys Santa had given him.

"Mom, you forgot to put the silver tea set on the table. We always use it for Christmas dinner," Troy said and looked up at the bare shelf. "Where is it?"

I hadn't thought anyone would miss it. I looked at Jimmy's mother who was watching me.

"Well, Santa asked if he could borrow the tea set," I said. "He was having a special Christmas party and he didn't have a tea set. I was very happy to loan it to him and told him he could keep it as long as he wanted to."

Jimmy's mom guessed what had happened and her eyes glistened with tears. We smiled at each other. We'd both been through some difficult times lately but we were both going to survive and thrive and move forward.

That Christmas was the most exhausting, stressful, and expensive one I'd ever had. It was also the best Christmas I'd ever had.

~April Knight

Chapter
9

The
Gift of
Christmas

There Will Be Family

The Snow that Couldn't Stop Christmas

Nothing encourages creativity like the chance to fall flat on one's face.
~James D. Finley

The phone beside my bed rang just after sunup. "Merry Christmas," my mother said in a less-than-chipper voice.

"Merry Christmas to you, too, Mother." I rubbed my eyes and tried to stifle a yawn. "You're up bright and early."

"I'm calling to tell you I can't come for Christmas dinner. My driveway's just too slick."

I got out of bed and cranked the window blinds open. Snow that had fallen two days earlier was still piled on the curb where the plows had pushed it aside, but the street in front of my house was clear and dry.

"Things look okay in my neighborhood," I said.

"Well they're not okay over here. What melted yesterday afternoon re-froze last night. It's such a mess that I'll never be able to get my car down to the main road."

Mother lived across town in the house where my siblings and I had grown up. A long, steep driveway made getting to her house tricky, even in good weather. In winter, huge hemlock trees that flanked the drive kept the sun from melting the snow even after most of the roads in town were clear.

Through the years, whenever bad weather threatened, my dad would park a car at the bottom of the hill so that we could get about town. We'd joke that we were like a family of mountain goats climbing up and down that snow-covered driveway, sometimes for weeks at a time.

Dad had died last spring, just a few weeks shy of my parents' fiftieth wedding anniversary. This Christmas was going to be hard for Mother. She couldn't spend it alone.

"I'll come get you," I said. "Just give me a few minutes to throw on some clothes and pop the turkey into the oven."

"Honey, your minivan can't make it up the driveway." I could tell that Mother was trying hard not to let her voice crack. "And you know I can't walk down to meet you."

My once physically fit mom had fallen off a stepstool last summer while taking bed sheets down from the clothesline. Her badly broken ankle hadn't healed well, making it hard for her to walk even on level surfaces. It would be impossible for her to make it down a steep driveway covered with ice and snow.

"We'll think of something," I said. "How soon can you be ready?"

"All I have to do is pack up the cornbread dressing." I could hear a lightness in her voice that hadn't been there a couple of minutes earlier. "And the pecan pies. I baked two this year."

"We'll see you in about an hour," I told her.

My three teenage children, now too fond of sleep to get up early on Christmas morning to see what Santa had brought, sprang out of bed when I hollered upstairs that their grandma needed help. Daughters Meg and Leigh volunteered to get dinner underway. Son James offered to go with his dad and me to help Mother down the driveway.

"It wouldn't hurt to wear your baseball cleats," George told him. "Sounds like her hill is pretty icy."

So off we went. Mother hadn't been exaggerating when she'd

said the driveway was treacherous. We parked the minivan at the bottom and gingerly made our way up to her house. How in the world were we going to get Mother back down to the car? Though she was barely five feet tall and weighed less than a hundred pounds, carrying her wasn't an option. The driveway was just too slick.

"Why don't you guys poke around in the garage and see if you can find something to help us get Mother down the hill?" I told my husband and son. "I'll go inside and help her finish getting ready."

There was little need for that. Mother, already dressed in coat and hat and gloves, was sitting on the couch with her overnight bag at her feet and a cardboard box on her lap. The smell of dressing and pecan pies wafted out from the box.

"Looks like you're ready to go," I said, hoping that George and James had run across something that would help her get down the hill. But they soon came tromping up the steps empty-handed.

"Sled's no good," James said. "Left runner's broken off."

"What about the wheelbarrow?"

"Not on this ice," George said. "We'd all end up breaking bones."

Mother pulled a tissue from her coat pocket and dabbed at her eyes. "I was afraid this would happen," she said. "I've brought you all the way over here and ruined your Christmas morning for nothing." She thrust the cardboard box at James. "Take this food home with you. I'll be okay here."

"Hey…" he said, a smile creeping across his face. "Do you have any more boxes, Grandma? Really big ones?"

Before Mother could answer, I was heading for the laundry room where she stored her recyclables. I didn't find a big cardboard box, but I found something even better—the extra-large plastic laundry basket she used when she hung sheets out to dry. Coiled neatly inside were three long strands of nylon clothesline she'd taken down before winter began.

"Good thing you've kept your girlish figure," I said as I carried the basket and rope into the living room. "Your coach awaits, Madam."

We took the laundry basket out to the yard and Mother climbed in, sitting cross-legged while we wedged her suitcase in beside her and settled the box of food onto her lap. The guys lashed a piece of clothesline to each side of the basket and one to the back. Then, laughing uproariously, we headed down the hill, with George and me guiding and James bringing up the rear with baseball cleats dug in to keep the makeshift sleigh from becoming a runaway.

We made it to the minivan without incident, unless you count one slightly smashed pecan pie. Which, nevertheless, was delicious. Especially when topped with homemade vanilla ice cream.

Ice cream made from a late December snow that didn't ruin Christmas after all.

~Jennie Ivey

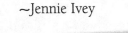

A True Treasure

When a child is born, so are grandmothers.
~Judith Levy

They say that the best gifts come in small packages. I confirmed this adage on Christmas morning 2007 when my daughter Samantha and her husband Craig presented Tom and me with our Christmas presents. For over an hour our family had been leisurely unwrapping our way through the festive mountain of gifts while nibbling on warm gooey cinnamon buns and sipping on coffee in our cozy family room, which was littered with shredded reindeer-decorated paper and mounds of crumpled tissue.

Christmas carols softly played in the background and miniature blinking lights reflected off the crowded colored balls and silver tinsel strands adorning the stiff pine branches of our seven-foot tree. All that remained to unwrap were two small 5x5 identical boxes neatly covered in simple red paper and tied with white bows.

Samantha handed me one box and gave her stepfather the other one. Unlike me, she seemed to see a difference in the two gifts. Facing one another we agreed to open them simultaneously. As we casually peeled away the thin covering, Sam and Craig's eyes were fixated on us like spotlights on a premier event. Under the paper was a simple white unmarked box. Since Tom was further ahead in the process, I happened to glance over at him and I noticed moisture filling the middle-aged creases around his brown eyes. Shifting my attention back to the square on my lap, I gingerly removed the lid from my box. Looking downward I saw a deep crimson frame with a matching soft velvet loop nestled inside the box. Within the perimeter of the white mat I observed a glossy black and white blurred image. For a fleeting moment I thought I recognized the outline of a small child but I was afraid to jump to conclusions and I continued to examine the photo.

"Mom, read the title!" Samantha anxiously exclaimed from the couch.

My eyes shifted below the picture and I focused on the bold black lettering which read "Grandma and Me." Tom had already read his message "Grandpa and Me" which explained his tears of joy. My heart pounded with excitement and suddenly I could not contain my flow of random questions as I squealed with delight.

"When did you find out?"

"Is it a boy or a girl?"

"When are you due?"

"Do you have morning sickness?"

Sam and Craig together laughed and explained that in early November they confirmed that they were expecting their first child. Since they wanted to make sure that they got safely past the first few weeks, they decided to make a Christmas announcement.

My son Rick was in on the secret too. The extremely close sibling bond between brother and sister has never allowed for any secrets. In fact, I later learned that he was the one who helped cover for her the night before during our traditional Christmas Eve dinner. Rick exchanged his sister's glass of white wine during the cocktail hour for ginger ale and secretly dumped out her goblet of red wine before dinner and poured in red sparkling grape juice from a hidden bottle that was purchased in anticipation of our traditional family toast. When we were all busy preparing the meal, he took over the task of cutting up the pungent cheese as Samantha secretly slipped away to ward off a wave of nausea. I had been oblivious to all of these surreptitious activities, as I was just happy to have everyone home for Christmas and I was busy while making final preparations.

That afternoon I hung our matching ultrasounds next to each

other in a special place on the third floor, and in the weeks to come I would often slip away and stand in front of them to make sure that my memory of that Christmas morning was not just a dream.

Seven months later, on July 21, 2008, our family gathered at the hospital to welcome into the world Max David LaBarbera. When I saw my first grandchild my heart pounded with the same excitement that I felt on that Christmas morning. As I held him in my arms I was mesmerized by his angelic face and his bright blue eyes, which looked up at me as we silently introduced ourselves. A shock of thick dark hair covered his pink scalp and I couldn't help but marvel at the miracle of his birth. While admiring my grandson, I felt the presence of Samantha's father, David, in the room and I knew that he was celebrating with us from Heaven while on earth his grandson was proudly given his name in his memory.

Christmas has always been a special and exciting time for me. As a little girl I often awoke in the early dawn and tiptoed downstairs before my three sisters were awake to sneak a peek at Santa's magical handiwork. The delicious smell of warm baked cookies, the pine scent from our freshly cut Scotch pine and the aroma of smoldering wood in the stone fireplace all permanently reside in my memory as reminders of the season. Numerous gifts have been wrapped and unwrapped over the years, but the true treasures have always been the recollections and mental snapshots of our shared family traditions over the years.

Christmas 2007 will forever be special for me. That year the joyous season of giving welcomed me into my next stage of life and reminded me of the miracle of the circle of life. The little red frame heralding the beginning of a new life will probably be my most precious Christmas gift ever. That gift of life will provide me with bountiful memories as Max David grows and matures and he will bring me perpetual joy and happiness as a new grandmother.

~Kim Kluxen Meredith

Lessons from My Grandparents

A grandparent is a little bit parent,
a little bit teacher, and a little bit best friend.
~Author Unknown

These days, I only get to return to my hometown about once or twice a year. On my last visit, my mom pulled me aside. "Remember to go through the boxes from your Grandma," she said. In other words, please, please take some boxes home so Mom would have more space.

Grandma had moved to a new nursing home a few months before and had pared down her belongings to fit her apartment. At almost ninety, she was preparing for the inevitable and wanted some of her most precious things to be given to the appropriate people. She chose these boxes for me.

I opened one and gasped. "The Santas," I said, and began to unwind the bubble wrap.

Grandma had grown up with images of the jovial Coca-Cola Santa Claus. Her enthusiasm for Christmas rivaled that of any bouncy child. She grabbed Christmas gifts on sale all year long—often misplacing them by the time the holiday actually arrived.

She encouraged me to start playing traditional carols in June or July. "Good music is good music all year long," she said. "There's no need to limit it to December."

When I was on summer break, she helped me to start making crafts to give as gifts to my uncles and cousins. More than once, she surprised me with bags of Styrofoam circles and sparkly pom poms. When my grandpa was sick and bedbound, we would sit in nearby chairs and work on little projects while Burl Ives crooned over the sound of fans and air conditioning.

Knowing her joy for Christmas, I always bought her Santa figurines. Despite my small allowance, I believed I was giving her something grand. As an adult, I realized the truth.

"Some of these are outright hideous," I muttered, already sorting through them to make a donate-to-charity pile. "Why did she keep them?" I held up one porcelain Santa Claus with runny mascara and almost nonexistent legs.

"Because you gave them to her," Mom said. She blanched as she pulled out what appeared to be a zombie Santa with googly eyes and stark white skin.

I never had a clue that I had given her such horrible gifts. Grandma gasped and exclaimed over every single one and gave the Santa Clauses a prominent place on her shelf year-round. She loved them. As a child, I hadn't questioned that love. At almost thirty, I suddenly realized how cheap, misshapen, and anatomically-bizarre they were, and I was ashamed.

After I returned to my own home five hundred miles away, I set my new stash of Santa Clauses aside. I got to thinking. I went into my box of my most special belongings, and I pulled out a letter from my grandpa dated December 31, 1990, just weeks before I turned eleven years old.

Dearest Beth,

Thank you for the writing tablet you gave me. It is practical and I needed it.

You are a young lady of good taste and judgment and I am proud to be your grandpa! I think you have a great chance to do some wonderful things, and I hope I get to see them happen.

Love,
Grandpa

P.S. Happy New Year to you.

He died nine months later.

My gift for him that year had been a small notepad of paper, unlined, plain. Probably cost no more than three dollars. But the letter he wrote on it? Absolutely priceless. I can't say how many times over the years I've pulled out that sheet. I've had some dark, despairing moments in my life, times when I really wished my grandpa had been available for hugs and counsel. But even with him gone, in that thank you note he told me something important: he believed in me.

My grandma has been widowed almost twenty years now. She needs a walker to get around. Her eyesight is too poor, her hands too shaky to do crafts. But she loves her holiday music and the sight of Santa Claus still makes her squeal. Looking back, I realize how much she and Grandpa taught me about the true spirit of the season.

Grandma always regarded Santa Claus as the symbol of Christmas's joy. But in my family, the central figure of Christmastime wasn't the man in the big red suit. It was Grandma. She was the one who organized us to sing together, who drove me all over town so I could find just the right presents for my parents and brother, who taught me how to make her traditional holiday stuffing just right.

Now she had gifted me with all of her beloved old Santa Clauses as she prepared for her own death. With my returns home so infrequent, I never knew if I would see her again. Every hug and kiss was precious. She knew I loved her, but beyond that, did she realize how she embodied Christmas for me?

It was time for me to write my own thank you letter for Grandma, just as my grandpa had done for me so many years before.

Dear Grandma,

I know Mom will need to read this to you since it's hard for you to see now. It's important for you to realize how much you mean to me, and how you really made Christmas into the most beautiful time of year.

Thank you for teaching me how to cluck like a chicken along with Christmas songs like "Jingle Bells." I still remember how we laughed so hard we cried.

Thank you for buying me such thoughtful Christmas gifts as I grew up. I know those years were hard, especially when Grandpa was sick, but you always made sure we had special things. It made it even more special when you misplaced them and found them again months later. How many other kids got to open Christmas gifts in March or July?

Thank you for teaching me the joy of holiday music all year long. It's a wonder I didn't wear out our old record albums and tapes. Right now a good quarter of the music on my iPod consists of Christmas music. That's your legacy.

Lastly, thank you for accepting all of those hideous, cheap Santa figurines I gave you. You were always so gracious, treating all of those dollar-store horrors like they were from Lladró. You and Grandpa taught me it wasn't about the cost of the gift, but the love behind it. I hope I can teach my son the same.

I'm proud to be your granddaughter. For me, you'll always be the spirit of Christmas.

Love,
Beth

~Beth Cato

Christmas with Phil Spector

To a father growing old nothing is dearer than a daughter.
~Euripides

he alarm went off at 4:45 AM on December 25th, 2009, but I had long been awake. My flight from JFK to LAX touched down nine hours earlier. I had that "first day of school" feeling. Mom fed the cat while my younger sister packed a cooler of refreshments for the day. We took off in Mom's car a little after 5:30 AM.

Usually, the family spent Christmases on a Hawaiian beach. Now we visited Dad in prison. Prison? How did this happen?

The trip to the maximum security Corcoran Prison clocked in at three hours. Having been turned away before, we called the prison visitor center hotline to make sure the inmates weren't on lock-down.

Mom turned on the radio "to listen to traffic," but it was really to drown out the silence. We drove by Magic Mountain and I remembered the Freefall ride from my high school trip, dropping fifty stories in half a second and leaving my stomach back at the top. That's how it felt driving to prison.

We made a pit stop at the county line in Bakersfield for one last restroom break: prison restrooms typically had no toilet paper or soap. I'd seen Himalayan outhouses that were cleaner.

The only things visitors were allowed to bring in were money, an ID, car key and an unopened pack of tissues. Sometimes I smuggled gum in my bra. Dressing for prison was a constant costume conflict, and I had to come prepared with a suitcase of clothes. Years prior, I rented an Easter Bunny costume and wore it to visit my dad in jail. Oh jail. Life was so simple then.

Regardless of the written rules, if a guard didn't like what you were wearing, you were turned away, kind of like not getting picked in line at a hot new nightclub. Halfway to the visitor center door, I realized my bra had the contraband underwire and had to rip the wires out right there in the parking lot.

Lately it had been taking us over three hours to get processed; usually it was half that. The guards mostly relaxed behind the counter, resting their big black boots on their desk with their big black sunglasses on, holding their big black guns. It looked more like The Terminator Convention at recess.

The guards called our names to go through security. I dumped my belongings in the plastic bin and walked through the X-ray machine, just like at the airports. After clearance, we walked through the electric gates and followed the yellow path to Dad's facility as the tower guard watched us with his rifle.

We took our table in the visiting room — much like a high school cafeteria, except for the prison guards armed with rifles, batons and mace. We bought Dad some fruit from the vending machines; the inmates couldn't get fruit at chow, as Dad called it. They fermented the fruit into alcohol, and some fermented the packs of barbecue sauce into wine. These guys were like Eagle Scouts, and I decided if I were ever trapped on an island, I'd want a California inmate with me.

Dad came out dressed in his best double denim. This was my tenth year spending Christmas at prison since Dad's murder conviction of his strip club partner. I was forty-one years old; I felt like I was fourteen.

When does this get easier?

My father, once so powerful, now treated like a caged animal, donned with shackles. "I'm still the head of this household," Dad would repeat.

I knew what we'd talk about during the visits. Dad rehashed the same stories over and over—his trial, the guards, his cellmate.

I glanced over at Mom—hunched over staring at the floor, squeezing hot sauce packets between her fingers. Mom's life was in limbo—prisons, attorneys, questions. Even with her holiday cheer sweater on, she looked defeated. Out of everything, I resented Dad most of all for that.

My sister was opening up the New York cheesecake we bought Dad in the machines. I used to buy my dad fine wines for Christmas. Now I sent him stamps and bought him vending machine food.

Dad looked over at Mom and squeezed her knee. Mom perked up and said, "Michael, why don't you ask your daughter how she's doing?" Since moving to New York City, I only saw Dad now a few times a year.

He reluctantly switched gears and asked me about my car. I'd been trying to pinpoint the cause of a slight vibration for months now. "Did you try cleaning the engine mounts?" he offered. "Yeah, I did that already and tightened up the exhaust as well." "You should really sell that car," he constantly said.

Just when we thought we'd gotten him to switch gears and have a conversation that didn't involve him, he jumped right back into his ranting. We continually hoped he'd ask us about ourselves.

Call me crazy, but I actually looked forward to one thing at prison—burritos in the vending machines. Forget about finding any worthwhile Mexican food on the East Coast. I got the meat and cheese burrito. It was called The Bomb, and had red flames on the wrapper.

I eagerly waited in line with other inmates, mostly sex offenders, to microwave my Christmas meal. I doused it with extra hot sauce and dug right in.

As I came up for air from The Bomb, I realized Phil Spector was across the room. I didn't recognize him at first without his big wig.

He looked more like Benjamin Franklin now. I politely smiled at Phil, bits of The Bomb stuck in my teeth.

"Inmate restroom break," a female guard brazenly broadcasted. Phil stood up and strolled by me. I smiled again. Dad said he had given Phil nail clippers when he first arrived, but now didn't speak to him much.

The guards announced visiting was over. Dad walked us to the door, squeezed me hard and said, "Take care of yourself, Lip. I love you." He called me Lip because I stuck out my bottom lip when I pouted as a child. I held back tears and gave him a big kiss.

Leaving Dad was like leaving your dog in doggy day care. We waved goodbye to him through the windows as the guards herded the inmates back to their cells.

The drive back home was quiet, as usual. We were still adjusting to Christmas with sex offenders, drug lords, murderers—and now Phil.

In the hallways back at work, a coworker asked me how my Christmas was. I hesitated and wondered if I should divulge the truth about prison, Phil Spector and The Bomb. Instead, I replied, "Fine, and yours?"

~Laurel Woods

The Problem
with Pickles

Sometimes, in a moral struggle, we discover the right thing to do—
just as, on some cold day long ago, we discovered mittens
pinned to our coat sleeve.
~Robert Brault, www.robertbrault.com

Every year about a week before Christmas, our small town church always had a special evening gathering called the "White Christmas" service, long before Irving Berlin immortalized the words in his pop music classic.

White was the color scheme. Almost always the weather cooperated by draping the outside world in a foot or two of it. Inside, the altar was covered with a white lacy cloth and the focus for the evening's activities was the presentation of offerings on the altar to be distributed to the needy.

The gifts were jars of home-canned fruits and vegetables, each wrapped in white tissue paper, caught with white ribbon around the jar lid then left to flower open at the top. Although individually they looked like albino pineapples, collectively they resembled a flock of white doves with upturned wings.

I loved helping my mother choose her special jars of tomatoes, peaches, and, when she was in a very generous mood, mixed pickles. She had a very high regard for her pickles. They had won a ribbon at the county fair, and she often used them as gifts for favored friends. Still she always had enough left to try to foist on me. I was not enthusiastic. Even as a seven-year-old, I preferred Heinz to hers.

Since my dad worshipped with *The Wall Street Journal* instead of with the Methodists, I was the only family member available to attend the service and help Mother lug her generous offering to the altar. I loved walking down the aisle with her, bursting with sinful pride, as if carrying the bounty had something to do with its creation.

This was my sole involvement in the service until the year I was seven, when I made a more distinctive contribution.

Mother was one of the few working women in our little town, and the night of the service that year, she called to say she would need to work late so would I please wrap the jars. This was a heavy responsibility because I'd always served as "sous-wrapper" before.

I'll be the first to admit that my albino pineapples did look hurricane impaired, but nothing broke and I got most of the paste out. And so what if they didn't exactly flower on top?

The service went uneventfully, though I noticed that when we approached the altar, Mother tried to find space in the background for our offerings. But what we lacked in artistic achievement, we compensated for in quantity.

As we drove home after the service, the conversation took an unfortunate — if not completely unforeseen — direction.

"By the way, Nancy, what were in all those jars?" she asked.

"Pickles," I responded nonchalantly.

"All of them?" she persisted.

"Uh huh," I admitted.

"Oh Nancy, you know those are my favorites."

"But I thought you would want to give your very best."

Long pause. We turned the corner by the schoolhouse and headed up the hill to our house past the Curnutts, and the Baileys and the Stoners. We were almost home when she finally replied.

"Yes, it was right for me to give my best. You did that for me," she said.

And then she added, "Just be sure you always do that for yourself, too."

~Nancy Bechtolt

The Cancer Christmas

Instead of being a time of unusual behavior, Christmas is perhaps the only time in the year when people can obey their natural impulses and express their true sentiments without feeling self-conscious and, perhaps, foolish. Christmas, in short, is about the only chance a man has to be himself.
~Francis C. Farley

The first Christmas after my father was diagnosed with brain cancer, I realized everything had changed. Up until his diagnosis, my father's life revolved around working. When I was growing up, I found that if he wasn't at the office, he was teaching me how to change the oil on our car, finishing my grandparents' basement, shushing us because he was listening to the stock reports, or forcing me to do fractions well before I understood them.

But he knew how to have fun, too. He was the one who picked us up and hurled us on the bed over and over again, while my brother and I bounced to our feet and begged for more. He showed us how to limbo under a broomstick. And, years later, when my first pregnancy ended in a stillborn baby girl, although he said little, he made her a blanket embroidered with her name and date of birth and death.

The summer of the following year, around his fifty-sixth birthday, my parents came to visit me and our new son, Max. Dad mentioned having trouble remembering people's names and having to work more slowly. Since I was an emergency room doctor, albeit on maternity leave, I asked if he wanted to come to the hospital to scan his head. He said no, his family doctor had referred him to a memory clinic.

On November 2nd, the scan showed a tumor too deep to remove. When he first heard the news, his first reaction was, "I guess this means I can't work." His second was to point at my six-month-old son, Max, and say, "I just wish I could watch this one grow up." His third was to tell me and my brother, "I've done what I needed to do. Take care of your mother."

By Christmas, the first treatments had already taken their toll. The anti-epileptic drugs gave him a rash. The high-dose steroids made him dizzy and hungry and moon-faced. And who knew what side effects came from the radiation. But he still kept nearly all of his hair and he looked much the same. He was just very, very tired.

I didn't realize how tired until my family came to visit for Christmas. Dad posed for pictures in the kitchen. He put presents under the tree. He accepted his stocking. He even offered to take care of baby Max, since his number one goal in life was to be useful. But when I searched for them fifteen minutes later, I found Dad sitting on the toilet lid while Max ripped handfuls of paper off the toilet paper roll and threw them on the floor, cackling with delight.

The environmentalist inside my breast cried out, "No! Toilet paper comes from trees!" The clean freak in me yelled, "What a mess!" But I bit my tongue. I realized that my father was too exhausted to carry Max or push toy cars on the floor with him. The most he could offer his beloved grandson was one treat his mother never allowed: destroying toilet paper.

I wish I could say that I laughed with them, but I wasn't that enlightened. I cleaned up the paper and carted Max away so my father could rest.

The following Christmas, my father was hospitalized. He'd fallen several times at home. He needed two people's help to stand up, so he couldn't even go home on a day pass. And I have to say, despite the candy cane decorations and the tinsel on the ceiling, it saddened my heart that my father was spending Christmas on the cancer ward. But when I brought Max to see him, Dad opened his eyes and started to play.

I was amazed. How could this man, who couldn't even sit up on his own, play with his nineteen-month-old grandson?

Each patient had received a small Christmas stocking filled with candy. The oncology nurse pulled a small candy cane out of Dad's. Max had never tasted a candy cane before, but he sucked on a small piece and smiled.

My father took a piece of candy cane into his own mouth. Then, using his lips, he pushed it back out toward Max.

Max giggled and reached for it.

Dad pulled the candy cane back into his mouth. Then, after Max gave up, Dad pushed it out again: peekaboo!

Max laughed and laughed.

I stood silently by the hospital bed. My father had lost nearly everything: his ability to work, his sharp intelligence and memory, and even his ability to walk to the bathroom by himself. But this holiday season, he had not forgotten how to love or how to make his grandson laugh.

And maybe I had learned something, too, because when Dad said he didn't want any presents this year, I understood. I asked my family to write letters to him instead. We gathered around his bedside and took turns reading stories about our time together and how much we appreciated him. Dad snuggled in bed and closed his eyes in order to concentrate on our words. And so, before he died in May, we were able to tell him exactly how much we loved him.

I can't say this was my best Christmas, because it was mired in sadness. But it did teach me the spirit of Christmas: love.

~Melissa Yuan-Innes

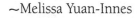

A Polish Christmas Eve Tradition

Homecoming means tradition.
~Author Unknown

"What are you doing, Grams?" my three-year-old granddaughter, Isabella, asks. I open an envelope and pull out four sheets of six by three-and-a-half-inch-long oplatek. She follows me around the dining room table as I break pieces off the blessed, thin, white wafer and place one small segment onto each dinner plate just as my mother and grandmothers had done in the past.

In our family, Christmas Eve would not have the magical quality that links our three generations to my mother, dad, grandparents and their parents if we did not break and share the oplatek at the onset of our meal. This Christian custom, sharing the sacred unleavened bread, has been preserved by Eastern and Central Europeans and passed down through generations. My four grandparents brought their memories and tradition to America when they migrated from Poland in the early 1900s.

"You'll see, Isabella. We are going to do something special."

The Christmas tree glitters in the living room, candlelight flickers throughout the house, voices and laughter resound from the adjoining rooms. My granddaughters, Katie and Jessica, carry in more wrapped presents to stack and wait to be opened.

Alicia, my seven-year-old granddaughter, runs into the dining room, joining Isabella and me. "When do we start, Gramma? I remember from last year. I love making the wishes."

Our entire family of twenty, including Shirley and Bob, my daughter-in-law's parents, gather at the home of our oldest son, Steve, his wife, Karrie and their four children, for our traditional Christmas Eve holiday.

"Do you think Santa will bring us that new game for the Wii?" Cameron asks in the other room.

"And a remote control helicopter?" Conner adds.

In their voices and enthusiasm, I slip back to my youth.

● ● ●

I couldn't wait for Daddy to come home from the post office where he worked so Christmas Eve would start. Some years he worked late. My sisters, brother and I itched with anticipation, eager to hear his steps in the hallway. I helped Busia, a Polish name for Gramma, ready the table and place a piece of the white wafer on each dish.

My mother stirred hot borsch in the large kitchen/sitting room located in the basement of my grandmother's house. She then carried a baked rice-and-apple casserole to the table while Busia placed three types of filled pierogie on serving plates: sweet cheese, potato/onion and sweet cabbage. I ran upstairs one more time to check if Santa had arrived.

The living room Christmas tree stood alone, twinkling, the absence of presents apparent. Red, green, blue, and yellow lights reflected in the windowpanes and lit the dark room in a soft glow. Silver icicles swung from the boughs, shimmering. I inhaled the evergreen scent. Would Santa Claus ever arrive?

"Tonya," my mother had called. "Daddy's home. We're about to begin. Where are you?"

I ran, tripped, bumped my knee, barely felt it and continued down the steps to join the family. Busia set the borsch tureen in the center of the table, wiped her hands on her apron and sat down. We all said grace together, and then Dad began the Christmas Eve ritual. He held his oplatek before my mother. As she broke a small piece off the wafer and ate it, he made his wish. "Good health, happiness and a long life, Lottie."

Mom extended her piece of unleavened bread to Dad. He held a small section between his index finger and thumb. They looked into each other's eyes. "Walter, I wish for you: love, the promotion you're hoping for, and good health." Dad then snapped off his tiny piece, and ate.

Everyone followed suit in a disorganized, grand commotion, everybody speaking at the same time. Uncle Louie walked to the opposite side of the table and made wishes to Busia, while Uncle Stas spoke and exchanged wishes with my sister, Terrie. The person who received a wish, made a wish back to that relative, then broke off a segment of the other's oplatek. We all asked God to grant the favor made for that particular loved one. My parents glided from one family member to another until they spoke to each person.

My mother beckoned, extending her oplatek toward me: "I wish you only happiness, good health, and a wonderful life."

"I wish that Santa would come," my little brother groaned to Uncle Stas.

As we sat down to partake in the meal, my uncle said, "You kids have to taste a little bit of everything."

Mary Anne and I looked at each other and made a face at the warm prunes and apricots.

After dinner, my sisters and I helped wash and dry dishes, never noticing that Dad slipped upstairs. My brother, Johnny, played with the Lionel train set on the other side of the basement sitting room.

Excited voices sounded from the stairway. "Quick! Come upstairs, kids," Dad called.

"I heard reindeer on the roof!" Uncle Louie shouted.

Off we ran, passing the living room filled with presents. My dad and uncles stood by the front door. "You took too long. I saw the reindeer pulling Santa and his sleigh in that direction, over those rooftops." Uncle Louie pointed to the right.

...

"Gramma, Gramma," my granddaughter calls, breaking into my reverie. "Katie is about to read about baby Jesus being born and we're going to sing Happy Birthday to him."

I place the last of the oplatek on a plate and go to the family room. I sit beside my husband, inhale the woody scent of the crackling fireplace that mingles with cinnamon candles. We sing. The grandkids clap.

When it comes time for dinner, we gather around the extended dining room tables. My husband, Dave, begins the wishes, holding his oplatek before me. "Good health, happiness. I pray we share a long life together." He kisses me.

I break a small piece of his wafer as my mother had, as my great-grandparents had. "I wish you good health and wish we live to see our grandchildren marry." He breaks off a piece of mine.

And so it continues. Voices blend. My youngest grandson, Cameron, eats the oplatek on his plate, the one he was to share. He looks glum as his brothers tease him.

I hug him. "You don't eat your own piece, Cameron. You break off someone else's piece and make a wish. Then, they break off a piece of yours and make a wish. That's how you get to taste it." I smile. "Let's start over. I'll give you a segment of mine."

Each person makes their way across the room to bestow wishes to each and every person, breaking oplatek with the person to whom they speak. When the ritual concludes, we begin our feast: ham, stuffed shells and assortments of salads and vegetables.

I have come full circle and now pass this gift of heritage and Polish tradition to our grandchildren.

In this instant, I hear my mother's voice in my thoughts as she held her oplatek to me.

"Yes, Mom. I've had a good life. I'm happy. Your wishes came true."

~Toni Louise Diol

The Grinch

If two stand shoulder to shoulder against the gods,
Happy together, the gods themselves are helpless
Against them while they stand so.
~Maxwell Anderson

I woke up filled with dread. My mother-in-law, Edna, was coming to Christmas dinner. Except for not being green, she could have passed for the Grinch. "Are you okay?" my husband, Bob, asked.

"Yes," I smiled bravely. After all, it was Christmas morning. "I'm fine. Really, I'm fine. It's Christmas, it's going to be a great day." I pulled my pillow over my face.

"Maybe there is a blizzard. Maybe the roads are closed," he said hopefully and looked out the window. "No, the sky is clear and blue and the sun is shining." He sighed, "She'll be here."

"It's going to be fine," I said.

Bob lay down and put his pillow over his face. We both lay there a few minutes.

"Are we trying to smother ourselves or are we trying to hide?" he asked.

"Hiding," I said.

There was the sound of a car horn honking and Bob looked out the window.

"She's here," he said. "She's four hours early! Who comes to dinner four hours early?"

"Your mother," I sighed.

We scrambled around getting dressed and headed for the door.

"Merry Christmas, Mom." Bob and his mother gave each other a pyramid hug and kissed the air.

"Hi, Edna," I said. "We're so glad you made it in time to join us for breakfast."

"Is that what you're wearing for Christmas?" she looked at my faded jeans and sweatshirt.

"No," I said. "I haven't had time to get dressed yet." I reached up and tried to smooth down my bed head hair.

"I knew from past experience neither of you would be dressed properly for the festive occasion so I took the liberty of bringing a dress for you and a sweater for my son." She handed each of us a sack.

Bob and I returned to the bedroom like two dutiful, scolded children and put on the clothing she'd brought.

Bob pulled on a red sweater with a large Christmas tree on the front of it. I squirmed into a green velvet floor-length dress that had stiff, itchy lace around the neck and sleeves. I would have loved the dress when I was twelve.

We stood side by side and looked into the mirror.

"Horrible," Bob said.

"Horrible," I agreed and scratched my neck where the stiff lace was poking into my jugular vein.

"We only have to wear them a few hours," he sighed. "But it will feel like an eternity."

Later we sat around the table and listened to Edna compliment my cooking.

"The turkey is dry. You cooked it too long. Don't worry, I'll just cover it with gravy. Is this that instant gravy that comes in an envelope? Never mind, I'll just eat the turkey dry. Are these sweet potatoes the canned ones? They are always so mushy. You could have saved yourself time and money if you'd just served frozen turkey dinners. Did you bake the pumpkin pie yourself? It looks a little pale. You should have put in more cinnamon and allspice. That's all right, I'll cover it with whipped cream. You didn't get the kind that comes in the plastic containers at the store, did you? I don't like that kind. I always make my own from thick, sweet cream," she said. "I should have brought some dessert. You forgot to make my famous green bean salad. I sent you the recipe. It doesn't seem like Christmas dinner without my famous green bean salad."

Bob and I remained silent. We both hate green beans.

It was time to open the gifts.

Edna handed a box to me and I opened it and found a sweater. A huge, enormous blue sweater.

"I decided to surprise you with a hand-knitted sweater," she said.

"Did you knit this?" I couldn't picture Bob's mother having the patience to knit a potholder, let alone a sweater.

"Oh, heavens no! I wouldn't waste my time knitting! I bought it at one of those craft shows. The lady was a genius with yarn. She made all sorts of clever things," Edna said.

I pulled the sweater on over my itchy dress. The sleeves were too long. In fact, I would have needed arms like an orangutan with my knuckles dragging the ground in order for the sweater to fit.

"Does it fit okay?" Edna asked.

I started rolling up the sleeves.

"It fits fine," I said.

"Are you sure the sleeves aren't too long?" she asked.

I rolled faster.

"No, they're fine," I said.

"Maybe you arms are too short," she said. "Does your family have short arms?"

"Yes," I said. "My family has freakishly short arms. It's a curse."

"I thought so," Edna said. "I'm sure the sweater would fit a normal person."

I gave Bob a look that said, "You'll hear about this later."

"That's not your only gift," she said and handed me a small box.

It was a knitted bathroom tissue cover which was made from the same yarn as my sweater.

"Go see if it fits," Edna said.

I stared at her for a long minute and then went into the bathroom and pulled the cover over a roll of tissue paper and brought it out to show her.

"Perfect fit!" she said happily.

Thank goodness rolls of tissue paper don't have freakishly short arms.

Bob opened his gifts which included a beautiful leather jacket, which had sleeves the perfect length, matching leather gloves and a hundred-dollar gift certificate at a book store.

I gave Edna a blouse, which she said wasn't her color and asked if I could exchange it and give her something else. I also gave her a bestselling novel which she said she'd already read.

Bob gave her a black shawl which she said was "devine."

I hadn't heard anyone use the word "devine" since... well, since ever.

We finished exchanging gifts and she left as suddenly as she arrived.

Bob and I changed back into normal, non-itchy, comfortable clothes and had some pie.

"I love you for putting up with my mother. I'm going to give you next year's Christmas gift right now," he said.

"What is it?" I asked.

"I promise to take you someplace, far, far away next Christmas. Mom will have to spend Christmas with my sister," he smiled.

"Thank you! It will be the best Christmas ever!" I wiped my eyes and sniffed, "And God Bless Us, Every One!"

~April Knight

Christmas Eve vs. Christmas Morning

We all grow up with the weight of history on us.
Our ancestors dwell in the attics of our brains as they do in the
spiraling chains of knowledge hidden in every cell of our bodies.
~Shirley Abbott

While I was growing up, there was one tradition in my family that always made me crazy. My father's side of the family was pure Swedish, and apparently in Sweden presents are opened on Christmas Eve. I never objected to any of the other Swedish traditions that Dad insisted upon. Who could find fault with a Christmas Eve smorgasbord laden with such delectable treats as Swedish meatballs, rice pudding and something we called Bacon Spaghetti (spaghetti with a sauce made out of bacon grease mixed with a can of Campbell's Tomato Soup and a little bit of flour—sounds terrible but tastes heavenly)? There was so much I loved about Christmas Eve, having the family sitting together under the soft glow of lights from the Christmas tree, eating until we were ready to pop, listening to Christmas carols on the radio. But after we were all finished eating and it was officially time to open the presents, I always felt a flash of disappointment mixed with a strong sense of disapproval. We were doing things too early and way too quickly as far as I was concerned. Once the presents were opened Christmas was over, a full twelve hours too early.

Having been born with a wide streak of conventionality, I was well aware of the fact that presents weren't supposed to be opened on Christmas Eve. Everyone knew (in America, at least—I still don't know what they think in Sweden) that presents were brought by Santa Claus during the night to be opened on Christmas morning. Not eve. Morning. A.M. After Midnight. Did anyone ever see a sticker with "Don't Open Until December 24th" printed on it? I don't think so. I couldn't understand why my family was so enthusiastic about opening the gifts on Christmas Eve. I knew my siblings watched the same television commercials that I did, the ones featuring the adorable children rushing down the stairs in their flannel pajamas to see what Santa had left for them during the night. Didn't they know we were doing things wrong?

But I could never persuade anyone else I lived with to see things my way. My siblings all liked opening gifts on Christmas Eve and my dad thought it was normal. My mother didn't care much one way or the other. I was the only hold-out in a family of early present openers. True, we had our stockings to enjoy on Christmas morning, but back when I was a child, stocking stuffers weren't nearly as interesting as they are now. In those days we typically got an orange, walnuts, some chocolate and a very cheap and small present from Woolworth in our stockings such as a fake Barbie doll or a small container of Play-Doh. Not exactly the stuff that sugar plum fairy dreams are made of.

Finally, one year, my persistent combination of whining, pouting and crying finally wore down my parents, brother and sisters to the point that everyone was willing to wait until Christmas morning to open our presents. "Just this once," my father said.

I agreed. I would have agreed to anything to be able to tell my friends that my family had finally seen the light and that we opened our presents at the proper time.

The days leading up to Christmas seemed extra long and extra special that year. As I opened each door on the Advent Calendar hanging in the kitchen and gazed lovingly at the tiny pictures of families doing cozy things like going caroling, baking Christmas cookies and waiting until Christmas morning to dig into their loot, my need for convention was finally sated. The closer we got to the 25th the more I hoped that everyone would love opening their presents on Christmas morning so much, even my Swedish father, that we'd make the switch permanent.

I awoke before anyone else that Christmas morning and crept downstairs to turn the tree lights on. Sitting underneath them, I waited for the rest of the family to make an appearance. And waited. And waited. To my chagrin, they all slept in that year, a scenario that I hadn't anticipated. Although I contemplated opening my presents by myself, somehow that didn't fit in with the Kodak Christmas morning I'd been mentally rehearsing since I was old enough to mentally rehearse anything.

My brother and sisters slowly straggled into the living room followed by my mother. My father was still sleeping off the effect of grog, a particularly potent Scandinavian drink. As we took turns opening our presents, it dawned on me that while I really did prefer opening Christmas presents on Christmas morning, it somehow didn't feel right for my family. We were Christmas Eve openers after all. That was how we'd always done Christmas and that was our tradition. I learned that year that traditions really shouldn't be shaken and rattled too much. Shaking and rattling traditions can change them and once they're changed, they're no longer traditions.

For the rest of my growing-up years, I never again suggested that we open our presents at any time but following the smorgasbord and before going to bed. But when I got married and my husband and I had our first Christmas together I made one thing very clear: the tradition in our family was going to be Do Not Open Before Christmas.

Not even on Christmas Eve.

~Nell Musolf

Santa Hats

I will honor Christmas in my heart, and try to keep it all the year...
~Charles Dickens

A number of years ago, I came up with the idea of taking the photo for our family's annual Christmas letter during an upcoming Alaskan cruise. We were planning a dog sledding "shore excursion" on top of a glacier, and I envisioned the snow as the perfect "Christmassy" backdrop.

In anticipation of the photo opportunity, I purchased some cheap Santa hats before we left home. I can't truthfully say that the rest of my family was excited about the idea of wearing Santa hats in August, while having their picture taken with other people watching; however, they did cooperate!

Our guide took photos of us, standing in the snow, with our dogsled teams in the background. The pictures turned out really well, and the feedback from family and friends about our "Santa hat photos" helped me decide to make wearing Santa hats in our Christmas photos an annual tradition!

We expanded our "family" Christmas photo the following year to include some of our "extended family." My husband, Ed, daughter, Brittany, son, Blake, and I, along with Brittany's ponies, Angel and Winnie, and Blake's dog, Sandy, all wore Santa hats.

During a Thanksgiving visit to New York City, we enlisted strangers to take our Santa hat Christmas photos in front of the Serendipity restaurant and the Statue of Liberty. Two years ago, we wore Santa hats in June, in Venice, Italy, for photos in a gondola, complete with gondolier.

We've expanded our Santa hat tradition to include photos with family and friends who visit during the holidays. People look forward to it. I've accumulated lots of Santa hats, so we always have plenty for group photos! One of our funniest group photos was when we made some new hats stand straight up. The cone shape made us look like elves! We have some great multi-generational pictures recording those memories for posterity.

This past Christmas morning, our family wore Santa hats and Christmas pajamas, while talking via Skype to my niece, Tricia, in Dubai, who was wearing matching Christmas pajamas. We took family "Santa hat photos," while holding a laptop with my niece visible on the screen.

My all-time favorite Santa hat photos were made while our family was sitting in our backyard hot tub, wearing Santa hats and shaving cream beards. (We ended up choosing to send a photo without the beards, but I have framed the photos together of us with, and without, the beards.)

This year, our "Santa hat photos" were taken on a zip line canopy tour in the Northeast Georgia mountains. We used duct tape to secure our Santa hats to our red safety helmets for several fun photos. Since there's no telling when or where our next Santa hat photo opportunity will be, our family is always ready. We keep the Spirit of Christmas alive in our hearts all year long!

~Jamie White Wyatt

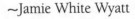

Chapter
10

The Gift of Christmas

A Christmas Carol

Miracle on First Street

He who sings frightens away his ills.
~Miguel de Cervantes, Don Quixote

We were a motley crew of carolers. We met at the little white church in Albany, New York. We represented an interesting mix of backgrounds with few similarities. Yet the camaraderie flowed between us with an obvious show of unity. We weren't just carolers, we were people knit together by a common thread. We were all children of the same Heavenly Father.

It was the week before Christmas and an ideal time to go caroling and hand out invitations to the church holiday program. A buzz of excitement filtered through the twelve of us, along with a lingering layer of unease which hung over the assembly. Christmas caroling was normally a fun and festive activity. Christmas caroling in an inner city, crime-ridden neighborhood presented a challenge that came with an element of danger. We prayed earnestly before we left the safety of the church building and headed out into the dark night. With a show of bravado we began a few Christmas tunes while joking about staying in the same key. We followed the lead of our pastor who resembled a jovial Santa sans the beard, with his arms full of an accordion instead of gifts. His music minister aka elf aka my husband walked beside him with his brass saxophone gleaming in the darkness.

The group walked from house to house with few responses to their singing. People refused to open their doors to strangers. Some peeked furtively through their window curtains. We continued to sing, becoming more courageous with our voices increasing in volume. Porch lights begin to flicker on. A few neighbors managed a tentative wave through the window. We reached a home where the children came to the door with their mother and a request. Could they sing with us? Delighted with the question, we welcomed the children to our group. More doors begin to open. Curious onlookers marked their progress down the street.

Children started to emerge from the houses and join us as parents observed the proceedings. Youngsters didn't play in these streets at night. There was the chance of being caught in a drug deal, being hit by a random gunshot or the horror of being abducted. This evening was different. Somehow, our little church group had chased away the shadowy figures. The children sensed the difference and reveled in their newfound freedom. The pastor matched the image of a pied piper as the little people followed him from house to house. The excitement grew; voices rang out clear and strong in the stillness of the night, singing ageless Christmas songs.

We finally stopped at a street corner. Our group presented a colorful blend of black, white, Hispanic, Puerto Rican, adults and children alike in a heartwarming circle of song. A police car drove by slowly. We waved and called out Christmas greetings to the policeman. He cracked a smile, gave a nod of approval and continued to navigate the streets. The children begin clamoring for certain favorite songs. "Play 'Frosty the Snowman!' Do you know 'Jingle Bells?'" Not the usual religious carols, but the songs certainly fit into the spirit of the season. The pastor's fingers flew over the accordion keys as he kept up the pace.

After several cheerful melodies there came a pause in the song requests. Then my husband began to play his saxophone. A soulful rendition of "Silent Night" echoed throughout the crowd. The adults grew quiet and even the children hushed. The notes rang out beautifully in this rough and hurting neighborhood. People braved the frigid winter air and stood on porches to watch and to listen. At that moment the atmosphere of danger dispersed and the light and perfect peace of Jesus Christ settled upon the little block on First Street. All became still in perfect accord to the words of the song, "Silent night, holy night. All is calm, all is bright." Only the sweet clarion call of the sax sounded in the quiet. After the last note reverberated through the air, silence remained for a moment. Then a child whispered, another child laughed and the adults joined in conversation once again.

Soon after, the children were safely escorted back to their homes clutching candy canes and Christmas cookies. We continued to hand out invitations as we made our way back to the church. At one of the final homes on the block an older woman came to the door with tears in her eyes. In a shaky voice, she confessed to the pastor, "In all my years of living in this neighborhood, no one has ever, ever come to Christmas carol here. God bless you, you have made my Christmas."

Lights now illuminated the streets, neighbors called out greetings to each other, and even the frosty air felt warmer. Because a small group of people overcame fear and allowed God to work through them, God's peace prevailed and His love flowed freely.

Truly, it was a Miracle on First Street.

~Cynthia A. Lovely

Merry Ex-mas

For centuries men have kept an appointment with Christmas.
Christmas means fellowship, feasting, giving and receiving,
a time of good cheer, home.
~W.J. Ronald Tucker

"Christmas comes but once a year" may be true for some, but not for my oldest daughter Dawn and her husband Rob. They celebrate four times every year they fly home to Kansas City for the brief holiday. With both sets of parents divorced and re-established, their tight schedule rivals St. Nick.

With the mind of an engineer, Dawn hatched a plan to streamline Christmas.

"Mom, Rob and I feel we need an arrangement to care for all our parents when old age sets in. But there's so many of you. The best we could do is one house and one nurse. You'll just have to deal with it and get along."

I should've known this just laid the groundwork for more to come.

Several months later came the call.

"Mom, remember my idea about you all living together when you got old? How about a trial run—say Christmas?"

The phrase "pregnant pause" must have come from a moment like this.

"Well...?" she plied.

"Whose house did you have in mind?" I asked.

"I've found a condo to rent in Winter Park, Colorado. There are plenty of bedrooms, a large kitchen, and it's in the middle of town. We could get away from each other if we need a break."

I stifled a "duh" and agreed to consider the option. It took a few days before I pitched the idea to my husband, John. The exact words I used escape me, but I know it started with "Honey, how much do you love me?"

Despite our differences, the parents involved in this reconfigured family group share one common trait, we love our kids. As for our spouses, they may be in line for sainthood. However, some say we all border on insanity. Whatever the cause, e-mails circled the net, schedules compared and consensus reached. Peace on earth and goodwill toward all with good intentions became the goal. We'd spend Christmas in Colorado with the EX-tended family.

Our five days of Christmas had three sets of parents, two sisters, one brother, one son-in-law, our dog Jessie, Barry and his lovely girlfriend—but no "partridge in a pear tree."

Why Barry? He and my son Clay were college roommates and he's like a second son. "I live in Denver and wouldn't miss this for the world," he said. "I'm also a lawyer and you may need one by the end of the week."

The Seattle kids flew into Denver and the rest of us loaded up a wagon, minivan and SUV and headed west. We stocked up on family-size portions at Costco and climbed the mountain to Winter Park. The weather and roads remained clear and we hoped to keep any squalls at bay.

Our two-story condo gave everyone their space, but we gravitated to the large country kitchen and shared homemade oatmeal and bagels every morning. My ex-husband's wife and I made a great team, I cooked and she did the dishes. We shared family Christmas cookies, holiday breads and homemade candy. On Christmas Eve, we filled each other's Christmas stockings with candy, free soap from the condo, ski hats, lotto tickets and toys from a local dime store.

Between skiing, *Scrabble*, and naps, everyone kept busy and congenial.

Always eager to tempt fate, the kids thought we should test the peace accord and try a family outing—an evening sleigh ride through the woods. The wait in line started the only family confrontation—but what's winter without a friendly snowball fight? We mugged for pictures and then hopped on board.

The large wooden sleighs, pulled by two dappled gray draft horses, had bench seats and the driver stood at the front. "It takes us twenty minutes to get to the bonfire. We've got hot chocolate and marshmallows waiting," he announced. "I challenge all my riders to sing 'The Twelve Days of Christmas' on the way back. Nobody's got it right yet this season."

The evening chill forced us under the wool blankets we'd each been given and we set out under a winter moon. Our sled took the lead, followed by one that held another family. Lisa, our youngest, led us in every holiday song she knew. Some of us had our own version, but everyone added their voice. We even barked "Jingle Bells." The family behind us remained silent except for one lone voice that sang along with us.

At the campfire, we laughed and sang some more, joined by our newly adopted family singer. His group didn't have much to say to each other.

"They lost their holiday cheer, so I'll share mine with you," he said and passed around his cinnamon schnapps to heat up our hot chocolate.

We charred our share of marshmallows and enjoyed the warmth and crackle of the burning pine. In the glow of the campfire, we huddled close and collaborated on our challenge. Everyone contributed, some more off-key than others, but we sorted out our leaping lords and milking maidens.

After we loaded up for the return trip, our driver turned around to say, "I don't know why families come out here for Christmas and can't get along—at least for the time they're here. You guys do it up right."

No one said a word. We just smiled at each other and then

became the first "family" to successfully sing "The Twelve Days of Christmas."

~Carolyn Hall

The Night
the Angels Sang

We are each of us angels with only one wing,
and we can only fly by embracing one another.
~Luciano de Crescenzo

I sat there, so alone, in the dark. The sweat was pouring off my forehead, mingling with the tears. The single strand of tiny twinkling lights on the bedraggled little plastic-needled Christmas tree from the Japanese store did nothing to lighten my mood. My pen wrote the words I struggled to share with my family, so far away. One page after another I crumpled the paper and tossed it aside. I really didn't want them to know how blue I was.

My mother had warned me when I left for the llanos (plains) of Venezuela. I could hear her voice now. "You aren't even old enough to vote! You have no idea what kind of pagans you will find when you get there!"

I almost thought maybe she had been right. However, the "pagans" were the other missionary family that lived in the house in front of me. They had some nerve! Here it was Christmas Eve, and while they had invited me to spend the holiday with them, I overheard them saying they wished they could spend the day alone. An intruder! That's what I would be. So I declined their invitation.

Actually, until tonight it had been pretty good. I was in charge of the young people from the church in Acarigua. Some of them were older than I was, but I didn't share that tidbit with most of them. They had shown remarkable talent as they prepared for a very special Christmas program at the church.

As I looked around my living room, there were still scraps of the plywood they had used to make the crèche, which sat so proudly on top of the church, lighted by a spotlight just above the star. Various paint cans, paint brushes and tools joined the mess, but I didn't feel like cleaning it up tonight. I might as well do it in the morning; I had nothing better to do.

The church had been filled to overflowing for the program. The youth had done a bang-up job of advertising it. A couple of the kids had written the drama they had presented, and they had done remarkable work.

But now it was over, and I was alone. I popped a music tape into the recorder, and familiar strains of English Christmas carols filled the room, but still left my heart feeling empty. It should be freezing cold. I should be drinking a cup of hot cocoa; the Christmas tree, a real one, should be glistening. My mother should be playing the little Conn spinet organ, with all of us singing carols along with her. There should be snow falling, or at least on the ground. The woods should have shadows shimmering through their branches, making you wonder if the wildlife was scampering about, celebrating the best night of the year in their own special way. But that was Christmas in Minnesota. And this was not! This was Venezuela, and the temperature was still almost 100 degrees, and it was almost 10 o'clock at night.

Suddenly, I thought I had fallen asleep and must be dreaming. Off in the distance I could hear someone singing "Noche de paz, noche de amor." Yes, it was the well-known sound of "Silent Night," but in Spanish.

I rubbed my eyes to see if I was awake or not. The sound grew louder, until it was right outside my little Quonset hut. I got up and went to the door, and there was the entire group of young people from the church. They were caroling, and it was my turn to be serenaded.

I hurried to invite them inside. I was going to turn the lights on, but they all insisted that I leave them off. They had never seen a Christmas tree before. Suddenly, even my pitiful little excuse for a tree seemed to glow so much brighter than before.

I went into my kitchen and got a big platter of the Christmas cookies I had baked for holiday visitors. They had never seen them, either, but they ate them with great gusto. I brought out ice cold lemonade, and we shared our joy together. The best part of it, to me, was that I was not alone. This was the life I had chosen, and it was the best life I could have dreamed of. It was just right.

As we talked, I told them what Christmas was like in Minnesota. They tried to envision snow, but it was impossible for them to comprehend it. Suddenly, the ever-present light bulb went off and I hurried back into the kitchen. I opened the freezer door, grabbed a heavy spatula and began to scrape the "snow" from the sides and the top of the freezer into a huge metal pan. I headed back to the living room, armed and ready to do battle. I set the bowl down on the coffee table, reached in and grabbed a handful of the "snow" and shaped it into a snowball. Soon others followed suit, and there, in my living room, with the fans running to keep it from being quite so hot, we had their very first ever snowball fight. The fact that the floor would be a pool by the time we were finished left me undaunted. It was well worth a little cleanup effort.

Just before they left, one of my best new friends, Crucita, came over and hugged me. "Vicente said he figured you were probably going to spend Christmas with the other missionaries, but if you aren't, we would love to have you come and spend the day with us."

The tears once again ran down my face. This time they were tears of joy, not of sorrow. I had never had a better invitation to anything, not even when she added "Vicente is going to barbecue the goat." They could have fed me anything and it would have been divine.

They had been there almost an hour. As they left, again singing Spanish Christmas carols, I went back and sat in my plastic-woven chair, smiled at my little spindle with its lights blinking at me, listened to the music on my tape recorder and began to write to my parents.

"Dear Mother and Daddy,
It is Christmas Eve. Tonight I heard the angels sing..."

~Janet Elaine Smith

The Nutcracker, Semi-Sweet

You can learn many things from children.
How much patience you have,
for instance.
~Franklin P. Jones

I took my boys, Ross, five, and Jack, twelve, to see *The Nutcracker*. I wanted to expose my miniature men to this classic Christmas ballet. Dancing in my head were visions of my spiffily dressed family waltzing, dignified, into the theater and feasting their eyes upon ballerinas magically transformed into snowflakes, angels and marzipan. But, it turned out, I was plum dreaming.

Sure, I considered the "sissy factor." I knew that at my boys' ages, I had a small window of opportunity to take them to *The Nutcracker* before they potentially deemed it "for girls." This could be my only year to take them to the production before the older son turned into a teenager and perhaps thought the title of the ballet meant something more, well, off-color. (Boys I knew in high school shamelessly named a pronounced dip in a popular sledding hill after this ballet.)

Prior to the performance, I asked Jack to change from tattered jeans and a T-shirt embellished with an orange juice stain into some "nice" clothes. You would have thought I asked him to don a tutu. He couldn't fathom why he needed to change. I explained that people dress up to go to the theater.

"What's the difference?" Jack argued. "It's like going to a movie. They turn out the lights, and you sit there." On he ranted about the injustice of wearing khaki pants and a sweater. I decided to compromise.

From Jack's closet I pulled new jeans and a clean T-shirt. Jack changed his clothes, but continued to bellyache as if he were being forced to wear Barney Fife's suit.

Meanwhile, unbeknownst to me, my preschooler was contemplating contraband to enrich his *Nutcracker* experience.

I glanced into Ross' bedroom and saw him looking admiringly in the direction of his hand—which wielded a six-inch screwdriver.

Ross looked up and asked, "Can I take this?"

By then, I had had enough testosterone tarnishing my pre-*Nutcracker* preparations, and I wasn't going to take it anymore.

"No!" I said sternly. "Put the screwdriver down. It's time to go."

"But I want to take it." Ross looked shocked that I would deny him a *Nutcracker* screwdriver.

"We don't play with screwdrivers, and we don't take them to *The Nutcracker!*" (They say we repeat to our children the same words our parents said to us. Not true here. My mother never told me I couldn't take a screwdriver to *The Nutcracker*.)

Once at the Long Center, Jack sat beside a little girl dressed in lace so stiff she could poke an eye out. Across the theater, I saw little girls in red velvet, green organza, frilly anklets, fur muffs and leopard tams. I looked at Ross next to me in the theater seat. His feet, in Spider-Man shoes, were dangling above the floor, and he was holding his… *Nutcracker* screwdriver!

"I told you not to bring the screwdriver!" I whispered frantically and looked around, hoping no one saw Ross' tool du jour.

Ross looked at me, his long eyelashes fluttering, and confessed. "I hid it in my pocket."

I seized the smuggled workbench-import and shoved it into my purse. As the house lights dimmed, Ross began to weep. I could see that he really needed the screwdriver to enjoy the performance. Call me crazy, but I relented. "You can have the screwdriver only if you keep it in your pocket," I said.

So, we settled in. With rapt attention, my sons watched *The Nutcracker*. And they enjoyed it. The ballet is not just about sugar plum fairies. It's also about a boy-endearing battle between mice and soldiers in which each soldier brandishes a sword—a long, sharp, metal object—very similar to a beloved screwdriver hidden deep and secretively inside my little boy's pocket.

So our family theater outing proved to be a different vision than the one I had originally conjured. It turned out to be better. Better because I smile when I think of my boys, one in jeans and the other in Bob the Builder mode, watching ballerinas pirouette.

~Angie Klink

The Touch It Tree

Life is really simple, but we insist on making it complicated.
~Confucius

My flashlight poked a tiny hole in the darkness. I stared into the cavernous attic at boxes stacked, like stalagmites, to the ceiling. "There's no way I can find the Christmas decorations in here." Sighing, I climbed back downstairs to check on the sugar cookies. Burnt.

I scraped the charcoal reindeers into the trash, along with my hopes of giving the kids a "normal" Christmas. With their dad in Iraq and their preemie brother Logan in and out of the hospital, the whole year had been a struggle. They'd given up soccer and play dates without much complaint. I wanted to make Christmas especially memorable for them, but these weren't the memories I was hoping for. At this rate we were headed for the worst Christmas ever.

"Hey, Mom! Look what I made!" Keith, my seven-year-old, bounded into the kitchen. He handed me a toilet paper tube angel. "We can put it on our tree."

"I made one, too, Mom!" Moriah, a year younger, was right behind him with more glitter in her hair than on her angel.

"Me, too! Me, too!" Even Haven and Everett, just four and three, came waving their cardboard creations like the big kids.

"When are we putting up the tree?" Moriah asked. "Victorya and Sarah Grace got theirs last week."

"Well, kids, we need to talk about that." My voice was shaky, and I could see in Keith and Moriah's eyes that they sensed what was coming. I looked away. "Mommy can't get the decorations out of the attic. Next year, when Daddy's home, we'll put up a big tree. Maybe we can even get a real one. But, this year..."

Moriah turned her angel over in her hands. She started to cry.

"I'm sorry, honey." I tried to console her with a hug, but "sorry" sounded hollow. She and her siblings had done without so much for so long. Was a tree so much to ask?

That night, after bedtime stories, I climbed back to the attic. I searched every pile of boxes until I found our Christmas collection. The tree box was taller than me, but I dragged it as far as I could toward the attic door, which wasn't even half the distance. I tried to wrestle it open, so I could throw the tree down piece by piece. The tape required a knife, though, and I wouldn't make the jump into the attic while holding a blade.

Defeated, I went to bed. "Lord," I prayed, "I know Christmas isn't about trees and ornaments, but would You show me how to help my children celebrate Your birth in a way they'll remember all their lives?"

At breakfast the next morning we talked about our favorite Christmas memories. "I like our 'Touch It Tree' the best," said Keith. "It's fun to rearrange all the ornaments."

"Yeah," added Moriah. "The big tree is for grown-ups to look at, but the 'Touch It Tree' is for us."

"You would be happy with just the 'Touch It Tree?'" I was surprised. Our "Touch It Tree" was a three-foot dime store special. The only ornaments we hung on it were safe for toddlers, and we encouraged all young family members and visitors alike to move the ornaments from branch to branch. It wasn't pretty or sparkly or even particularly Christmas-y. But they loved it more than I realized.

Thanking God for the remarkable idea, I left our breakfast table for one more trip to the attic.

That evening, Moriah lead us in "Oh Touch It Tree," sung to the tune of "O Tannenbaum" with lots of humming when we couldn't come up with rhyming words. Each child nestled his angel in its branches, and I read the Biblical account of angels telling the good news of Jesus' birth.

"You know what, Mom?" Keith asked as I tucked him into bed.

"Tell me."

"I think this is the best Christmas tree ever."

"Me, too, Keith. Me, too."

~Mary C. Chace

Holy Family

May the spirit of Christmas bring you peace,
The gladness of Christmas give you hope,
The warmth of Christmas grant you love.
~Author Unknown

It was a white Christmas, an unusual event in Chattanooga, Tennessee. Snow had fallen, and then ice had fallen longer. The trees appeared to be painted white and coated in crystal. The whiteness of it all glowed on that Christmas Eve, but for me there was little celebration. It was a Christmas without family, everyone having gone their separate ways this year. Even my friends were all away visiting relatives. I decided, having nothing else to do, to go to Midnight Mass.

My church was a growing church with many young families, so the main Christmas liturgy was held on Christmas Eve at 5:30. That way all the little people got home and into bed at a reasonable hour and didn't have to leave the festivities around their family Christmas trees to go to church on Christmas morning. All obligations fulfilled, families were free to celebrate the birthday of Jesus in the comfort of their own homes. All of which is to say, I generally made a point of attending the 5:30 celebration because I loved the togetherness and because Midnight Mass in my parish was not ever very well attended. But since I couldn't be with my family this year, I wasn't much in the mood for a big crowd.

I told myself the small group would suit me just fine this year.

After all, small liturgies passed more quickly. A night owl, I could get Mass over with and sleep in on Christmas morning. With nowhere to go, and no one expecting me, I would be free to pass the day just like any other day, only I wouldn't have to work.

If I had been a little more truthful with myself, I might have admitted I didn't want Christmas to be like any other day. I wanted celebration and song. I was lonely. My dogs, Oreo and Sleeper, whom I loved beyond measure, were great company, but I still longed for a few nieces and nephews and loud family dinners with sports and parades blasting from televisions and carols coming from the piano. The truth of my loneliness edged up beside me a time or two, but I shrugged it off. If I paid the feelings much heed, I might not get through the holiday without tears.

Around 11:30, just as I was leaving home for church, the power went out. Thank goodness for gas heat, I thought. I knelt and hugged my dogs. "I'll be back soon, guys!" And I was off to Mass.

The ice storm in the city had evidently knocked out power everywhere. Even the streetlights were dark. When I arrived at the church, I was grateful for the bright moonlight to guide me inside. Once there, my eyes beheld a lovely sight. Someone had lit candles all over the sanctuary to provide a bit of light and warmth for anyone venturing out on this icy, snowy night. The effect was very moving. The nuances of the light dancing around the crèche in the front of the church actually made my eyes well up a bit.

I took my place in the very last pew of this church built to hold hundreds. Soft guitar music played from somewhere near the front of the church, but there was no choir to accompany the lone musician at her post. I heard the strains of "Silent Night" and the loneliness I'd tried to hide from earlier crept back into my brain. It couldn't be helped. I pushed the feeling down once again.

When Mass finally started, there were eighteen people scattered about the church, every worshipper a study in the quiet of Christmas. From our farflung seats, we sang a mournful "O Come All Ye Faithful," and Mass began. Scripture was proclaimed, responses were offered.

People upped the volume on the usual "Thanks be to God!" and I realized everyone else felt as disconnected as I did. The pastor spoke quietly during the homily, telling us how, on another quiet night two thousand years ago, a Savior was born, and how the world had never been the same.

There was great beauty in the liturgy, in the calmness and quietness of a barely populated room lit only by candlelight. There was also great peace, and my worries about a lonely Christmas diminished with the familiarity of liturgy. When it came time for the Sign of Peace, a miracle happened.

Every single liturgy I had attended in ten years at this church was the same in this respect: the Sign of Peace was of the utmost importance. People left their pews and walked up and down the aisles every Sunday, every weekday, hugging their friends, offering them peace, stroking faces, patting backs, offering the love of Christ to one another. This Christmas morning, we all did the same. Eighteen of us converged near the front, from all the corners of the church. Our faces lit up as we recognized friends we had worshipped with for years who had been hidden in the dimly lit sanctuary. We shared hardy hugs. Older couples who had attended Midnight Mass since they were children, and single younger people with a need to acknowledge the miracle of Christmas became reacquainted. We all knew one another; we just hadn't been near enough anyone else to recognize the fact. Everyone seemed somehow relieved to realize during the Sign of Peace that they were among friends. When we sat down again, we sat together, in the front of the church, in the first two pews. We were together. We shared in communion. Hands were joined and held, in a solemn recognition of Holy Family, and I realized these were more than friends. I was with family after all. None of us was alone for the holiday.

When Mass ended, the eighteen of us stood in that beautifully lighted church and, yes, joyfully sang "Joy to the World!" as though we really meant it.

Every Christmas Eve after that, the church has been lit by candles. More people come every year.

~Marla H. Thurman

Christmas Through Your Eyes

I hold you in my arms,
your tiny warm breath soft upon my cheek.
You gaze in wonder at the lighted tree.
Your eyes drink deep this newest sight.
I see the lights of Christmas twinkling in your eye,
a hundred gleaming stars,
each a present of the future,
wrapped in sparkling possibility,
soon torn open with headlong glee.
Each day an undiscovered country,
raced through in breathless wonder.
Each moment a new treasure,
grasped in both hands and tasted.
You laugh, with the sudden joy of infant humor.
The stars dance and twinkle in your eye,
and glitter through the sudden mist in my own.

~Ronald A. Dimmer, Jr.

The True Sounds of Christmas

Kindness is the language which the deaf can hear and the blind can see.

~Mark Twain

Christmastime always brings surprises, but two years ago proved by far to be the most memorable. That particular holiday season came wrapped in a heartwarming lesson from the elderly.

As Office Manager of an assisted living facility, I worked at the front desk, an open office area within the Great Room lobby. On this particular December afternoon, the tedious task of sorting mail was a little more enjoyable from my view than other days. Peering over my desk, I thought the high-ceilinged Great Room was especially beautiful. Church volunteers circled the festively decorated room, distributing holiday sheet music to each elderly resident. Scanning the merry crowd, I witnessed many residents who warbled what few words they could remember and decipher from the sheet music resting in their shaking hands. Hot chocolate steamed from cups offered by the dietary staff. Residents clasped star-shaped cookies and candy canes as the piano music resounded throughout the room.

My eyes drifted back to my desk. A package wrapped in brown shipping paper addressed to Charlie sat before me. Because he was one of the most social and well-liked residents at the facility, I knew he would be in the Great Room in the midst of all the festivities.

Residents gravitated to him each morning as they began their day looking for his caring guidance. With his usual charm, he kindly greeted and assisted those in need of direction as they decided which activity to partake in.

A disharmonious rendition of "We Wish You a Merry Christmas" echoed through the room. Thinking these Christmas carols were the loveliest music I had ever heard, because it came from the elderly community I had grown to love, it suddenly occurred to me that Charlie was nowhere to be found. Puzzled, I headed down one of the nearby hallways, package in hand. I hummed the tune of one of the carols, believing I was displaying true holiday spirit until I approached Charlie's doorway. I was quite unprepared for the sight I was about to behold.

I detected his familiar voice and stood quietly to listen. With his back to me, Charlie sat in his wheelchair facing his bed. Upon his bed lay the sheet music the volunteers had shared with everyone. Alone in his room, Charlie was singing the Christmas carols quite loudly and off key with his arms dancing in front of him.

I moved across the room coming into his sight so as not to take Charlie off guard. Never intending to interrupt the song, I looked at him, then down at the sheet music, and once again at him. Sadness overcame me, knowing he was in his room singing the same tunes as the others, yet not participating with them. He spotted me but continued the performance in his distinctive Charlie voice coupled with his soft, kind smile. Stopping abruptly when he glanced my way a second time, he caught a glimpse of the return address label on the package I forgot I had been holding. Grinning, he uttered, "Wait."

His fingers fumbled as he opened the parcel from the catalog company and carefully removed the packing material. Inside was a brand-new, shiny, black cordless microphone. He blurted, "This Christmas gift is for the residents so they can hear what is going on in the Great Room with its tall ceilings."

It was then that I realized this man's compassion. With tears falling softly down both his cheeks and mine, I tenderly patted his arm and nodded in agreement. I was deeply moved by his truly selfless

Christmas gift, for Charlie has been totally deaf since he was a young boy.

Each time that microphone carries the voices of our entertainers, guests, and residents throughout the facility, I silently thank Charlie for teaching me the true sounds of Christmas.

~Maryrose Armato

Out of the Mouths of Babes

There's nothing that can help you understand your beliefs more than trying to explain them to an inquisitive child.
~Frank A. Clark

The Christmas Eve church service was pretty late for a five-year-old to attend, but my little nephew Phillip insisted he wanted to go. He solemnly promised, crossing his heart with a big, exaggerated "X," not to get cranky.

His mother, my sister, thought that keeping him up late before the "big day" might be a good way for everyone in the household to get a little extra sleep in the morning, so she agreed to take him with us.

Phillip entered the church solemnly, holding onto one of each of our hands. As we entered the sanctuary, everyone we encountered nodded and smiled to us, and especially to Phillip. Many friends said a cheery holiday hello in hushed tones. Some waved from where they sat. We found a spot for the three of us in the second pew and settled in.

Wide-eyed, Phillip watched as the story of the immaculate birth was reenacted by the older children from the Sunday School. He delighted in the children dressed as shepherds and wooly sheep, and a small gasp escaped him as the angels, sporting glittering halos, gathered around the manger.

The moving ceremony concluded with the lighting of individual candles. Row by row, the ushers lit the first person's candle, and the flame was carefully passed along. My sister and I kept a sharp eye on Phillip as he reverently held his candle upright with both his little hands.

The lights were dimmed, and we all stood as one, preparing to sing an a cappella rendition of "Silent Night." Just one chord was struck on the organ to signal the start of this final hymn.

Deeply moved by the spirit of the evening, and awed by flickering of so many candles, at the sound of the organ Phillip quickly opened his mouth and burst into song as only a jubilant five-year-old can do: "Happy Birthday to you..."

The congregation stifled their laughter and quickly joined him, singing, "Happy Birthday, dear Jesus..."

And that would have been a perfectly suitable ending to this story, had Phillip not capped it by tugging insistently at my sleeve as the song's conclusion. "Jannie," he loudly whispered. "Jannie, does Jesus have the same birthday as Santa Claus?"

A woman in the pew in front of us turned around and smiled. She crouched down to Phillip's level, patted his hand and whispered back, "Yes he does, Phillip. He most certainly does!"

~Jan Bono

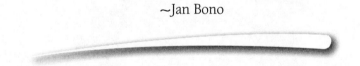

The Gift of Christmas

Good Gift Hunting

A Christmas Shopping Spree

Children are a great comfort in your old age —
and they help you reach it faster, too.
~Lionel Kauffman

"Dashing through the snow in a one-horse open snake." The loud voice of four-year-old Lorne joined the carolers in the mall. I smiled and wiped ice cream drips from his chin. I was ready to call our Christmas shopping spree complete when my energetic son darted into the Santa Claus line. Oh well, I thought. This afternoon was Lorne's turn to shop alone with me and choose his presents for our family while Daddy babysat the other kids.

Lorne squeezed every last second out of our Mommy-and-me time until we finally wandered outside. A sea of vehicles assaulted my eyes and I hoped I'd remember where I'd parked my car. I thought back to when we arrived at the mall and what Lorne asked to purchase first — "a big screwdriver that Daddy really needs." (I didn't inquire what had happened to the big screwdriver Daddy already had.) Using this as my clue, I figured I must have parked by the tool section of Sears. So off we tromped in that direction. No car.

Okay, I thought. Maybe I parked closer to the bookstore because a board book for our baby was his second gift. We hiked up and down columns of automobiles that were beginning to look all alike. No car.

I knew we didn't park near the toy store. But since we'd spent a long time in that place choosing a ball for his brother and a Barbie doll dress for his sister, we staggered in and out of rows that seemed to be getting longer and longer. No car.

A mall security guard pulled up beside us in his little cart. "Merry Christmas! Can I help you?"

"I can't find my car," I said.

"No problem. Hop in and we'll drive around."

Lorne looked worried. He pulled me down and whispered in my ear, "Is that policeman going to un-rest us?"

I assured Lorne all was well and we climbed into the cart. As soon as I sat down, my feet sang the Hallelujah chorus since they'd been complaining for some time. Up and down, in and out, and around and around we drove. No car.

"I hate to tell you this, but car thefts have been up lately," said the security guard.

I groaned and thought this was a terrible way to start the holiday season.

Lorne pointed. "There's Daddy's car again."

"Stop!" I yelled. My memory shifted into gear. I mumbled an explanation about how my husband's car had been parked behind mine at home and instead of moving it, I'd taken his, and I was sorry I'd taken up so much of his time, and we'd gone by my husband's car about twenty times, and I really appreciated his help, and…

The security guard stared at me. I could tell he thought my candy cane was a couple of stripes short.

Lorne and I jumped into our car. "Why didn't you tell me Daddy's car was parked there?"

"You didn't ask me," was the answer.

I flipped on the radio and we started toward home. "We Wish You a Merry Christmas" filled the air.

"We all want some icky pudding," joined the high little boy voice from the back seat.

~Sharon Landeen

Did Father Know Best?

Any man can be a father. It takes someone special to be a dad.
~Author Unknown

"What do you want for Christmas, Lori?" my husband asked our teenage daughter as she sulked on our remote farm in Missouri, after we arrived from Florida for our holiday vacation.

There was a long pause before she mumbled, "I want a boyfriend. Everyone at school is paired off, except me."

My heart ached for my daughter. She was beautiful, athletic, an honor student, and president of her class. Were the boys intimidated?

Jim busied himself with maintenance projects before Christmas. Storms had blown shingles off the roof; a large limb blocked the lane to the farmhouse; and holes in the siding invited mice.

"Hop in the pickup and ride to town with me before it snows," he asked one cold, gray morning. "I need supplies from the hardware store."

While Jim lost himself in the tool aisle, I slipped into the general store next door, where I found a warm, flowered nightgown for Lori to open on Christmas. Later, Jim and I met at the truck and stored our purchases in the back.

"I bought a cute nightgown for Lori," I shared as we drove back to the farm.

"I found the perfect gift for her too," said Jim with a mysterious smile.

On Christmas morning, Lori undid the festive red bow adorning the colorful Christmas paper and squealed as she held up her new nightgown.

"I love it!" she exclaimed. "I've been freezing on these cold nights."

Then she picked up another present with her name on it, that I hadn't wrapped. Jim must have taken care of that one. Lori unknotted the twine, pulled back the brown paper, and stared at the box in her lap.

"What's this?" she asked her dad.

"You told me you wanted a boyfriend for Christmas," Jim explained. "I didn't know where to get one, so I did the next best thing, and bought this present for you at the hardware store."

I leaned over and read the lettering on the box, then gasped in disbelief. In large print were the words STUD FINDER.

"Explain this to me Dad," Lori insisted, as she rolled her eyes.

"Well," Jim began as he cleared his throat, "a stud finder is a device that helps carpenters find supporting stud boards in walls, so they will have a sturdy place to put nails. In your case, it may help you find a boyfriend."

Jim laughed.

Lori and I didn't think it was funny.

~Miriam Hill

I'm Dreaming of a White Elephant Christmas

We should give as we would receive, cheerfully, quickly, and without hesitation; for there is no grace in a benefit that sticks to the fingers.

~Seneca

In my family, re-gifting during the holidays is a mandate — not a secret we try to hide with fluffed up bows and new wrapping paper. We call it giving "white elephants," which means you give something you already have. To clarify, it doesn't have to be something given to you that you've never used. It can be something you've inherited or something you have that another person has always admired.

It can't have been bought within the past year.

I should add also that the annual white elephant gift exchange doesn't apply to my entire family. It's between five women and three different generations: my mother and my aunt, my sister and I, and my niece.

What started as a cost-conserving measure a few years ago is now my favorite Christmas ritual. On Christmas Eve day, we all gather at my house for a private girls' lunch with fresh fruit, coffee, and light appetizers.

Then, we sit back and the unwrapping begins. We often give

each person several gifts. There are a few different categories under which our white elephant gifts qualify, and new ones are invented when the occasion arises:

"Teachable moment gifts" are gifts that impart wisdom, history and even hilarity from times past. A few examples:

Silver dollars: My mother gave these to all of us; the coins dated from the mid-twenties. Turns out, my paternal grandparents (who never went anywhere before or after this trip) won them in Las Vegas in the 1940s after driving cross-country with another couple.

Art-deco bowl: My aunt gave this to my sister, who laughed so hard she almost wet her pants. As a little girl, she remembered my maternal grandfather using it as an ashtray for his stinky cigars and my grandmother yelling, "It's not an ashtray, Jim!" To which he'd chuckle and reply: "It sure looks like a dang ashtray." She threw a pound of hamburger meat at him to illustrate her point.

Milk glass candy dish: My aunt gave me this beautiful piece that belonged to "Granny," my great-grandmother. Unfortunately, Granny wasn't too popular. She spent her declining years cutting people out of her will—and adding them back in—depending upon who she deemed deserving.

Santa Clauses: When my sister and I were growing up, my mom collected Santa Clauses and would display them on the mantle. We were usually with her when she bought them at department stores and Christmas shows. She had nesting Santa dolls, a Santa with hinged wooden legs, tall, skinny Santas and short, fat Santas—each of them with a story. We were delighted last year when Mom started passing them down and now display these Santas in our own homes, occasionally arguing over who has the best ones.

"Gotta have" gifts are gifts that you get to beg for from the person who owns them. Think of it as intimate window shopping coupled with genuine harassment.

Mosaic soup tureen: My mother gave a beautiful soup tureen to my sister one Christmas as a white elephant. I whined about that tureen for an entire year until my sister finally gave it to me the next year. It was a wonderful surprise, as I'd forgotten how much I'd wanted it. It now sits in grand splendor on my dining room table.

Silver bracelet: After about six months of flattery, my sister finally took the hint and gave my mom the beautiful silver bangle she'd been admiring.

Boutique towel: My niece gave me a fuzzy wrap-around towel for my birthday just two months before Christmas. I could tell how much she loved it when she gave it to me; she fingered the fabric and showed me the trim and how to fasten it. It dawned on me this eighteen-year-old young woman spent every weekend dolling herself up and would put it to much better use than I, whose evenings are often spent playing *Chutes and Ladders* and cooking frozen chicken nuggets from a bag.

"Useful gifts" take a lot of thought. It isn't always easy, but it is interesting, and you remember a lot about the person as you struggle to find a great white elephant. My aunt, who lives in Texas, just started joining our group for Christmas two years ago, so it's always a challenge to find something she'll really like. The challenge has made my sister and me pay closer attention to her interests and our correspondence during the year.

Truthfully, our white elephant gifts are just a cover. The real gift, in fact, is the story that accompanies each item, old or new—where and when you got it and how it reminded you of the recipient.

The white elephants always get us talking and connecting in a way we simply might not have done over store-bought gifts. On that day before Christmas, we are three generations of women, catching up, growing up, and learning a bit more each year about what makes us family.

And, really, isn't that what the holidays are all about?

~Christa Gala

The Ring

To give and then not feel that one has given is the very best of all ways of giving.
~Max Beerbohm

It was the most unconventional gift a sister could give a brother. As I clutched the tiny box in my hand, I wondered how my brother was going to react and if he would cry. I didn't want him to cry, because if he cried, I would too, and the task at hand was already playing with my emotions.

My older brother Jason and I were never close. There is a seven-year age difference between us and as far as I was concerned growing up, we were living on different planets. The few memories I have of him were of him terrorizing me and making me cry.

When our parents divorced and our household divided, he went to live with our grandmother. I didn't miss him. When our father remarried I adopted my stepbrother as my brother.

When I was sixteen, my nephew was born. What resulted was a tradition of me and Jason getting together with his son and our relatives every year for Christmas and in the summer for a picnic. Now, instead of seeing Jason never, I get to see him twice a year. This doesn't leave much time for bonding.

Jason is a good person, with a good heart. He has ambitions and dreams, but seems to keep getting the short end of the stick. He has such bad luck that if he didn't have that, he wouldn't have any luck at all. His job barely pays enough and with vehicle repairs and his financial obligations to his son, his wallet is empty.

Right before Thanksgiving, Jason told me not to buy him a Christmas gift.

"I can't afford to buy you one, so don't get me one," he told me over the phone. He explained the financial shortfalls he was experiencing. He had less than $80 and needed to buy parts for his truck so it would pass inspection. And he didn't know how he was going to do it.

I contemplated his request for weeks. I didn't need a gift from him, but I had the money to buy him a gift and I felt he deserved one. After all, I was buying for my sister. Why not him? I struggled with a gift idea.

A week before our annual family gathering, our mom informed me that Jason and his girlfriend of two years were engaged.

"He said he can't afford to buy her a ring, but they're going to get married anyway."

In that moment I realized I had exactly what my brother needed — a diamond engagement ring.

After a failed relationship, I had tried to hock the ring for cash but no one was interested. So for nine years it sat in my jewelry box unloved. Now it was going to have a home.

I slipped a note inside the jewelry box: "I hope this brings you a lifetime of happiness."

I kept waiting for the moment to catch him alone. Attention from the rest of the family was not what I was seeking. In fact, I didn't even want anyone to know, but every time he walked in or out of a room, there was someone following him.

I was getting restless and nervous and the box was burning a proverbial hole in my pocket. I sat with my hand inside my coat fingering the silver ribbon I had lovingly tied around my precious gift.

I was lost in my thoughts when I realized my brother had vanished.

"Where's Jason?" I asked his fiancée nonchalantly.

"In the shed," she answered.

I bolted for the door and for a minute I thought she was going to follow me, but she didn't.

I caught Jason outside, alone, and presented the box to him.

"She doesn't need to know it came from me."

My brother cried. I cried.

~Valerie Benko

Christmas Gifts for Nanny and Grandpa

Each day comes bearing its own gifts. Untie the ribbons.
~Ruth Ann Schabacke

"Grandpa, what do you want for Christmas?" I asked. Every day I asked Grandpa the same question and every day he gave me the same answer. "A thousand dollars and a white elephant," he said.

I was nine years old then. Our grandparents lived around the corner and were like another set of parents to us kids.

They knew how to make each of us feel important. Grandpa built a treasure chest with a lock and key for my seventh birthday. It was about thirty-six inches wide, eighteen inches tall and painted pink, my favorite color. In a large family it's important to have your own space—a place to hide your favorite games, crafts and mementoes from sisters, brothers and cousins. This instantly became my place.

Nanny sewed dresses for us girls and taught me how to embroider. I had bought Nanny a handkerchief for Christmas at the five and dime store and embroidered a rose with bright red thread and the word NANNY in green lettering on the corner. All the crafts I had made for the rest of our family were wrapped and tucked away except Nanny's. I loved holding the handkerchief up and admiring the stitching.

One afternoon, I opened my chest intending to count the coins in my peanut butter jar bank for Grandpa's gift. I saved the two-cent refund from every soda bottle I returned to the store. Just as I reached for the bank, my younger cousin, Harriet burst into my room and knelt down beside me. She spotted the handkerchief on top of the *Monopoly* game. "Where did you get that pretty handkerchief?" she asked.

"I bought the handkerchief for ten cents and embroidered it," I boasted.

Harriet tried to grab the hanky but I pulled the lid down almost pinching her fingers. "You can't touch it," I shouted. "It's a surprise for Nanny for Christmas."

She left the room pouting.

Our neighborhood girls' club met that Thursday and voted to ask one mother to buy a Christmas present with money collected from our weekly dues and we would draw a name for the winner. "You have to go home and get two cents or your name will not be added for the drawing," one girl told me.

At home I threw myself on the bed, torn between giving up the pennies and saving them for Grandpa's gift. Christmas music rang from the house next door where all the girls had gathered. It didn't seem worth missing out on all the fun. I tugged on the peanut butter jar bank. It slid down under a box of paper dolls. Hanging onto the cover, I yanked it free then emptied it on the bedspread and counted twenty-three cents. Unwillingly, I removed two pennies and dropped them next door into the coffee can holding the club's savings.

"I will buy Grandpa's gift today," I decided later, fumbling for my bank in the chest. The *Monopoly* game tipped upside down, and play money scattered. While replacing the money neatly in the *Monopoly* box, I stared down at my hand. I was clutching a thousand-dollar bill. All along a thousand-dollar bill lay in the treasure chest Grandpa had made. I set it aside. But where would I find a white elephant?

I flipped magazine pages in search of a picture of a white elephant but found none.

Two days before Christmas, I strolled over to our neighborhood girls' club. With all the festivities, I had forgotten about the mystery gift. An older girl walked over to the tree and retrieved a tiny package from between the branches. "It's time to draw a name for the winner. Everyone's name is in here," she said. "My little sister will draw the name because she isn't part of our club."

The three-year-old reached into a paper cup with her chubby fingers and pulled out a name. "Let me have the paper," the older sister ordered.

All six of us girls waited, hoping to hear our name called. All eyes were on the scrap of paper.

"Phyllis," she read. "It's you, Phyllis. You won."

"Open it," the voices chorused. "Let's see what it is."

I tore the red tissue paper off the tiny parcel and opened it. "Wow! It's beautiful," I managed. I stared at a child's necklace with white beading and a small pendant hanging from the center.

"Put it on," my sister, Carol, yelled.

"Yes, try it on," Harriet chimed in.

"Not now. Later. I'll keep it in the box. I don't want anything to happen to it."

When our party ended, I raced home, unlocked my treasure chest and carefully placed the necklace safely inside.

That night I returned to my room closing the door behind me. When I was certain no one was in the hallway outside, I pulled out the thousand-dollar bill. It fit perfectly in the jewelry box.

On Christmas morning, I ran all the way to Nanny and Grandpa's house clasping their gifts.

When Nanny opened the handkerchief, she had no idea that I had embroidered it. "You stitched this by yourself?" she asked.

"Yes," I grinned.

"I will treasure this forever," Nanny said, squeezing me.

Grandpa held the large carton in his hand and read the tag. "To Grandpa. Love, Phyllis." In his usual jovial way, he shook the parcel, turned it upside down and tried to guess what it was.

"Open it," I teased.

His blue eyes glowed like a child's. "What is this?" he asked. "Another box? You're making me work for this."

All eyes centered on Grandpa when he continued to unwrap two smaller boxes inside the larger ones. Lastly with arthritic finger, he opened the jewelry box. He began to chuckle—a real deep chuckle that made his eyes water. "What is it?" Carol asked.

"Just what I wanted. A thousand dollars and a white elephant," he said. He looked at me with tenderness and love. Words did not come. Tears were streaming down his cheeks when he gave me a great big hug.

I picked up the jewelry box with the thousand-dollar bill and lifted it to inspect the tiny white elephant pendant that I had clipped from my white beaded necklace. I thought about the two pennies I had trouble parting with a week ago. What if I had chosen to keep them? Another girl would be wearing the necklace with the white elephant pendant around her neck. Two cents could never buy the joy Grandpa, Nanny and I shared on Christmas Day in 1947.

~Phyllis Cochran

Gramma's Christmas Store

Nobody can do for little children what grandparents do. Grandparents sort of sprinkle stardust over the lives of little children.

~Alex Haley

In the early years of raising our family Tom and I suffered a lot of financial disappointments and we had to cut way back on Christmas for our children. When their friends were writing lists of Christmas "wants" we encouraged our children to write out lists of what they might create to give to others. It seemed like a good plan, but I often worried that they might be missing out on some of the excitement of the holidays.

Each year as a family project we put our heads together and came up with gift ideas that we could make. We had to be very creative as even our craft supplies were limited. Our ideas sprung from whatever materials we could find inexpensively. We filled the weeks before Christmas making toys and baubles for friends and relatives.

One year we painted rocks to become ladybug paperweights for adults and pet rocks for kids. Another year we sewed up little lamb bean bags from woolly fabric we'd been given and wrapped them to give to all the cousins. We made jam for aunts and uncles from the wild blackberries growing around our house. The kids collected seashells and pebbles and glued them onto boxes for their grandparents and we gleaned apples from the neighbors' trees to make homemade applesauce and apple bread for friends. But when it came to gifts for their siblings or Mom and Dad, the kids were stumped. Anything they could dream up and create in our little duplex would be discovered mid-project.

Our home was tiny and secrets were difficult, besides the fact that the kids were still little and needed a lot of help with their projects.

As Christmas Day loomed, I dreaded the moment when the children would ask if they could go and buy a gift for their brothers, sister or dad. I'd get a lump in my throat and fight back tears. The money just wasn't there for anything but absolute necessities.

My mom had been living near our family ever since my dad died. I had supplied her with her only grandchildren and she reveled in her role as Gramma. She was careful never to impose on our family or insist on her way, so I was surprised one day in December when she knocked on our door and asked to have the children for an hour or so.

"What's this all about, Mom?" I asked.

"Oh, you'll see!" she teased, while winking at my toddler. The four kids giggled as they filed out the door and climbed into her car. It was obvious that this was a conspiracy! "We'll be at my house, so don't worry," she hollered as they drove away.

When the children arrived at my mother's home they were each given a shopping bag and told they were about to enter Gramma's Christmas Store. Here they could shop for gifts for everyone in the family. My oldest child worried that they didn't have any money to pay for their items, but Gramma assured him that the only payment required was a hug and a kiss. With all worries set aside the kids stepped into a child's paradise of merchandise. Neatly laid out around the room on every chair, on the coffee table, and lined up on the counter were delightful items to "purchase." The grown-up items like earrings, pens, and sunglass holders were in one section, while the stuffed animals and bouncy balls that appeal to children were in another. The chair seats displayed their wares especially well because they kept everything at eye-level even for the youngest child. The gift items were wonderful, appearing to be all shiny and new, but

Gramma had bought most of the items at garage sales throughout the year and stashed them away for this day.

One by one she helped the children pick out something that would be "just right for Mommy" and "Oooo, Daddy will love this!" Then came the harder part of choosing something for each other and slipping the gifts secretly into their bags. All four children took their job of Christmas shopping very seriously and often tugged on Gramma's pant leg for advice. It was a fabulous afternoon made only better by the cookies and milk she offered. To wrap up the day, Gramma helped them wrap up their gifts, tucking away their secrets until the big day.

When Christmas morning finally arrived the kids were far more excited to see others open the gifts they had selected for them than they were to open the gifts with their own name on the tag.

The boys would tease, "You're gonna love what I got you," and shake a package in front of each other's faces, while my daughter would gently pull out a wrapped item from under our scrawny little tree and say, "Mommy I got this for you!" As each gift was unwrapped under watchful eyes, the giver and the receiver would each gasp with delight and run to hug one another. Tom and I could only watch with tears welling up in our eyes and gratefulness swelling in our hearts as we realized that Christmas spirit had come to our home after all thanks to a lot of help from Gramma and her magical Christmas Store.

~Lindy Schneider

The Long Ride Home

Coincidence is God's way of remaining anonymous.
~Albert Einstein

The journey started with my purchase of a 1987 Nissan Pulsar T-top, the perfect sexy car except for one thing—the powder-blue body. Easy to fix, right? Paint it black. But what began as a simple paint job soon developed into a new friendship and a discovery beyond my imagination.

My quest to turn this little car into a sleek, black, speed machine led me to Archie, a local mechanic and body man. Unlike me, Archie breathed, smelled, and dreamed about cars; all cars—fast, old, muscle. His passion for life and easy smile were contagious, and many afternoons I looked forward to just shooting the breeze with him. We'd talk about everything from family to sports to politics.

One day, while we were chatting away in his shop, Archie shared his excitement about a fast, old car he found online. Moments later, he pulled up the site, and before I knew it, the two of us were having an intelligent talk about—of all things—muscle cars. Internally, I laughed at the picture of me—a fifty-two-year-old widower and longtime federal office employee—sitting in a hot, stuffy garage discussing muscle cars with a fifty-something man who was as excited as a kid with a new Christmas toy!

I mentioned that Archie's smile was contagious, but his excitement must have been too. Perhaps that's why, two nights later when my favorite show turned out to be a re-run, I sat down at my computer and pulled up Archie's online site. Eight o'clock on a Thursday night, and I was looking at muscle cars for sale!

The site listed twenty-six pages. By the time I reached page six, I was bored and ready to call it quits when a blue '65 Mustang caught my eye. My younger brother-in-law, Scott, once owned a car just like it. Out of the blue, only weeks earlier I had thought about that car. I even contacted Scott's dad to see if it still sat in his barn, only to discover Scott sold it several years earlier. Though he loved the car, Scott never found the time to fix it up. So, when I saw that Mustang and read that the car sat for nearly thirty years in a barn, I was curious. Could this be Scott's old car?

Of course, I called the number listed in the ad. And after a few questions, I was certain it was my brother-in-law's old car. Chills ran down my spine. Okay, so what's the likelihood that I'd recently thought of that car and then accidentally found it online? The car price sounded reasonable; the car just needed some bodywork, but, hey, I knew Archie. The only real glitch was another potential buyer planning to purchase the car in two days.

I needed to make a quick decision, but my intentions that night hadn't included buying another car. To be sure I had the right vehicle, I contacted Scott's sister, Tammy, in Montana. Minutes later, after questioning her, I was convinced.

I called the seller back and bought the car. What a great surprise this would make for my brother-in-law, now confined to a nursing home. Scott suffered a work-related accident two years earlier that resulted in a coma and rendered him paralyzed with little hope for recovery.

With excitement I called my sister-in-law again and explained my plan. Dead silence. After a moment she said, "Bruce, the first owner of that car was not Scott. It was a hand-me-down. Dad bought that car for Tracy, and she learned how to drive on that Mustang."

My head started spinning. Tracy, my wife, died five years ago.

As I talked to Tammy, another idea popped into my head. Instead of simply showing Scott the car, I would put that Mustang into top condition and then give Tracy's first car to her dad. With Christmas just months away, that would make a great present.

Then I had yet another thought. To add to my gift presentation to Tracy's dad, I would place the Mustang key in a special ornament box—one that Tracy gave him. When she was alive, each Christmas for ten years, Tracy bought her dad a Hallmark car ornament. The year she died, the Hallmark series abruptly stopped. Two weeks before that Christmas, I remembered Tracy's tradition, and decided I would complete her dad's collection since she was gone. I scouted the whole state until I found that year's ornament.

For this Christmas, we'd wheel Scott to the nursing home parking lot to see the car, and we'd hand Tracy's father his last gift to open—the Hallmark ornament box with the car key inside. To Tracy's mother, we'd present a scrapbook that contained pictures of the car's progressive makeover as well as a picture of sixteen-year-old Tracy standing in front of her first vehicle.

My heart overflowed with warm thoughts, and I was awed as I acknowledged that only God, full of power and mystery, could possibly bring such details together over many years and miles.

Now, I just needed to pick up the car, located in Riverdale more than eighty miles away, and get it to Archie. I called the seller to make arrangements. He just "happened" to be driving to Bismarck the next day, and since he owned a trailer, he agreed to haul the car to the body shop. Surprisingly, he still had the original title to the car—the one with my father-in-law's name.

I chuckled over how all the pieces were falling into place and couldn't help but see God's hand in the connections.

But one more surprise remained for me. Out of curiosity, I asked the seller how he found the Mustang, especially since Riverdale was over seventy miles from Flasher, where Scott lived. He explained that he hounded Scott for two years after he saw the car in an old barn. He'd made the original trip to the barn because he received an out-of-the blue call about a different antique car—a 1946 Chrysler

Windsor. When he was looking at the Chrysler, he saw the Mustang also parked there.

My ears perked up. Eight years earlier, I convinced my father-in-law to sell an old car he inherited when he bought his farm. I had made dozens of phone calls to antique car dealers in order to sell the vehicle. The car? A 1946 Chrysler Windsor. Yes, I was the man who contacted the seller, who now owned the Mustang. Now years later, I bought it back in memory of my deceased wife, to cheer my disabled brother-in-law, and as a present for my father-in-law.

Yes, my journey began with me purchasing the wrong color Nissan Pulsar. But the adventure continued until one very special blue '65 Mustang concluded its long ride home.

~Bruce Rittel as told to Georgia Bruton

The Last Saturday Before Christmas

The Eskimos had fifty-two names for snow because it was important to them;
there ought to be as many for love.
~Margaret Atwood

It was the last Saturday before Christmas and I was working. Ugh! Working! Okay, it wasn't that bad, working. After all, I was a teenage girl, employed in the mall, selling clothes. It was a dream gig. Seriously. But it wasn't how I wanted to spend that day. I wanted it to be special. Like I said, it was the last Saturday before Christmas.

So, I was kind of mopey and unChristmasy, and thinking this Christmas was going to suck because I had a crush on a boy and he obviously didn't crush on me back and the feeling was kind of, you know, crushing.

But then, Hell-o! I looked up from the new shipment of sweaters I was folding and there was Aiden Cooper.

Aiden Cooper! My crush.

Merry Christmas!

I smiled, trying not to stumble over my own feet. "Hi!"

He smiled back, looking surprised. "I didn't know you worked here."

Obviously he wasn't like me. He didn't replay every word we ever said to each other over and over again in his brain—because

I told him I worked here. I remembered telling him—two weeks ago, in my kitchen, the night he came to my house after he coached my little brother's hockey game. Oh well. I couldn't expect him to remember everything I ever said to him. Unlike me, he had a life.

"Can I help you find something?" I asked, realizing I'd been unconsciously wringing the sweater I was holding. I did my best to straighten it out, at the same time trying to sound professional and sales-associate-like.

"Well, there's this girl," Aiden said. "I'm just starting to get to know her...."

Instantly, I knew he was talking about Irelan Gates. I'd seen the two of them together at school lately. Ugh! They were becoming a couple; I knew it! My best friend, Sara, said they weren't, but I knew they were. Man! In less than a nanosecond my heart took a spastic turn from total elation to complete depression. I definitely didn't need this. Not on the last Saturday before Christmas.

I swallowed, still trying to sound professional. "And you want to get her something, right?"

Aiden nodded.

"Something nice," he said. "Something that lets her know I think she's great, but won't scare her off. Like I said, I'm just getting to know her."

I bit my lip, hunting for an idea—anything. So, my Christmas was massacred—that didn't mean his had to be. I was a sales person. What could I show him? My eyes darted around the store, searching, pleading.

That year we decorated our store with red and green gift bags, then stuffed them with Christmasy-type tissue paper. The look was festive, fun. Gazing around now gave me an idea.

"You can take one of our green bags," I told him, snatching one from the display I'd put together that morning, "and fill it with red gifts."

I went around the store, helping him find inexpensive, yet fun, red things. We ended up with stuff like a red camisole and red Christmas socks and mittens and some cute little candy cane earrings—stuff like that.

"Do you think she'll like it?" he asked.

"Of course," I said.

"Would you like it?" he pressed.

The question kind of jabbed at my heart. I'd watched him deliberate about the gifts. I saw that he cared about the things he was buying. He obviously liked Irelan a lot.

"Yeah," I told him softly. "I'd like it."

When my shift was over, I felt even more anti-Christmas. It was sad because I love this season, love the feel of it. I knew I needed to do something to lift my spirits. But ugh! As I left the store, I found Aiden talking with some of his friends right outside the door. That wasn't going to do it for me—lift my spirits. I started to walk away.

"Hey Melanie," he said, leaving the group to walk beside me. "Want to get a hot chocolate?"

Okay, so suddenly my spirits were lifted. "Sure," I said.

The mall was packed and the lines were long. I found us a table while Aiden bought us hot chocolate and donuts. When he took off his jacket, I couldn't help smiling. He was wearing the tie-dye shirt I helped my little brother make for him, as a "Merry Christmas, Coach" type thing. We'd spent an embarrassingly long time laboring over it.

"Nice shirt," I said.

He smiled, looking pleased. "Thanks."

He did a little turn, so I could get the full effect. "I mean—thanks for the compliment," he said, then he looked into my eyes. "And thank you for the shirt. Your brother said you helped him make it. That was nice of you."

He played with the lid to his hot chocolate for a moment. "I have to tell you something," he said. "I knew you worked here. You told me—that night, in your kitchen. I've been coming by every day," he confessed, "hoping to catch you here. I never came at the right time though, not until tonight."

My stomach felt all fluttery, like there were a million butterflies flitting around in there, doing the happy dance. "Well, I'm glad you made it tonight."

He smiled, kind of shy-like. "This is for you."

He handed me the green bag with the red gifts. Suddenly my spirits were soaring. Suddenly I knew, this was going to be an epic holiday, one I would cherish. I could tell by the last Saturday before Christmas.

~Melanie Marks

A Gift of Love

You can give without loving, but you can never love without giving.
~Author Unknown

I helped Momma onto the plane in Houston, Texas and watched as she shivered and pulled her sweater tighter around her. The chemotherapy she took each month for ovarian cancer made her cold most of the time.

Later that week at work, I noticed a fellow employee, Dorothy, as she sat crocheting on her coffee break. An idea popped into my head. I could make Momma a lap afghan. I poured a cup of coffee and joined Dorothy.

"Do you think I could learn to crochet?" I asked.

"Sure, anyone can do it," she answered.

"I don't know," I said. "It's a job for me to sew on a button."

"Get a crochet needle and some yarn and bring it to work tomorrow. On our lunch hour I'll show you how to do some basic stitches. You can practice and see if you really want to learn."

Later that evening I called Sandra, my younger sister. "Guess what?" I said. "I'm going to make Momma a lap afghan for Christmas. Dorothy at work is going to teach me to crochet."

"This I've got to see," Sandra said. "Cozy, I know how you hate to sew. I remember some of the hissy fits you threw when you were taking Home Ec in school."

"Just wait, I know I can do it," I answered.

"You'd better get with it," Sandra said. "You have only four months to get it done."

"Don't say anything to Momma. I want this to be a surprise."

"My lips are sealed," Sandra said. "It will be a surprise to me as well."

The next day at work, armed with my crochet needle and some yarn, Dorothy taught me how to do a single crochet stitch and make a chain. The next was the double crochet stitch.

After a couple of days I was ready to start. Dorothy wrote out the instructions. She crocheted a couple of rows so I would have something to check on.

I decided on some thick, heavy yarn. I picked burnt orange, orange, and mahogany for the colors. Each one of the three tiers would be a different color.

Eagerly I plunged into my first encounter with crocheting. I should have this done with time to spare, I thought. Well it may take a little longer, I muttered to myself as I pulled out stitches, counted, and recounted.

I finally finished the first tier, the burnt orange, and began the orange. It looked good as I hooked the orange onto the burnt orange with my accurate stitch.

I marked the days off the calendar. A week behind my planned schedule, but now I had the hang of it.

About halfway through the orange tier, I took the afghan to work to have Dorothy check it. Dorothy the perfectionist, looked it over, adjusted her glasses and looked again. My stomach did a flip-flop when she said, "Look on the fifth row, about in the middle."

I didn't want to look. If Dorothy saw something, I was in big trouble. I counted down and there were two little gaps where I had counted wrong. I saw it now, but the nights when my eyes nearly crossed and my neck ached, I let the mistakes slip by.

"Do I have to pull out the five rows that I finished?"

Dorothy nodded. "Here, I'll pull them out and get you started again." I didn't want to get started again.

At home I forced myself to work on the afghan. The third time

I pulled out the same stitches, I flung the afghan to the floor and kicked it. "Just quit," I yelled. "Forget it Cozy, Momma doesn't know about it."

I stared at the crumpled orange pile on the floor. I wanted to leave it there, but I couldn't. With trembling hands, I picked it up. "I won't quit," I whispered. "I've worked too hard on Momma's Christmas present and I'm going to finish it."

I closed my eyes and lifted my problems to God. "Lord, here I am again. Will I ever learn? I know, without you I can do nothing. Help me finish this afghan, and let it be a comfort to Momma. Thank You and I love You, Amen."

I worked on the afghan every evening and on the weekends. Before I began I would ask the Lord to calm my spirit and give me patience.

I carefully checked each completed row. I pulled out stitches, counted and recounted. The task did not become easier. Many times I counted to ten, taking long deep breaths to keep my temper from flaring.

As I continued I felt an inner peace knowing that Jesus was with me.

Momma's appointment in Houston was on December 20th. I pressed toward completion of her present. On December 15th, I took the last stitch on the last row. I let out a loud yell. "Thank You, Lord, thank You." I held the afghan tight and danced around the room.

On December 19th, Sandra and Momma came to Amarillo to fly to Houston. I had the present ready.

"Here, Momma," I said. "I know you'll be back before Christmas, but I want you to open this now."

Gently, she removed the bow and ribbon and opened the box. "Oh, Cozy, this is beautiful," she said, holding up the afghan. "I love the colors. Who made it for you?"

"I did, Momma, I made it for you."

Sandra shook her head. "I can't believe it. Will you make me one?"

"Nope, my crocheting days are over."

Momma sat down and spread the afghan over her lap. It reached to her ankles. "This is just what I need." Tears filled her eyes as she stroked the afghan. "Cozy, this is truly a gift of love."

Later, at the airport, I watched Sandra push Momma in a wheelchair to the boarding area. Momma turned toward me, smiled, and patted her three-tier lap afghan.

On December 20th, when they gave Momma her chemotherapy, they discovered a blood clot in her leg and hospitalized her.

My older sister, Babs, and her family lived in Houston. They spent Christmas day with Momma and Sandra at M.D. Anderson Hospital. I was not in Houston to celebrate the birth of our Lord Jesus Christ with Momma and my sisters, but part of me was there in the three-tiered afghan spread across Momma's lap.

~Helen Luecke

Three Times the Love

All women become like their mothers.
That is their tragedy.
No man does. That's his.
~Oscar Wilde

"How come you got the purple one?" Judy asked as she looked at the red dress in her hands.

"I don't know; ask Mom," Chris shot back.

Mine was pink. I always got pink. Everything Mom bought us was exactly the same, except for the color that is.

We had three Barbie dollhouses on Christmas morning. Those came out of the box from the factory ready-made, so Mom put a colored bow on top of each one so we'd know which house belonged to whom. Three Cook 'n Bake sets another Christmas. Three four-foot-tall walking dolls, each with a red, pink or purple ribbon in her hair.

"Mine won't walk right," I complained the day after the holiday.

"Neither will mine," Judy said right back.

"Well, we'll have to take them to the doll doctor," Mom replied. And she packed them back in their boxes. Mom did her best to keep us three girls happy, but sometimes, it was just out of her hands.

Chris was three years older than me, and Judy was two years younger. Chris was tall with thick, wavy blond hair. I was all legs, with pigtails and bangs. Judy was short with straight dark hair and brown eyes. We couldn't have been more different in looks, yet Mom insisted on dressing us all alike, except in different colors. We looked like colored eggs at Easter: Chris in blue, Judy in yellow and me in pink; but for Christmas we all had red and green dresses, hair ribbons and bows in exactly the same red and green pattern.

Around the house, Mom considered us her own little cleaning crew. "Dust first, then vacuum," she always said. "That way, when the room is done there won't be footprints in the carpet." Like I really cared about footprints. Someone was going to walk on it sooner or later! But we didn't argue. We just did it Mom's way.

She always bought us the nicest things, but made sure that we received equal amounts of gifts (the same number of boxes under the tree every Christmas) or the exact number of cookies divided equally between us. No one ever had more or less than the others. She taught us good manners and responsibility, but we were always testing the limits of Mom's patience, and spent many an afternoon stuck in our bedrooms for time-outs. I'm sorry to say that we didn't always respect the gifts Mom and Dad gave us.

It was another "Christmas of the Same Gift." This time it was the year of the bikes. Shiny two-wheelers. Judy had a little trouble reaching the ground when she sat on her bright red one, but my long legs touched easily from the seat of my new pink cruiser. Chris was older and had perfect control when riding her bright purple bike. They all looked the same, except for the color of course, so we decided to see who could be different.

Off we went to the neighbor's driveway. Our driveway was flat, but the neighbor's was up a small hill. It was just tall enough to climb up with our bikes and then have a contest to see whose bike would make it down the driveway and across the road. With no one on it.

"Ready…" We were all poised at the top near the garage holding our bike by our side.

"Set…" We lined up the front and back wheels as straight as could be, holding the bike steady.

"Go!" Then we pushed the bike forward. Off it would go, straight down the driveway. About halfway down it would start to wobble, like a spinning top running out of steam, tipping first to one side and then the other. We were all screaming, shouting, giggling with delight, hoping our bike made it across the street first. Most of the time they crashed at the end of the driveway, but sometimes, oh how sweet those times were, a bike made it down the drive, across the road, and into the ditch on the other side.

"Hooray! I win!" Judy exclaimed one day.

"You won this time," Chris replied. "Let's do it again."

Years later, Mom found out about our childhood bike-capades. She just shook her head.

We grew up as a threesome, Chris, Judy and me. Mom did her best to keep us all in line. When one of us had a time-out, we all had a time-out. That's just the way it was. Mom braided our hair every morning before school and fixed us brown bag lunches that we grabbed on our way out the door each morning. Sometimes, we were mad at the way Mom dressed us the same, gave us the same gifts every Christmas, and put the same amount of money into savings bonds on every birthday. But we got three times the love that just one child would normally receive.

Now that we're all grown up with children of our own, we don't dress alike anymore. Sometimes I even miss it. But a recent phone call brought it all back to mind.

"Hey, what are you getting your kids for Christmas this year?" Judy asked one day.

"I'm getting them the same thing—PlayStations," I responded. "How about you?"

"Remote control cars. All the same kind, just different colors," Judy said.

Yup, we got three times the love—and a ton of memories to go with it.

~B.J. Taylor

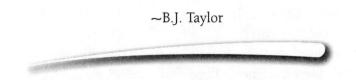

Presents
Under the Tree

The cat is domestic only as far as suits its own ends.

~Saki

Each Christmas, Mom insists upon giving presents to my cat Bubba. She wraps a myriad of silly little gifts and puts ribbons and bows and tags on them, as if the cat cares. But he seems to enjoy the fluffy little toys on strings and the plastic balls with bells inside. And just like a kid, sometimes he plays with the bows and paper almost as long as he plays with the toys.

Of all the gifts, however, I think he especially looks forward to receiving the traditional little cans of cat food Mom always tries to disguise by wrapping them in various colors of paper. She knows I don't normally give my cat canned food, but since Mom always finds a coupon she can use, and I'm the only kid who has a cat, Bubba is the obvious recipient.

A few days before Christmas last year, Bubba and I had a picnic dinner in the living room. With the twinkling tree lights as the backdrop, I opened a can of Fancy Feast and emptied it onto a cut-glass saucer. He dined on a placemat decorated with a pretty Christmas design while I sat beside him on the floor and ate a tasty turkey and dressing microwave meal.

We enjoyed our "quality time" so much that the following night I repeated the experience. Bubba was thrilled! He gobbled up his dinner in no time flat and nosed around the packages to see if there might be more gourmet meals tucked away for him.

But the next night I had other plans, and for several days he got only his regular dry cat food in his regular bowl at its regular place. On Christmas Eve, however, I again reached under the tree to get out another ribbon-tied can. Imagine my surprise, and dismay, to discover Bubba had brought his own special offering to the banquet table.

Among the gifts, I found irrefutable evidence that on the night before Christmas, at least at my house, "Not a creature was stirring, not even a mouse."

~Jan Bono

Chapter 12

The Gift of Christmas

The Star of Bethlehem

The Nativity Set

So, like a forgotten fire,
a childhood can always flare up again within us.
~Gaston Bachelard

I hurried into the department store, glad to be out of the bitterly cold December weather. Just inside the store I stopped at a display of nativity sets. Bins of individual figurines sat beside the shelves holding the complete sets. My Christmas shopping list quickly disappeared from my mind as I stared longingly at the display.

I had always wanted to have a nativity set as part of my Christmas decorations. Yet years of holidays had come and gone and owning my own set remained nothing more than a desire. I always told myself that some day I would get one. I just didn't know when. Usually all the sets I saw and liked were beyond my budget. The most beautiful ones were delicate and breakable, which would have been impractical in a house with children.

But the prices attached to these bins were affordable. My hopes soared as I began sorting through the containers of pretty yet unbreakable pieces. I started wondering if I could find all the figures needed to make up a complete nativity set. Excitedly I picked up Mary, Joseph and baby Jesus. Next I pulled out a few different shepherds and three unique wise men. Then I found a donkey, sheep and even camels. Finally I discovered an angel. I put them all into my shopping cart and began searching the shelves for a stable, but all of them were part of full sets. Undaunted I completed the rest of my shopping and purchased all the affordable figures. I could keep looking for an inexpensive stable or get someone to nail a few rough boards together to represent one.

Eagerly I headed home with all my Christmas surprises and treasures. Later that afternoon I gathered the children around the Christmas tree and began to tell them about Mary, Joseph and Baby Jesus while I placed them under the tree. Then I told them about the shepherds on the hillside and the choir of angels who announced the birth of the Christ child. I added the shepherds and a few sheep to my display while I told how they eagerly hurried to Bethlehem to see this amazing event for themselves. I stood the angel close by, as if watching protectively everyone surrounding the manger. I told them about the wise men who came from the East to worship the newborn King and added three figures along with their camels. Finally I placed the donkey and cow behind the holy family to complete the scene. My youngest watched every move.

As I finished telling the story my three older children scattered to activities that more fully captured their interest. I headed to the kitchen to make supper but glanced back to admire my new, long awaited nativity set. I saw my two-year-old, special needs daughter lying on her tummy staring intently at the scene. I continued to watch quietly for a couple minutes. Soon her little hand reached out and began to rearrange each piece. Baby Jesus remained in the centre but she moved Mary and Joseph even closer. Then she moved the shepherds, sheep, wise men and camels until all were crowded around the manger holding the baby. Finally she turned them until all were gazing in adoration at Jesus. Completing her task she got up, noticed me and smiled before coming to take my hand and pull me toward the Christmas tree. She possessed an almost negligible vocabulary, but no words were needed to let me know how important this set already was to her. I realized she understood the Christmas story she listened to repeatedly at Sunday School and at home.

Each day, until we put the decorations away after New Year's, she spent time lying in front of the Christmas tree looking at or rearranging the pieces. Baby Jesus always remained the central figure. I enjoyed watching this often repeated task and the huge smiles that always accompanied it. Several more years disappeared before I found a little, rough wooden stable to add to the scene but that didn't seem to matter to her. All she needed to act out the Bible story of Christmas were the figures themselves.

The years passed and each year my youngest daughter eagerly waited for the Christmas decorations to fill the house. She thoroughly loved this holiday season. Smiles wreathed her face especially when the nativity set made its appearance under the tree. It became her self-appointed job to arrange it until she was satisfied that all eyes were on the baby in the manger. She also continued to sit and listen to the Christmas story from the gospel of Luke as many times as someone would read it to her.

Tasks that we often take for granted proved difficult for her to learn. By the time she turned ten she had finally learned to read and received a children's Bible as her Christmas gift. As soon as she opened it she brought it to me so I could show her where to find the Christmas story. Over and over she read the words all by herself. This brought her so much pleasure and filled my eyes with tears of joy.

My children grew up and the oldest three married. Our family continued to expand with the addition of grandchildren. It had become our family tradition for my youngest daughter to arrange the nativity set under the tree each Christmas, a chore she relished. If anyone moved it around she'd go over and gently replace all the figures to her liking. One year as I took out all the decorations, I wondered if the time had come to upgrade the nativity set to a fancier one. While we decorated the house I voiced my thoughts only to quickly be met with total rejection by my youngest daughter.

"A new fancy one will be breakable. How will all the nieces and nephews play out the Christmas story? They have to be able to play with it and move them around. You have to keep this set. It has to go under the tree," she said with a worried look on her face.

I realized the intensity of her desire for my grandchildren to have the opportunity to enjoy the simple pleasures she had experienced year after year and I gave in. The original set stayed.

Over the years I have added other decorations that depict the Christmas story from the Bible. Yet none of them holds the special place in her heart that my original purchase does. This first visual representation, which made the story come alive for her, needs to remain part of our family tradition. My desire for a nativity set had a wonderful ripple effect within my family, but mostly with my youngest who continues to surprise and amaze me.

~Carol Harrison

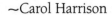

The Making of a Tradition

The best of all gifts around any Christmas tree:
the presence of a happy family all wrapped up in each other.
~Burton Hillis

Our Christmas tradition began the year my father died. We buried him ten days before Christmas. The day before his death, we had closed on our new home. Just five days before Christmas, I was sitting amid unpacked boxes, exhausted from grief and the trauma of moving, with tears leaking from my eyes. Try as I might, I could not stop crying.

"Let's skip the Christmas celebration this year," my husband Ted suggested. "The kids and grandkids will understand."

"Nooooooo," I wailed. Yet, relief flooded my being. No decorations (even if I could find them). No tree to put up. No stockings. No gifts to wrap. No cookies to bake. No turkey to roast. The thought of all that needed to be done overwhelmed me and my leaking tears became a steady downpour. I both wanted and did not want our Christmas gathering. Ted joined me among the boxes and held me tight.

In the end, we compromised. A tabletop tree already lighted. Dinner from Luby's. No stockings. No gifts. Just the gift of being together. Just each other. When my granddaughters arrived and saw the sad state of Grandma's Christmas preparations, disappointment flickered across their faces. Then, Amanda perked up as an idea came to her. "Let's gather cedar branches and yaupon with berries on the limbs. It will be just like the old fashioned Christmases." Off to the nearby woods skipped two happy girls intent on helping Grandma out. The greenery and berries they collected and placed on my mantel served as the manger for baby Jesus. That was the extent of our decorations.

On the day of our celebration, we sat in a circle and listened to Ted and two of our granddaughters read the story of the birth of Jesus from the family bible. The presence of family soothed me. Still, when I spoke of my dad, known as Bud to all of us, my voice was thick with emotion. It seemed to me that we needed to comfort one another. So, without giving it a great deal of thought, I announced, "Let's pray for each other. Just say a prayer for the one next to you." And, so we did. We joined hands and cried and prayed and laughed too. It was a hard Christmas, but we were family.

It is said that for traditions to be worthwhile, they must be in a constant state of evolution. If they are to flourish, they must grow. When the next year rolled around, my son Vince called. "Mom, I was thinking about our Christmas get-together last year and the prayer stuff was really great. Are we going to do it again this year?"

"Yeah, I was thinking about it."

"What would you think if I brought my guitar, and we sang some Christmas carols?"

"Great!"

So, in addition to praying for one another, we added music to our Christmas devotional. We rearranged the words of a favorite hymn so they read, "And, they'll know we are family by our love." Of course, we sang "Happy Birthday" to baby Jesus also.

After several years, it was suggested that we draw names instead of just praying for the person next to each of us. We seemed to be creatures of habit and always sat next to the same person. This way, we could expand our prayers to include those we had not previously prayed for.

I considered this to be a great idea and decided we should hang the names on that original tabletop Christmas tree. We passed a basket around so each person could draw an ornament (with name attached), pray for that person, and then decorated the tree with it. Eventually, we decided to undecorate the tree when I realized there wasn't much I could do with twenty-some-odd identical Christmas ornaments each year. So we began with the tree decorated with the named ornaments and then, after prayer on the day of our gathering, went home with that person's name, with the instruction to pray for that person in a special way throughout the year.

Our celebrations became thematic. One year, I attached the names to snowflakes and we pondered how God made us all unique. Another year, the ornaments were Christmas trees and we read a story from a children's book about how the Christmas tree gives its life, just as Jesus did. We learned about the star that lead the wise men to Bethlehem and that we are all stars in God's eyes. We've discovered the Christmas legends of the poinsettia and the candy cane, each story leaving us with something to contemplate.

Our rituals once took place inside our home, but since that fateful year when my dad died, we've built a gazebo on the other side of the stream that flows behind our home, with a bridge providing the crossover. Now we process to the gazebo, singing Christmas hymns with the youngest child (now a great-grandchild) carrying the image of the baby Jesus to place in his manger there. South Texas weather usually cooperates, but we have been known to wrap up in blankets as well.

As your family grows, it becomes inevitable that eventually some will not be present. Somewhere along the line, we began to pray for and remember those who could not be there and those who had died. One year, we decided to remember these absent ones by lighting a candle for them. Problem was that we were outside and gusts of wind would not allow the candles to stay lit. After a number of tries, my son Pat laughed. "Just like Bud to pull a trick like this on us." Naturally, the story telling commenced.

Not only did our family celebrations grow in numbers with marriages and new births, but it also included others. When my best friend died suddenly, her daughter and her family came to participate. When a young college student lived with Vince and his wife for a semester, she became part of our Christmas family.

While parts of our tradition continue to develop, other segments remain solidly the same. Ted and the grandchildren continue to read the Christmas story from the bible. It is always the first piece of our celebration.

I believe we are making memories for these young ones. And, I also think my dad would be so proud to know that his family focuses on things that are truly worthwhile at Christmas—the birth of Jesus, prayer for each other, and family.

~Nancy Baker

Kaylie's Christmas Prayer

If you count all your assets, you always show a profit.
~Robert Quillen

Another festive December is here but what is there to celebrate? Fighting back tears, I drive my courageous daughter to the hospital. Rebekah has cystic fibrosis and must be hospitalized often due to lung infections. You would think that I would be used to frequent hospitalizations by now. But it is so near the holidays and my daughter has never been quite so sick. Rebekah has pneumonia and bronchitis. Her doctor said, "Rebekah might be hospitalized throughout the entire Christmas holidays." So she needed to be prepared for a long stay. Rebekah must have strong antibiotics and receive numerous breathing treatments to clear her congested lungs.

But how can Rebekah be in the hospital during December? Distraught, I focus on all of the yearly family activities my precious daughter will be missing, including decorating our Christmas tree. Will Rebekah improve and get well enough to be out of the hospital in time for Christmas Day?

December is a time of celebrating. My family has wonderful traditions. But since Rebekah is in the hospital, how can we participate? My daughter will miss family parties, school festivities, last-minute shopping, driving around and looking at Christmas lights, decorating our traditional holiday cookies and the Candle Light Christmas Eve Celebration at our church. I am depressed as my husband and I carry Rebekah's luggage to the small sterile room that will be her home for at least the next two weeks.

Although the situation is dreary, Rebekah has an amazing attitude. She openly shares her faith in God with each doctor and nurse. She is a college senior and will graduate in the spring. However, this semester was physically demanding and has taken a toll on her fragile health. She is unable to sleep without sitting up. And, she coughs constantly.

Although Rebekah is positive, I focus on the negative. Our house is not ready for Christmas… no tree, no lights, no treasured decorations are displayed. And because I have a new full-time teaching position, I have not even purchased one single gift for Christmas. As I sit outside the hospital room, my tears flow freely.

My amazing daughter makes the best of the situation. Rebekah plays Christmas music in her hospital room, reads the Bible, and watches Christmas videos. But I keep focusing on all that we are missing due to the hospitalization.

Finally two days before Christmas, Rebekah has improved enough to be released from the hospital. But, she still has the IV PICC line in her arm and is required to administer daily IV medications for two additional weeks. Once we arrive home, we hurriedly unpack Rebekah's luggage and my family quickly puts up the evergreen tree and a few decorations. Due to time constraints, we only put on the minimum amount of lights and tree decorations.

The next day, my husband and I go shopping and buy all the presents in one day and frantically wrap the gifts and put them under the tree. I look at the remaining unused decorations and one box marked FRAGILE. I know what is in the box… it is the Nativity set. But there is no time to unwrap and set out our beautiful Nativity figurines. Memories flood my mind as I gaze at the box. I recall that each year since my two children were small, we read the Christmas story from the Bible on Christmas Eve. Each child would move a figurine as my husband read Scripture describing the beautiful angels, hard working shepherds, and baby Jesus. Exhaustion sets in. I decide the contents of the box can wait as I slide it in a corner. I go to bed exhausted.

Although Christmas Day arrives, I feel no joy. We go to my sister-in-law's lovely home for lunch. As always, her house is beautifully decorated. Christmas music plays in the background and our entire family is there, including my niece and her children.

We sit down to a festive meal with all of our holiday favorites... roasted turkey and cornbread jalapeño dressing, cranberry sauce, mashed potatoes, green beans and a variety of desserts including pecan pie, pumpkin pie, and fudge. The table is beautifully set with gorgeous Christmas china and scented candles. My daughter is so happy and grateful to be part of this holiday event.

Before we begin to eat, my husband is asked to say the prayer. But to our surprise... my niece's spunky four-year-old daughter, Kaylie, proclaims, "I want to say the prayer." So, we all giggle and give her permission to pray thinking Kaylie will be praying for lots of toys for herself. However to our delight, Kaylie says, "Thank you God for Christmas because we can celebrate Jesus' birthday." Suddenly, I fight back tears as I realize that I haven't even thought about the birth of Jesus this entire Christmas season.

I smile and silently thank God for Kaylie's heartfelt prayer which focuses on the birth of our Lord and Savior, Jesus Christ. But, Kaylie isn't through. During the meal, she proceeds to ask each adult, "Did you know that we are celebrating Jesus' birthday today?" And in response each adult laughs and says, "Yes!" To our amazement in the middle of the meal, Kaylie proclaims, "Let's sing 'Happy Birthday to Jesus' to celebrate." We each swallow our mouthful of turkey and dressing quickly and begin singing a loud and off-tune version of the "Happy Birthday" song to Jesus. Kaylie's sparkling eyes watch gleefully to ensure that each adult is singing. We pass her approval. Later in the meal, Kaylie requests that we sing to Jesus again. And so we do. Kaylie's holiday wish is granted.

Finally, the dinner is over and all presents are unwrapped. We hug relatives and leave. Once at home, we unload our Christmas gifts and goodies and I sit to ponder the day's events in front of the fireplace. I notice a box in the corner. I open the box marked FRAGILE! I gently un-wrap the Nativity figurines and place them on the coffee table. And I realize that during the hospitalization, I was busy dwelling on negative thoughts and the activities that we were missing. Instead, I should have been thinking about all of God's blessings. Gazing at the nativity scene I suddenly have an overwhelming peace and I experience the joy of the season. I pray and praise God for the blessings of my family and Rebekah's improving health but most of all I thank God for the gift of eternal life. The prayer of a four-year-old child helps me again focus on the reason we celebrate Christmas... the birth of Christ... and I whisper, "Happy Birthday, Jesus."

~Marilyn Phillips

Mary and Me

The moment a child is born, the mother is also born.
She never existed before. The woman existed, but the mother, never.
A mother is something absolutely new.

~Rajneesh

I'll never forget the year Mary, the mother of Jesus, became a real person to me. Up until that time she'd always been a character in a story. A beautiful story, to be sure, but a story nonetheless. Even though I grew up in church and believed the telling of the biblical account of Jesus' birth, I didn't have a personal connection with Mary or Joseph, the shepherds or the wise men. They were simply names and people mentioned in a wonderful tale told every year at Christmas.

Not even when I played the role of Mary in our church's performance of the Nativity Story did the actual woman come to life in my mind. I was thirteen years old and was terrified I'd forget my lines or screech off-key notes in my solo. I certainly had more important things to concern myself with than pondering the life of a woman who'd lived nearly two thousand years before me.

After I married I bought a crèche for our first Christmas. It was a cheap set made in China and wasn't very fancy. Baby Jesus' blond hair bothered me so much one year that I had to paint it brown. My mother's crèche, the one I remember from my childhood, was beautiful in a simple, elegant way. The pitched roof, the little music box, the tiny ceramic lamb. It had always fascinated me as a child, but most particularly the figurine of Mary. The artist who created her did an amazing job. Her face was sweet and serene as she gazed lovingly at the baby Jesus nestled in his manger. Her blue outer robe and lighter-colored gown had just the right folds in them as she knelt beside her newborn son.

But it was her lovely hair that held my gaze year after year.

Long, brown, wavy locks flowed down her back to her waist. She wore no head covering and I always got the impression that this was how Mary looked when she was at home with her family, relaxed and comfortable. I'm not ashamed to admit I coveted that beautiful hair. Oh, how I wished I had hair like Mary.

I remember how surprised I was to learn Jesus' mother was probably a teenager when she gave birth to him. Tradition in those days was for women to get married or betrothed, as Mary was to Joseph, in their early teen years. Knowing how immature and silly I was as a young teenager, I marvel that God found favor with Mary and gave her the amazing honor of bringing His Son into the world.

But Mary was still simply a character in a story to me. A ceramic figurine with lovely hair. It wasn't until Christmas of 1990 that she became a living, breathing woman in my mind and heart. That Christmas I was pregnant with my firstborn son. He was due in March and though I wasn't exactly "great" with child, I felt a kinship with Mary unlike anything I had ever experienced before. I could picture her placing her hand on her protruding belly to feel Jesus' movements in the same way I felt my son move. I could imagine her talking to him, sharing her fears and wonder at this miracle of life. I knew the feel of a baby in my womb the same way Mary had.

That year Mary moved from the pages of the Bible into my world. I rejoice with her each Christmas over the birth of her son. I understand her panic and fear when she and Joseph found Jesus in the temple in Jerusalem when he was twelve years old. He'd been missing for three days, or so they thought, and I can relate to the whirl of anxious thoughts that went through their worried minds. I grieve with Mary each Easter when I think of how she had to stand helpless as Roman soldiers nailed her son to a cross and then watched him die a horrific death. The pain of her mother's heart is imprinted on my own.

This Christmas I'll take out the five crèches I've collected over the years. I'll arrange them just so, making sure my favorite—the one my husband bought me—is prominent in the living room. Even the Chinese crèche with blond-painted-brown-haired Baby Jesus has a place. I'll gaze at each one in the twinkling lights of the Christmas tree, marveling at the simple beauty of the Christmas family. Marveling that Jesus willingly left heaven to come to earth as a tiny baby. Amazed that angels announced the great event to a group of lowly shepherds.

But always, always, I'll lean in close to look at Mary's face. I'll study it, wondering what she was thinking, what she was feeling those many years ago. I see her peaceful smile. I warm to the love in her eyes as she gazes at her son.

Mary was a woman, a wife, a mother. A daughter, a sister, a friend. She lived, she loved, she laughed. She cried, she mourned, she died.

She was definitely not just a character in a story.

~Michelle Shocklee

A Serendipity Christmas

He changed sunset into sunrise.
~Clement of Alexandri

"Good morning, Karen—Merry Christmas!"

Stirring under the covers after her greeting, the familiar refrains that had filled the air for the past several days fell upon my ears. But instead of joyful Christmas carols and the jingle of sleigh bells, it was the toots, horns and beeps of the Intensive Care Unit for heart patients. I was recovering from quadruple bypass surgery, an unexpected gift of life I'd received as a result of a heart attack just days before.

I smiled at my attending nurse as she tenderly ministered to my needs. "I think today you're going to be transferred to your own room. Then your whole family can come to visit with you and stay as long as you'd like."

What a gift that would be! No more twenty-minute visits staggered over the day with only one visitor at a time. I pictured my precious loving family gathered around my bed and thanked God for the gift of each one, praying it would really happen. A few hours later, my prayer was answered.

As I settled into my new surroundings, I reveled in the tranquility of having a place all to myself for the remainder of my stay and rejoiced in anticipation of the gaiety in celebrating Christmas Day with my family. Soon my room filled with loved ones, their arms loaded with packages adorned with holiday trimmings. How wonderful to have my husband, David, my children, and my grandchildren enfolding me in their hugs and kisses.

"Before you open your presents, Mom, I brought you a special treat. This will be your 'turkey dinner,'" Susan said with a grin as she set the frothy milkshake on the bed stand.

Laughing with delight, I took a long-awaited sip through the straw, relishing its rich chocolate taste. I had craved the milkshake for days and it was like ambrosia to me. I took my time savoring its luscious flavor and the unexpected gift of my daughter's thoughtfulness.

Knowing their turkey dinner was waiting for them at home, we soon said goodbye. As the stillness settled in around me, I reflected on the days I'd spent in the ICU. Despite the constant static of monitors keeping guard, I had experienced an inner peace and serenity that only God could provide in the midst of unsettling circumstances.

My mind meandered to what David had said when we first learned I wouldn't be home for Christmas. "It really doesn't matter does it? We have Christmas in our hearts all year long."

Christmas in my heart—I recalled the joy of when I discovered the reality of Jesus. God's gift of salvation was a marvelous, phenomenal present with my name on it. His promise to cleanse me and forgive was beyond my comprehension, yet the gift of his love had filled me completely as I allowed him to permeate my heart. As I drifted off to sleep, I thanked God for the greatest unexpected gift of all, wrapped in the person of his son.

~Karen R. Kilby

Honk If You Love Christmas

*To perceive Christmas through its wrapping
becomes more difficult with every year.*
~E.B. White

Honestly, I must admit that Christmas is not one of my favorite times of the year. I realize this statement may come as a shock to many who are reading this admission from a minister, so I suppose an appropriate explanation is in order. My unenthusiastic attitude concerning Christmas has nothing to do with a "Scrooge Complex Syndrome" nor am I parsimonious when it comes to gifts or spending. No, my displeasure with Christmas has more to do with the increasing attention given to the secularization of the season and the gradual diminishing of the spiritual.

So, for several years I had my own private protest and I blatantly refused to give in to the tinsel, toys, and trees facet of Christmas. That was—until—well—my three granddaughters came along.

This year my youngest called me to ask, "Granddaddy, you got lights on your house?" To which I responded, "No, sweetie, I'm protesting the lights, trees and decorations because they're too secular and take away from the true meaning of Christmas!" Yeah right! Think that's what I said? Oh no—at that precise moment my attitude toward Christmas decorations changed. I sprang into my sleigh and sped off to buy decorations at my local Walmart. And buy I did! My entire house is now covered from the foundation to the roof. Every bush, tree, and plant has so many lights that when you turn them on the little wheel in the electric meter spins at approximately 10,000 rpms! Now I've got friends, neighbors, church members, anybody and everybody driving by my house just to admire the spectacle of lights.

Okay, so I compromised my convictions and jumped headlong into the Christmas rat race. I admit that I went a tad overboard buying more toys than the girls need, and decorating my house with way too many lighted icicles.

That was when I realized what an influence my Christmas protest was having on others. I had no idea that anyone, other than close family and friends, knew about it. Honestly, I had neighbors standing on their lawns watching me put up those lights, staring at me with a sort of sick fascination. Some appeared obviously disgusted, wagging their heads back and forth and clucking their tongues in cheek. Some cheered and gave me the thumbs-up sign. A few even yelled, "Hey Harold, what's up with the light thing—you giving up the fight?" One lady was more pointed, because she said, "You just watch, you'll fall off that ladder and break your neck!"

I was a little confused by that one because she sounded more like she thought I was compromising my convictions and would be divinely punished for my sin of stubbornness. I did stumble once and fell against a huge wind chime that my wife had hanging on the porch. When the clanging, ringing, and clapping ceased, I couldn't help overhear my neighbor across the street laughing. Finally he asked, "Why have you decided to put up lights this year?" I responded, "Because of little blue eyes about the size of quarters!" He replied, "It's strange how those grandkids can make you do weird things, isn't it?" Hmm, he has a point!

Now that I'm into it, I've noticed the various techniques that we Southerners take when we decorate our houses during the Christmas season. For many, this process begins by putting up our decorations immediately after Halloween and taking them down on January 2nd.

But there are always those who are an exception to the take-down rule. Once their decorations are up and glowing they never bother taking them down again—ever!

Personally I've always believed that Christmas decorating ought to be one of those projects that requires much planning. After all—if you're going to decorate, at least do it right! One of my pet peeves is how many people seem to attack Christmas decorating with no master plan, decoration design, or forethought! They just string multicolored lights unevenly along the property line fence or throw net lighting over the old car that has been sitting on concrete blocks for years, as well as other immovable objects. They take strings of lights, duct tape, and baling wire and go crazy outlining the windows, doors, tractor, lawnmower, mailbox, etc. My personal favorite is when they just bundle them up in a huge wad, stand back and throw them as high as they can to the top of a tree, and allowing them to fall on whatever branch they land. Then they simply plug them into a 150-foot electrical extension cord and "wham" they're lit and ready for the season!

So what is the point of all this? For one, my personal opinion concerning certain aspects of Christmas as absurd has not changed. My fascination with Christmas still centers on the *person* of Christmas and not the *presents* of Christmas. There is so much more to this special day than meets the eye. If our Christmas jollity is merely limited to festive ornamental celebrations, then we miss the real reason for the season—namely the birth of the Savior, Jesus Christ.

For me this is how I explain all the lights, glitter, and so on to my granddaughters. Jesus Christ is indeed the light of the world. I want them to be reminded of the Christ of Christmas every time those huge blue eyes see a Christmas decoration—even if they are strung unevenly along a barbed wire fence!

~Harold D. Fanning

The Stocking Stuffers

Every evening I turn my worries over to God.
He's going to be up all night anyway.
~Mary C. Crowley

It was December 24, 1980. I was newly divorced with two sons: Curt, eight, and Chris, twelve. I had struggled to keep them in Our Savior Lutheran School, which was just three blocks from my house. And I was broke. Very broke. I had a job, which covered the food, tuition, and house payments. But little else. Child support had turned out to be a mythical joke.

My first Christmas alone was a struggle. Throughout the year, I had clipped coupons to put presents under the tree. It was called "refunding" and I would receive a dollar here and there in return for buying specific products. Just that afternoon, I received $5 cash as a result of eating mountains of frozen pizza. It was 6 o'clock when the mail finally came to bring me that $5.

The boys were spending Christmas Eve with their father and I was busy locating items to put in stockings. In my planning for Christmas I had somehow neglected to think about the treats to fill the stockings. I had no apples, oranges or candy canes. But I did have the newly arrived $5.

I weighed my options. I could drive to the store and get the stocking items. There was little gas in the car. Truly a bad idea as the $5 would go entirely for the stocking stuffers and the gas tank would be even lower. Plus, then I'd be late, and probably miss completely the Christmas candlelight service at Our Savior.

I decided to walk to the church. I felt pretty sorry for myself as I passed well-lit homes with whole families doing all the normal things. It seemed everyone had company but me.

The church service was beautiful as always, even when the four Onishi boys started coughing behind me. They sure cured my feeling of being alone. I slipped the $5 into the collection plate as I prayed for stocking stuffers and gave thanks to God for all my blessings. My sons were healthy and the only thing I was worried about was stocking stuffers. I had to laugh. They would simply have to do without the food items normally found in their stockings.

As I exited the service I noticed a table laden with small brown lunch bags. Brent Kranig, a friend of the boys said, "Here, take one of these for Chris and Curt," as he handed me two bags. I walked home with the bags, feeling emotionally enriched from the candlelight service. Tears filled my eyes as I looked at my neighborhood anew. I was so fortunate to live in such a community. Many single mothers lived in apartments. I gave thanks all the way home. I was indeed fortunate.

I tossed the bags on the kitchen counter and retrieved the handmade stockings. I scrounged the cupboards but found only chocolate chips. Then I decided to peek into the lunch bags and see what was in there. Each bag held an apple, an orange, a candy cane, and a Snickers bar. Everything I needed to put into the stockings was provided.

I knew then and there that being single would not be the catastrophe I feared. With God watching over the little things like the Christmas stockings, I knew He was in total control of our life.

~Linda Burks Lohman

Love in a Book

When we put our cares in His hands,
He puts His peace in our hearts.
~Author Unknown

hirty thousand square feet of space! Over forty thousand items to look at! I am only five feet six inches tall, probably more square feet of me than I would like, but honestly, the task ahead was monumental. I was standing in the Christian bookstore in the city where I live. The size of the store reminded me of a Walmart Supercenter. On one side was the music and video department, then an area for children's toys and books, church supplies, cards, gifts, jewelry, pictures, teacher's educational resources, stationery, office supplies, books… a person could get dizzy just visualizing the store layout.

It was Christmas, my favorite time of the year, and I was on assignment to pick out the perfect gift for my older son Jeff. We have a rather large family and several friends that seem like family to us, so shopping for gifts begins early. This is when I am finally appreciated for being "the list" person in the group. I try to jot down ideas for gift giving throughout the year when I overhear someone mention something they wish they had. But this particular year I fell short of ideas and was now standing in our local Christian bookstore trying to decide what to get Jeff that would be meaningful.

This was definitely one of those "going shopping with God" moments. After all, He knows everyone better than I do and what they need. So I prayed as I entered the store that God would some-how direct me to the perfect gift. I stood just inside the front door poised and ready, waiting for some kind of direction.

"Can I help you find something?" asked one rather puzzled store clerk who had been watching other shoppers rush by me.

I guessed that she and several others had noticed I was heading nowhere. How do you tell someone, "No thanks, I'm just waiting for God to direct me?"

Well, I surmised, while I'm standing here I might as well use the common sense I have been given. Let's see—Jeff teaches men at his church—what would help him in his studies? Immediately a thought came—a concordance. Of course! A concordance would be the perfect study guide for anyone teaching the Bible. I would be lost without mine. This would be easy. So I headed to the book area and the study resource section in particular.

In disbelief I peered over the section entitled "Concordance." Several years ago when I purchased mine there were only a couple of choices. Now they were lined up row after row screaming, "Pick me, pick me!" Different shapes, different colors, different translations, different formats, different prices.

Another quickie prayer for help shot up, "Oh Lord, which one?"

With that, one of the concordances seemed to come alive. I was almost certain I saw it inch its way forward from the rest of the pack on the shelves. At any rate, it caught my eye. For no other reason than it stood out to me, I walked to the checkout counter with the winner.

Christmas Eve arrived. The shopping was done and I placed Jeff's gift along with the others under the family Christmas tree. Part of our family always gathered together for dinner and devotions the night before Christmas in anticipation of the Christmas Day festivi-ties. Gina, Jeff's wife, started the tradition of a family candlelight ser-vice in their home each Christmas Eve as we reflected on the Story of Christmas.

"Name something you learned this past year," Gina instructed, "and then something you want to learn this next year."

As usual, Jeff waited until the others were finished.

"I learned this year that God can bring good out of anything," he said. Then he cited several instances where God came through for his family, his work, and his service at church.

"This year," he continued, eyes staring at the floor he was sitting on, "I want to see God's hand in my own life personally. I want to have my eyes open to see His love for me. I want to slow down and take more time to see Him in the blessings He brings into my daily life."

We all nodded in agreement and wished the words had been our own. It was a desire we all could relate to, but Jeff made it his personal prayer.

Christmas morning began too early, as it does in most homes full of younger children (and grandchildren). An elaborately planned breakfast was gulped down in a hurry. There were gifts to open and messes to make! There were screams of joy, wide-open mouths and "you really shouldn't have" to be heard. I watched as the gifts were distributed to each family member. It was then I saw my gift to Jeff peeking out from under the others—this time content not to inch its way forward.

"I hope he won't be disappointed with our gift," I whispered to my husband Larry. A book is usually one of those "I hate it" or "I love it" kind of gifts. But in my heart, I knew he would graciously pretend to like it even if he didn't. After all, I'm his mom!

As usual, Jeff waited until everyone else was finished before opening his gifts: a CD of his favorite artist from his younger son; a sweater from Gina; cologne from his daughters. Red licorice—who threw that in?

Our gift was left until last—a simple concordance from the Christian bookstore. Wrapping paper torn aside and lid removed, Jeff lifted the chosen concordance from its captive box. He paused silently for a short moment and then with tears rolling down his face looked to heaven and began to thank God.

"I was in the bookstore several weeks ago," he explains. "I've always wanted a concordance and spent some time looking through several of them. Although I wanted to buy one, I kept thinking of all the other things our family needed that were more important. So I put the one I liked back on the shelf, hopefully, to buy it down the road."

"That's amazing!" Larry said, giving my hand a tender squeeze.

"Yes, but you don't understand," he continued. "Of all the rows of concordances I looked at, the one I chose is now the one I'm holding in my hand!"

We were reminded once again in a personal way of the Christmas story — God's gift given as an expression of His love for us. This year His love was found in the gift of a book.

~Patti Ann Thompson

Be Careful What You Wish For

May the sun shine, all day long, everything go right, and nothing wrong.
May those you love bring love back to you,
and may all the wishes you wish come true!
~Irish Blessing

"Be careful what you wish for, you might just get it." What I wished for more than anything in the third grade was to play the lead as Mary in the class's Christmas play. For once in my life, I wanted to be the star. I had never been "a star" in any sense, not at school and certainly not at home where there were already ten noisy, hungry children. Sure, I was loved and cared for, but there, amid all the many chores required of farm living, I was basically one more mouth to feed.

Plus, I was a backward, reticent child. Until I was on stage. I had already been assigned minor parts in different school plays throughout the years. Despite my painful shyness, by the third grade I had figured out that while I might not shine elsewhere I could act.

Our teacher, Mrs. K., decided every child in class would audition and the best one for the lead would be selected. Still, I wasn't worried and was so excited at the prospect of the forthcoming play that I not only learned Mary's part, I memorized all the roles. I felt knowing all the parts would give me a better shot at getting the part.

On the afternoon of the auditions none of the boys seemed eager to try out for the role of Joseph but several of us girls were anxious to be picked as Mary. There were, I knew, several good contenders, but aside from knowing that I was able to act, I also had long beautiful ash-blond hair. Sure, Mary probably had dark hair but I knew Mrs. K. would consider how well my hair would look in the part.

After the auditions were over I secretly thought that mine had been the best presentation, especially if Mrs. K.'s smile was anything to go on. I was certain that the applause, the adoration of the crowd would soon be mine.

I literally skipped home that day only to discover that Aunt M., who was visiting with her youngest son, had discovered that he had head lice. All of us would have to have our heads medicated to avoid a breakout, and, to be safe, Aunt M. planned to cut our hair.

"No!" I cried, and tried to run.

Aunt M. immediately grabbed me and I was the first child forced to succumb to her ministrations. Aunt M. always thought of the quickest way to get the job done. So her method was to put a bowl on my head and cut around the edges of the bowl. Unfortunately for me we had only small shallow bowls, so I ended up with an extremely short and ugly hairdo.

As I looked dismally into the mirror that evening I felt too numb to even cry. I didn't stand a chance now of being selected for the role of Mary in the class Christmas play.

The next day Mrs. K. tried but wasn't entirely successful at hiding her shocked look when she first saw me. My only comfort was some of the other kids, boys and girls, had also had haircuts, but none had hair as short and ugly as mine. A few minutes later, Mrs. K., sighing, took out a list and announced that Katie, who had short thick hair, would be playing Mary and that Don, who still had a normal head of hair, would be Joseph.

On the evening of the play we all had to stay after school for dress rehearsal before the actual play was presented to the proud parents who would be attending later. I knew Mrs. K. had requested everyone stay so that no one would feel left out. Still, as part of the "props committee" I didn't have much to do, other than help move the chairs back and out of the way.

As Katie took her place as Mary in front of the classroom, I tried to tell myself I would enjoy the play no matter what. However, when I saw Katie I was smitten with jealousy. The sensation was so strong I suddenly had to blink back hot, angry tears.

"That should have been my part!" I wanted to cry. "I should have been Mary!"

In the meantime, the other actors had taken their places, all except Don who was to play Joseph. He had had to go home that afternoon for some family errand, but had told Mrs. K. he would be back in time for dress rehearsal.

That's when Mrs. K., along with the rest of us, got the bad news. The principal, who was lingering to see our Christmas play, came in and told us that when Don got home his mother had discovered that he had head lice and had shaved Don's head. And now Don was refusing to participate in the play.

None of us, I knew, would have particularly cared about Don's looks, since there were already several boys sporting crew cuts or bald domes due to the same problem. However, remembering the first day of school after my "bowl cut," I could sympathize. I knew how Don felt.

"Oh no!" Mrs. K. cried, tears welling in her eyes now. "What will we do?"

Her eyes desperately searched the faces of the other boys. "Do any of you know the part of Joseph?"

The boys looked down and shuffled their feet.

"We'll have to cancel the play," she said, pulling a tissue from her pocket and dabbing at her eyes. She looked at the principal. "We won't have time to let parents know not to come but we can still serve them cake and punch."

I couldn't stand it. I tugged at the teacher's sleeve. "Mrs. K.? I do."

She looked down, irritated. "You do what?"

"I know Joseph's part. I memorized all the roles when I auditioned for Mary."

Mrs. K. seemed past astonishment.

"Her hair is certainly short enough," the principal said.

"Okay," Mrs. K. finally said happily. "The play is on again."

And that's how I eventually got exactly what I had wished for, the lead in the third grade Christmas play. Sure, it wasn't the role of Mary but when the play ended I stood in front of the classroom, just as I had dreamed. And the sound of the applause was no less gratifying because I had ended up playing Joseph, due to my short, ugly, blunt bowl cut.

It is amazing how things work out sometimes. Although I think they ought to change that old saying, "Be careful what you wish for, you might just get it." Instead, it should be, "Wish and dream for anything and everything you want, but whatever you do, for goodness' sake, be specific."

~Marijoyce Porcelli

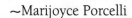

A Christmas Angel

All God's angels come to us disguised.
~James Russell Lowell

Growing up, I liked to put the glistening golden angel treetop ornament on the family Christmas tree. Mom would lift me up until I could reach the very top branch of the tree. And after the angel was in place, I'd wonder aloud if angels really did exist and say that I wished I could see a real Christmas angel.

"All God's angels come to us disguised," Mom often said, and she'd always assure me that we all have a guardian angel looking over us and that miracles do happen.

When I grew up and had a family of my own, we crafted a paper cone glistening golden angel treetop ornament using glitter glue, sparkles, sequins and lace. Each year, as I admired the creation that adorned the top of our Christmas tree, I still wondered about angels... until December 1978.

I was enjoying the hustle and bustle of the Christmas season, even though I had to find a way to buy gifts for family and to make ends meet within a meager budget.

One afternoon in between waiting for batches of Christmas cookies to bake, I prepared twenty-four Christmas cards for mailing to friends and relatives that lived on the East Coast. Inside one dozen cards addressed to friends, I tucked short notes and a family photo, and in the remaining dozen cards for family, I included Sears

Roebuck gift certificates or JCPenney gift certificates or new, crisp twenty-dollar bills.

I was elated that I'd been able to pinch pennies by inserting gifts inside a Christmas card instead of spending extra money for shipping packages across the country. And I was grateful for not having to stand in line at the post office, as I'd done in previous years.

It was a cold and rainy winter day, with no sign of it clearing anytime soon. I watched the wind hurl rain against the kitchen windows; I didn't relish driving five miles to the post office to send my cards. I decided it'd be more convenient to drop the cards into the mailbox located in front of an insurance office only three blocks from my house. I hurried to make the last mail pick-up at 5 PM.

When I arrived in the insurance company's parking lot, I parked as close to the mailbox as I could, opened the car door, pulled the hood of my raincoat down as far as it would go, and ran for the mailbox. The cold rain stung my cheeks. I tried to brace myself against the gusty winds, but I lost my balance and dropped the plastic bag containing the twenty-four red envelopes.

"Oh, please... please... someone help me," I pleaded. My heart sank, as I watched the envelopes soar through the air, there was no way I could recover the envelopes. And there wasn't any money left to replace them or the gifts inside.

The storm raged on as I lay sprawled on the pavement. I sobbed uncontrollably, trying to ignore my skinned right knee wracked with pain.

Suddenly, the rain and wind died down, the dark sky brightened and only a light rain fell. I was able to stand and I was surprised my knee no longer hurt. As I reached down to rub my knee, one of the red envelopes landed at my feet.

Then, in the distance, I watched as a tall, blond-haired man dressed in a pale gray jacket and matching trousers, retrieved red envelopes from the pavement and stuffed them inside his jacket. Before I could take a step, the tall young man decked in light gray, with the gentlest blue eyes I'd ever seen, stood before me. He nodded, smiled slightly, but did not speak. He unzipped his jacket and handed me a stack of red envelopes.

"Oh, thank you, thank you," I squealed tearfully as I sorted through the envelopes. "They are all here."

However, when I looked up, I was dumbstruck; he was nowhere to be seen. An icy shiver ran through me. He wasn't walking in the parking lot, and the same three cars remained that had been parked there before I fell.

Then I recalled those words, "All God's angels come to us disguised," and a sense of peace and joy washed over me. Indeed, a Christmas angel came to my rescue that day.

~Georgia A. Hubley

Meet Our Contributors

Monica A. Andermann lives and writes on Long Island. Her work is widely published both online and in print with several credits in the *Chicken Soup for the Soul* and *A Cup of Comfort* collections. When she is not writing, she most enjoys spending time with family and friends.

Deborah Y. Anderson is a freelance writer from the Midwest. She has written for *Cross Times*, Focus on the Family, and published in numerous other publications. Deborah is also a monthly columnist for *Christian Fiction Online Magazine*. She is working on her first novel. You can reach Deborah via e-mail at DAnderson955@aol.com.

Using his extensive experience in producing films, videos, and television commercials, **Max Elliot Anderson** brings that visual excitement and heart-pounding action to his adventure and mystery books for readers eight to thirteen. Readers say that reading one of his books is like being in an exciting movie. Learn more at www.maxbooks.9k.com or contact Max via e-mail at Mander8813@aol.com.

Maryrose Armato received her Bachelor's Degree, majoring in English at Bradley University. She was a high school English teacher and a junior college Writing Lab Instructor. She moved to Florida with her family, where she fell in love with the senior population while working at an assisted living facility.

Nancy Baker resides in College Station, TX, with her husband and Golden Retriever. Upon retiring, she pursued her lifelong love of writing and has been published in numerous national magazines and anthologies. She has three children, eight grandchildren, and nine great-grandchildren, all a source of inspiration for her.

Jessica Beach is an author and volunteer coordinator living in the Pacific Northwest. She's traveled the world and worked with humanitarian and mission organizations. She enjoys cooking, sewing, gardening, and singing.

Nancy Bechtolt wrote a travel column, "Ikimasho" (Let's Go) for an English language newspaper when she lived in Japan from 1971-76. She summers in Chautauqua, NY where she has won several poetry prizes. Currently she is working on a collection of personal Christmas stories. E-mail her at bechun@aol.com.

Valerie Benko is a writer living in western Pennsylvania. She has been published in multiple anthologies including *Chicken Soup for the Soul* and *Patchwork Path*; in *All You* magazine and online at storiesthatlift. com, coolstuff4writers.com and whisperingtree.net.

Jan Bono taught school for thirty years on the Long Beach peninsula in southwest Washington State. She now works as a life coach, writing coach, Law of Attraction presenter, and freelance writer, with numerous articles and several books to her credit. Check out her blog at: www.daybreak-solutions.com/blog.

Amy Brady holds a Bachelor of Science degree from the University of North Carolina-Charlotte. She enjoys motorcycle touring, Celtic music, golf, writing, and collecting antiques. Amy recently retired as Sergeant from the Charlotte-Mecklenburg Police Department after thirty years. She plans to continue writing stories about the job and the road. Please e-mail her at ahbrady@aol.com.

Christine Brooks is a freelance writer who lives in western Massachusetts with her family and very opinionated dog, Harley. She has published several essays in magazines across the world and her second book, *Letters to M*, will be out in 2010. Please visit her online at www.fourleafclover.us.

Sue Cameron is a grammy of eight, a Bible teacher, speaker, and author. She has written for Christian publications, newspapers and nearly a dozen devotional books. Sue's fiction won an EPA award in 2009. Find her CD, *Praying for My Husband and Marriage*, at www.letspraytoday.com. Please e-mail her at grammysue@gmail.com.

Richard Todd Canton is an educational assistant at Truro Junior High. He also hosts a local television show. Writing is his passion. For more information about Richard visit www.toddcanton.com.

Barbara Carpenter is the author of *Starlight, Starbright*; *Wish I May, Wish I Might*; *The Wish I Wish Tonight*; and the memoir of Dr. Secundion Rubio, *Without a Quarter in My Pocket*. This is her third *Chicken Soup for the Soul* story published. Contact her at www.starlightseries.com and www.becblog.com.

Mary Catherine Carwile took a leap of faith in her mid-fifties, becoming a flight attendant even though she feared flying. This thrust her into a newfound confidence. She has written and published two books, her second being, *Heartstrings and Pink Ribbons*. Learn more about Mary at www.MaryCarwile.com.

Beth Cato's essays have been featured in *Totts* magazine, *The Ultimate Cat Lover*, and two previous volumes of *Chicken Soup for the Soul*. She's also an associate member of the Science Fiction & Fantasy Writers of America. Her website is www.bethcato.com.

Mary Chace, a seasoned military wife and homeschooling mom, enjoys making memories with her favorite pilot Douglas, and their six children. An honors graduate of Southwest Baptist University in Bolivar, MO, she now freelances from the family's California home. She may be reached via e-mail at mary.chace@gmail.com.

Phyllis Cochran is a published freelance writer and lives in Winchendon, MA with her husband, Phil. In her nonfiction stories, Phyllis draws from personal experience. Her work has appeared in book and national and local magazines. Her book, *Shades of Light: A Mother's and Daughter's Pathway to God* was published in 2006.

Courtney Conover is a writer and author who often cracks under the pressure of having to find the perfect Christmas gift. Her likes include yoga, cheering on her alma mater, the University of Michigan, and more yoga. She lives in Metro Detroit with her husband, Scott. Visit her at www.courtneyconover.com.

Brenda Cook is a veteran teacher with thirty-two years of classroom teaching experience. She enjoys reading, writing, traveling, and spending time with family and friends. Brenda is also actively involved in Women's Ministry at her church and participates in various mission opportunities.

Donna D'Amour is a freelance writer living in Halifax, Nova Scotia. Her writing has been published in *PhotoLife*, *Saltscapes*, *Living Healthy in Atlantic Canada*, *The Globe and Mail* and *The Chronicle Herald*. Her essays on everyday life were published in *Colouring the Road* by Lancelot Press in 1995. Contact her via e-mail at damourwriting@yahoo.ca.

Ron Dimmer writes and teaches in southeast Michigan. He and his talented wife Linda are currently seeking a publisher for their picture book manuscripts. Their two wonderful boys continue to provide them with inspiration and ideas. You may contact Ron via e-mail at radimmerjr@hotmail.com.

Toni Louise Diol, of Polish ancestry, married forty-five years, grandmother of ten, former pre-school director and pediatric office manager, writes poetry, short stories and has published a narrative poetry book: *Roses & Lollipops*. She does presentations to teach and motivate journaling to preserve history for future generations. E-mail her at mylollipops@comcast.net.

Although blind, **Janet Perez Eckles** thrives as a Spanish interpreter, international speaker, writer and author of, *Trials of Today, Treasures for Tomorrow—Overcoming Adversities in Life*. From her home in Florida, she enjoys working on church ministries and taking Caribbean cruises with her husband Gene. She imparts inspirations at: www.janetperezeckles.com.

Helen Eggers is delighted to have her fifth story in the *Chicken Soup for the Soul* series. She's anticipating the upcoming nuptials of her son Michael and his Rose. Gardening, quilting, writing, fishing, yoga and living with her beloved husband Shawn fill her heart and days. E-mail her at hjs01234@aol.com.

Harold D. Fanning is a minister in Alabama. He is married to Deborah and they enjoy traveling and antique collecting. He has written two books: *Life In the Skillet: And Lessons Learned Along the Way* and *Life Along a Dirt Road*.

Susan Farr-Fahncke is the founder of 2TheHeart.com, where you can find more of her writing and sign up for an online writing workshop! She is also the founder of the amazing volunteer group, Angels2TheHeart, the author of *Angel's Legacy*, and contributor to over sixty books, including many in the *Chicken Soup for the Soul* series. Visit her at 2TheHeart.com.

Judith Fitzsimmons works as a freelance writer in middle Tennessee. Her greatest joy is spending time with her daughter.

Christa Gala lives in North Carolina with her husband and son. A professional writer, she holds a Bachelor of Arts degree in Journalism from UNC-Chapel Hill and a Master's degree in English from North Carolina State University. Christa is always looking for great White Elephants and funny stories. Learn more about Christa at www. christagala.com.

Ron Geelan is a full-time financial services professional and part-time freelance writer. He lives on Long Island with his wonderful wife and two beautiful children. Ron enjoys running, bicycling, coaching Little League and spending time with his family. E-mail him at rgeelan@optonline.net.

Judith H. Golde is a music teacher in the Buffalo Public Schools. She co-authored *The Music Teacher's Survival Guide* manual and has also been published in the *Buffalo News*. Judy's family is an endless source of inspiration for her writing and she treasures their love and support. Contact her via e-mail at goldenotes11@aol.com.

After her twenty-year nursing career, **Pamela Goldstein** turned to her passion—writing. She has completed three manuscripts, two plays, and several of her short stories have been published in anthology books. She produces/hosts the "Boker Tov" radio show, and is heard worldwide on the Internet. E-mail Pam at boker_tov2002@yahoo. ca.

Carolyn Hall is a freelance writer and speaker. She gives presentations on how to capture your memories for non-writers. Her book, *Prairie Meals and Memories: Living the Golden Rule*, captures her adventures and recipes from growing up on a small farm in Kansas. She can be reached via e-mail at chall711@gmail.com.

Carol Harrison has her Bachelor of Education from the University of Saskatchewan and her Distinguished Toastmaster designation. She is an inspirational speaker and the author of the book *Amee's Story*. She enjoys family time, reading, scrapbooking and speaking. You can e-mail her at carol@carolscorner.ca or visit her website www.carolscorner.ca.

Janet Hartman's articles, stories, and flash fiction have appeared in national magazines, online, and in three anthologies: *From the Porch Swing*, *This Path*, and *Making Notes: Music of the Carolinas*. She is the 2010 guest columnist for the Long Ridge Writers Group. For more, see www.JanetHartman.net.

Laurel Hausman lives in northern Virginia where she teaches high school mathematics. She is a multiple contributor to *Chicken Soup for the Soul* books. Hobbies include quilting, gardening, and reading, and she is working towards becoming a full-time writer. Please e-mail her at laurelhausman@aol.com.

Dana Hill is a bartender, a passionate cook and a freelance writer living in Oakland, CA. She writes several columns for www.examiner.com, and is currently working on a memoir of her experiences during a long career in the airline industry. Please e-mail Dana at danahill@att.net.

Miriam Hill is a frequent contributor to *Chicken Soup for the Soul* books and has been published in *Writer's Digest*, *The Christian Science Monitor*, *Grit*, *St. Petersburg Times*, *The Sacramento Bee* and Poynter Online. Miriam's manuscript received Honorable Mention for Inspirational Writing in a *Writer's Digest* writing competition.

April Homer is a happy stay-at-home mother of four children. Her children are constantly making witty remarks that keep her and her husband rolling in laughter! She loves to write in her spare time and her silly children make great material!

Georgia A. Hubley retired after twenty years in financial management to write full-time. She's a frequent contributor to the *Chicken Soup for the Soul* series, *Christian Science Monitor* and various other magazines, newspapers and anthologies. She resides with her husband of thirty-two years in Henderson, NV. Contact her via e-mail at geohub@aol.com.

Jennie Ivey lives in Tennessee. She is a newspaper columnist and the author of three books. She has published numerous fiction and nonfiction pieces, including several stories in the *Chicken Soup for the Soul* collections. Contact her via e-mail at jivey@frontiernet.net.

Jennifer Lee Johnson is a writer and editor based in Baltimore, MD. You can see more of her work at www.jen-johnson.com.

Kara Johnson is a freelance writer living in Boise, ID, with her husband Jim, and their dog Barkley. She enjoys reading, traveling, playing outside, and soaking up all of life's greatest blessings!

Susan Karas owns and operates a successful business with her husband. She enjoys reading and gardening in her free time. She has two grown children, and two dogs. Susan is a regular contributor to *Guideposts* magazine, and has been published in many other publications.

Ben Kennedy was born in Baltimore, MD. After surviving thirty years there, he now makes his home in Charleston, SC. He is a father, a husband, a stand-up comedian, an actor, and a natural storyteller (not necessarily always in that order). Please visit www.bigbenkennedy.com.

Karen Kilby resides in Kingwood, TX, with her husband, David. A Certified Personality Trainer with CLASServices, Inc., she's also a speaker for Stonecroft Ministries. Karen enjoys sharing her life experiences and has several short stories published in *Chicken Soup* *for the Soul* books as well as other publications. E-mail her at krkilby@kingwoodcable.net.

Angie Klink authored the children's books *Purdue Pete Finds His Hammer* and *I Found U.* She is published in *Chicken Soup for the Sister's Soul 2, Republican's Soul,* and *Our Fathers Who Art in Heaven.* She won an Honorable Mention in the 2007 Erma Bombeck Writing Competition. Learn more at www.angieklink.com.

April Knight enjoys galloping her horses on the beach and visiting her grandchildren in Australia. She is also an artist and freelance writer. She loves people who can make her laugh and believes no dream is too big to achieve and life is a great adventure. Contact her at moonlightlady1@hotmail.com.

Jess Knox has been published in several *Chicken Soup for the Soul* publications. She graduated from the University of Southern California in 2007 with a degree in screenwriting and is currently the VP of Publicity for OmniPop Talent Group in Los Angeles. Feel free to e-mail her at knox.jess@gmail.com.

Heidi Krumenauer is thankful for a long career in upper management with a large insurance company. In her spare time, Heidi has authored eight books and contributed to more than a dozen others. Heidi and her husband Jeff raise their two sons, Noah and Payton, in southern Wisconsin.

Madeleine Kuderick lives in Florida with her husband and two children. Her stories appear in *Chicken Soup for the Soul, A Cup of Comfort* and other anthologies. She holds a Master's degree from Saint Leo University. She is a member of SCBWI and a graduate of the Institute of Children's Literature. Learn more at www.madeleinekuderick.com.

Cathi LaMarche is a novelist and essayist. She has a master's degree and teaches English and writing. Residing in Missouri, she shares her home with her husband, two children, and three spoiled dogs. She is currently working on her second novel.

Sharon Landeen, mother, grandma, and retired elementary teacher, believes that working with children helps keep her young. She stays busy volunteering at schools, being a 4-H leader, and making blankets for Project Linus. She also enjoys traveling, reading, and following the University of Arizona's basketball team.

Michelle Langenberg is an editor, award-winning poet, teacher, Master Reiki healer, and artist in layout, oils and watercolors (as M. B. Lange). She believes we all, as God-empowered miracle-makers, have the power to bless, and she lives by the "law of kindness." Learn more at www.langefinearts.com or e-mail her at chelleashes1@yahoo. com.

Linda LaRocque is the author of several award-winning plays. Her numerous short stories have appeared in *Guideposts*, *Signs of the Times* and other *Chicken Soup for the Soul* books. A retired self-employed interior designer, Linda writes from her South Haven, MI home.

Mary Laufer is a freelance writer living in Forest Grove, OR. Her nonfiction has appeared in several anthologies, including *Chicken Soup for the Soul: Empty Nesters*, *Patchwork Path: Grandma's Choice* and *A Cup of Comfort Devotional for Mothers and Daughters*. She hopes to publish a collection of her work.

Teresa Lockhart is a high school journalism teacher and a freelance writer. She and her family enjoy traveling and attending Red Sox games. She is working on her first young adult novel. She has a passion for encouraging teenagers to find their potential.

Linda Lohman has a BA in English from Sacramento State University. She has previously been published in *Chicken Soup for the Soul: Thanks*

Mom, *Reader's Digest*, *The Sacramento Bee*, *Sacramento News & Review*, and *Solidarity*. Retired, she enjoys Red Hat friends and beading. You may contact her at laborelations@yahoo.com.

Cynthia A. Lovely is an upstate New Yorker involved in church ministry, freelance writing and music. Previous publications include *Romantic Homes, Poets & Writers* and *Living Light News*. A serious readaholic, she is currently working on a contemporary woman's novel in Christian fiction. Please e-mail her at cllyrics@gmail.com.

Helen Luecke is an inspirational writer of short stories, articles, devotionals and poetry. She helped organize Inspirational Writers Alive! (Amarillo Chapter). She lives in Amarillo, TX, with her husband Richard. They have two grown sons and four grandsons. Helen enjoys doing volunteer work, visiting with her grandsons and writing.

Amanda Luzzader received her Bachelor of Science degree in Family Finances from Utah State University. She is now a full-time stay-at-home mom, enjoying spending time with her husband and two young sons.

Kelly Starling Lyons is a children's book author whose mission is to transform moments, memories and history into stories of discovery. Her books include chapter book, *NEATE: Eddie's Ordeal*, and picture book, *One Million Men and Me*. Her next title, *Ellen's Broom*, debuts in 2012. Find out more at www.kellystarlinglyons.com.

Leigh B. MacKay received his BA from Amherst College and his MALS from Dartmouth College. He taught English for thirty-six years—twenty-six years at The Westminster Schools in Atlanta, GA, before retiring in May of 2007. Leigh enjoys traveling, playing golf, reading, and relaxing. Please e-mail him at LBM1004@hotmail.com.

Tina Marie is the wife to an awesome husband and the mother of two great kids. This is her fourth *Chicken Soup for the Soul* story. She is blessed beyond measure.

Melanie Marks mainly writes for children and young adults. She's had over fifty stories published in magazines such as *Highlights* and *'Teen*, as well as five books published including a young adult novel. Melanie is married to a naval nuclear submarine officer and blessed with three incredibly terrific kids. Contact her via e-mail at bymelaniemarks@comcast.net.

Dana Martin is a writer/editor living in Bakersfield, CA, with her husband of twenty-two years and their three (nearly grown) children. Dana has her BA in English and is president of Writers of Kern (a branch of the California Writers Club). Dana enjoys Christmas, editing novels, and watching her son play professional baseball. E-mail her at Dana@DanaMartinWriting.com.

Sara Matson is a freelance writer who lives with her family in Minnesota. Her daughters, now ten, enjoy painting their toenails; her husband, now wiser, never allows them to paint his!

Donna Meadows is the mother of six adult children. She worked for many years as an elementary school librarian and hopes to write a children's book someday. She loves reading, traveling, gardening and especially reading to her grandchildren. Please e-mail her at meadowsdonna@hotmail.com.

Kim Kluxen Meredith lives in Lancaster, PA, where she teaches Spanish. Her first inspirational/self-help book, *Listen for the Whispers: Coping with Grief and Learning to Live Again* was published in July 2010 by Cable Publishing. Please visit her website at www.kimkluxenmeredith.com.

Randy Joan Mills is a retired Special Education teacher whose passions include her daughter, Kelsey, her son and new daughter-in-law, Cory and Ashley, traveling with her husband, Bruce, especially to Ireland, tutoring former students, and scouring garage sales every weekend for her annual Christmas project. She can be reached via e-mail at millsgang4@juno.com.

Janet N. Miracle is a retired teacher and library media specialist living in Kentucky with her husband Carson. She received a Bachelor's Degree from the University of Maryland and Master's Degrees from Eastern Kentucky University. The mother of three grown children and two grandchildren, she enjoys gardening and traveling.

Kelli Mix is a freelance writer living in Carrollton, GA, with her husband and two young daughters. She is author of *The Game Day Poker Almanac Official Rules of Poker* and numerous articles for various publications. Kelli is an active board member for CASA, an advocacy group for foster children.

Martha Moore is a retired high school English teacher. Besides writing for Chicken Soup for the Soul, she is an award-winning author of young adult and middle-grade novels. She lives in Mansfield, TX, with her husband and younger son. Her older son, Peter, still has his Christmas stocking.

C.G. Morelli's work has appeared in *Highlights for Children* (winner of a 2010 AEP Award), *Ghostlight* magazine, *Long Story Short*, *House of Horror*, *Jersey Devil Press* and *Fiction at Work*. He is the author of a short story collection titled *In the Pen* (2007).

Lisa Morris-Abrams has been an educator for the past twenty-one years and a writer for a lifetime. In her spare time she enjoys gardening, writing, spending time with her family and loving her three Labrador Retrievers. Lisa is currently working on an educational book for teachers, which should be out by next spring. Please e-mail her at lovealab@aol.com.

Nell Musolf is a graduate of Northeastern Illinois University. She currently lives in Minnesota with her husband and two sons. She enjoys reading, writing and watching old movies with her husband. You can reach Nell at nellmus@aol.com.

Risa Nye is a California native. She is co-editor of the anthology *Writin' on Empty: Parents Reveal the Upside, Downside, and Everything in Between When Children Leave the Nest.* Her essays and articles have been published in several newspapers, magazines, and anthologies, including three *Chicken Soup for the Soul* books.

Suzanne Rowe Ogren is a writer/actress living in the Chicago area. She has written personality profiles and travel pieces for regional and trade magazines, was ghostwriter on a celebrity autobiography, and is currently working on her first novel. Her writing blog can be found at http://srogren.blogspot.com.

Ann Peachman has studied theology and gerontology and currently works enriching the lives of frail elderly. She is a widow with three grown children and one granddaughter. She loves to write, and is working on her first novel. In her spare time, she scrapbooks. Please e-mail her at peachie01@sympatico.ca.

Marilyn Phillips, a teacher, has articles published in three *Chicken Soup for the Soul* books. Marilyn has three books sold by Christian Cheerleaders of America. Her website is www.mphillipsauthor.com. Marilyn lives in Bedford, TX, with her husband, Nolan. They have two grown children, Bryant and Rebekah.

Marijoyce Porcelli is a freelance writer who has had work published in many different publications. She is also the author of the books *Rages of the Night* and *A Southern Woman's View of Life* (www.lulu.com/windchimebooks).

Joe Rector is a freelance writer who has published several pieces of work in books and magazines. He writes features for a local newspaper and maintains the blog www.thecommonisspectacular.com. Contact Joe for more information on his writing at joerector@comcast.net.

Recently, **Carol McAdoo Rehme** presented her adult children with their treasured childhood sleds — rescued from the sale of the family cabin. A veteran freelance editor, author, and ghostwriter, she publishes prolifically in the inspirational market. Carol has coauthored seven books, most recently *Chicken Soup for the Soul: Empty Nesters*. www. rehme.com.

Denise Reich practices flying trapeze, loves rock concerts and travels as often as possible. Her writing has appeared in various publications in the USA and Bermuda, including *Chicken Soup for the Soul: What I Learned from the Cat*, *Pology*, *Hitotoki*, and *The Royal Gazette*.

Bruce Rittel, father of two girls, resides in Bismarck, ND. To honor his deceased wife, he founded Tracy's Sanctuary House, a temporary home for families facing traumatic medical situations. For more information visit: www.tracyssanctuary.com. His sister, Georgia Bruton, published writer and editor, lives in Florida with her husband. Contact information: gjbruton@yahoo.com.

Courtney Rusk received her Bachelor's in English and Master's in Adult Education and Educational Leadership, with honors, from Northwestern State University. She teaches twelfth grade in Pineville, LA. Courtney loves spending time with her two children Jobey and Aubriana and her husband Greg. Feel free to e-mail her at courtleerusk@yahoo.com.

Lindy Schneider is an award-winning artist and illustrator. Her work has appeared in national magazines, textbooks and children's books. She is also the author of several children's books and co-authored the book *101 Ways to Live Better on Less*. She can be reached via e-mail at lindy_schn@yahoo.com or at www.lindysbooks.com.

Shannon Scott works as an administrative assistant and writer of the Coweta County Family Entertainment section of Examiner.com. Her background is in Public Relations and Marketing. She spends her free time reading and being with her family. Her close-knit family and children, ages four and six, give her ample material for her writing.

Marilyn Shipe is a freelance writer from Greenville, SC, a member of the American Christian Fiction Writers and is currently working on her first historical novel set on Sanibel Island, Florida. She also enjoys writing poetry, has published devotions online with www.christiandevotions.us and enjoys cooking, knitting, gardening, and scrapbooking.

Michelle Shocklee is an award-winning author of historical and contemporary Christian fiction. She lives with her family in Central Texas. Visit her website at www.michelleshocklee.com.

Candace Simar is a poet and writer from Pequot Lakes, MN. She enjoys writing a weekly online devotional, Sweet Honey from the Rock, and has published two historical novels, *Abercrombie Trail* and *Pomme De Terre*.

Janet Elaine Smith was a missionary in Venezuela for nine years, and it was a wonderful experience—except for the first Christmas. Her dreams have been realized with the publication of twenty-one books, most of them novels. *Rebel With a Cause* chronicles her time in Venezuela. Her website is www.janetelainesmith.com.

When **Mary Z. Smith** isn't penning praises to her heavenly Father for publications like *Chicken Soup for the Soul*, *Guideposts* and *Angels on Earth*, she can be found gardening or walking her Rat Terrier Frankie. Mary and her husband of thirty-three years reside in Richmond, VA, enjoying visits from their children and grandchildren.

Marisa Snyder earned a Bachelor's in Science at Kutztown University

(1992) with dual certifications in elementary and special education. She loves teaching, learning, reading, and especially writing! Though she is visually impaired, she opened her own boutique and enjoys her community. She is engaged and adores her family. Contact her at marisasboutique@yahoo.com.

Mother of one daughter and twin sons, **Marie Stroyan** is Gramma to Alex, Patrick, and Thomas. She finds her joy in the simple pleasures of life: family and flowers. At Christmastime, her favorite holiday, Marie decorates in soft blues and peaceful greens to create thoughts of a sacred, Silent Night.

B.J. Taylor loves being the middle daughter, even if she did have to always wear pink. She writes for *Guideposts* and has been published in many *Chicken Soup for the Soul* books. B.J. is married to a wonderful man. They have four children and two adorable grandsons. You can reach B.J. at www.bjtayloronline.com.

Patti Ann Thompson is an award-winning freelance writer, speaker and author. She is a 2001 honors graduate of Emporia State University. Patti Ann resides in Shawnee, KS, with her husband Larry and enjoys traveling, interior decorating and writing. She can be reached at pattiannthompson@gmail.com or www.pattiannthompson.com.

Marla H. Thurman lives in Signal Mountain, TN, with her dog Sophie. Marla is currently working on several nonfiction projects and hopes to publish an ebook soon. E-mail her at sizoda1@gmail.com.

Paula Maugiri Tindall, RN finds inspiration through personal life experiences and nature overlooking the lake she resides at in south Florida, writing her first book. Paula was previously published in *Chicken Soup for the Grandma's Soul* and *Chicken Soup for the Soul: Count Your Blessings*. Contact her via e-mail at lucylu54@aol.com.

David Vaughn received Bachelor of Arts degrees in Youth Ministry and also in Mathematics from Harding University and his Masters from Abilene Christian University in 2002. His greatest passions in this life are his wife and sons. He has been in Christian ministry for twenty years. Please contact him at dvaughn14@gmail.com.

Nancy Vilims enjoys volunteering at her church. She also teaches computers to senior citizens and plans, purchases needed food, cooks and facilitates for 75-150 meals at the community Open Door Supper once a month. Knowing the miracle of a loving gift, Nancy is pleased when she can serve others.

Donna Duly Volkenannt lives in Missouri with her husband Walt and their grandchildren Cari and Michael. When not carpooling or driving to sporting events, she reviews books for Bookreporter.com and pecks away at her young adult novel. Please visit her blog http://donnasbookpub.blogspot.com or e-mail her at dvolkenannt@yahoo.com.

Beverly F. Walker lives near Nashville, TN, and loves writing, photography and scrapbooking pictures of her many blessings—her grandchildren. She is published in various *Chicken Soup for the Soul* books and in *Angel Cats: Divine Messengers of Comfort*.

Samantha Ducloux Waltz is an award-winning freelance writer in Portland, OR. Her personal stories appear in the *Chicken Soup for the Soul* series, *A Cup of Comfort* series, and numerous other anthologies. She has also written fiction and nonfiction under the name Samellyn Wood. Learn more at www.pathsofthought.com.

Pam Wanzer writes of her life experiences as a young widow. Her first published book is a gift book for someone who recently lost a loved one. When at a loss for words, her simple book says it for you. Find her book and other inspirational stories at www.aninterruptedlife.com.

Stefanie Wass's essays have been published in the *Los Angeles Times*, *The Seattle Times*, *Christian Science Monitor*, *Akron Beacon Journal*,

Akron Life & Leisure, Cleveland Magazine, The Writer Magazine, A Cup of Comfort for Mothers, A Cup of Comfort for a Better World, and nine *Chicken Soup for the Soul* anthologies. Visit her website: www.stefaniewass.com.

Alan Williamson is a nationally published humor writer whose work explores the human dilemmas of everyday life. Shunning the complex issues and thorny global conundrums of the day, he chronicles the personal quirks, snags and convoluted capers that are grounded in real-life experience. Alan can be reached at alwilly@bellsouth.net or http://unauthorizedinsights.blogspot.com.

Los Angeles native **Laurel Woods** lives in New York and works for MTV by day. By night, she writes a memoir about her family's strip clubs, Catholic schooling, a psychotic parrot, and her convicted father's life sentence. Her dream is to score a coffee date with Carrie Fisher. www.laurel-woods.com.

Jamie White Wyatt loves to laugh and share "Joy on the Journey." She is a writer, editor, speaker, Bible teacher, event/retreat planner, and ballroom dancer. Originally from Florida, Jamie, her husband, and two children, live in Georgia, where Jamie has owned several businesses, including a bridal shop. E-mail: rockhavenw@me.com; www.dancingonthejourney.blogspot.com.

Melissa Yuan-Innes dedicates this essay to her father, James Yuan. She would like to thank the doctors and nurses at The Ottawa Hospital and Saint-Vincent Hospital for their care. Melissa is an emergency physician who writes and cares for her family outside of Montreal, Canada. Learn more at www.melissayuaninnes.net.

Meet Our Authors

Jack Canfield is the co-creator of the *Chicken Soup for the Soul* series, which *Time* magazine has called "the publishing phenomenon of the decade." Jack is also the co-author of many other bestselling books.

Jack is the CEO of the Canfield Training Group in Santa Barbara, California, and founder of the Foundation for Self-Esteem in Culver City, California. He has conducted intensive personal and professional development seminars on the principles of success for more than a million people in twenty-three countries, has spoken to hundreds of thousands of people at more than 1,000 corporations, universities, professional conferences and conventions, and has been seen by millions more on national television shows.

Jack has received many awards and honors, including three honorary doctorates and a Guinness World Records Certificate for having seven books from the *Chicken Soup for the Soul* series appearing on the New York Times bestseller list on May 24, 1998.

You can reach Jack at www.jackcanfield.com.

Mark Victor Hansen is the co-founder of Chicken Soup for the Soul, along with Jack Canfield. He is a sought-after keynote speaker, bestselling author, and marketing maven. Mark's powerful messages of possibility, opportunity, and action have created powerful change in thousands of organizations and millions of individuals worldwide.

Mark is a prolific writer with many bestselling books in addition to the *Chicken Soup for the Soul* series. Mark has had a profound influence in the field of human potential through his library of audios, videos, and articles in the areas of big thinking, sales achievement, wealth building, publishing success, and personal and professional development. He is also the founder of the MEGA Seminar Series.

Mark has received numerous awards that honor his entrepreneurial spirit, philanthropic heart, and business acumen. He is a lifetime member of the Horatio Alger Association of Distinguished Americans.

You can reach Mark at www.markvictorhansen.com.

Amy Newmark is Chicken Soup for the Soul's publisher and editor-in-chief, after a 30-year career as a writer, speaker, financial analyst, and business executive in the worlds of finance and telecommunications. Amy is a *magna cum laude* graduate of Harvard College, where she majored in Portuguese, minored in French, and traveled extensively. She and her husband have four grown children.

After a long career writing books on telecommunications, voluminous financial reports, business plans, and corporate press releases, Chicken Soup for the Soul is a breath of fresh air for Amy. She has fallen in love with Chicken Soup for the Soul and its life-changing books, and really enjoys putting these books together for Chicken Soup's wonderful readers. She has co-authored more than four dozen *Chicken Soup for the Soul* books and has edited another three dozen.

You can reach Amy with any questions or comments through webmaster@chickensoupforthesoul.com and you can follow her on Twitter @amynewmark.

Thank You

We owe huge thanks to all of our contributors. We know that you poured your hearts and souls into the thousands of stories and poems that you shared with us, and ultimately with each other. We appreciate your willingness to open up your lives to other Chicken Soup for the Soul readers. And we loved hearing about how you and your families celebrate Christmas.

We could only publish a small percentage of the stories that were submitted, but we read every single one and even the ones that do not appear in the book had an influence on us and on the final manuscript.

Putting together this special gift collection was a team effort. We owe special thanks to our assistant publisher, D'ette Corona, our webmaster and editor, Barbara LoMonaco, editor Kristiana Glavin, and editor Madeline Clapps for reading all the stories that were submitted and helping to shape the manuscript, edit it, and proofread it.

We owe a very special thanks to our creative director and book producer, Brian Taylor at Pneuma Books, for his brilliant vision for our covers and interiors.

Improving Your Life Every Day

Real people sharing real stories—for nineteen years. Now, Chicken Soup for the Soul has gone beyond the bookstore to become a world leader in life improvement. Through books, movies, DVDs, online resources and other partnerships, we bring hope, courage, inspiration and love to hundreds of millions of people around the world. Chicken Soup for the Soul's writers and readers belong to a one-of-a-kind global community, sharing advice, support, guidance, comfort, and knowledge.

Chicken Soup for the Soul stories have been translated into more than forty languages and can be found in more than one hundred countries. Every day, millions of people experience a Chicken Soup for the Soul story in a book, magazine, newspaper or online. As we share our life experiences through these stories, we offer hope, comfort and inspiration to one another. The stories travel from person to person, and from country to country, helping to improve lives everywhere.

Share with Us

We all have had Chicken Soup for the Soul moments in our lives. If you would like to share your story or poem with millions of people around the world, go to chickensoup.com and click on "Submit Your Story." You may be able to help another reader, and become a published author at the same time. Some of our past contributors have launched writing and speaking careers from the publication of their stories in our books!

Our submission volume has been increasing steadily—the quality and quantity of your submissions has been fabulous. We only accept story submissions via our website. They are no longer accepted via mail or fax.

To contact us regarding other matters, please send us an e-mail through webmaster@chickensoupforthesoul.com, or fax or write us at:

Chicken Soup for the Soul
P.O. Box 700
Cos Cob, CT 06807-0700
Fax: 203-861-7194

One more note from your friends at Chicken Soup for the Soul: Occasionally, we receive an unsolicited book manuscript from one of our readers, and we would like to respectfully inform you that we do not accept unsolicited manuscripts and we must discard the ones that appear.